# NUCLEAR BOMB IN GANGA

# NUCLEAR BOMB IN GANGA


**RK YADAV**

*Former Officer of R&AW*

*Indian External Intelligence*



PRABHAT PAPERBACKS

*Published by*
**PRABHAT PAPERBACKS**
An imprint of Prabhat Prakashan Pvt. Ltd.
4/19 Asaf Ali Road,
New Delhi-110 002 (INDIA)
e-mail: prabhatbooks@gmail.com

ISBN 978-93-5521-472-0
**NUCLEAR BOMB IN GANGA**
*by RK Yadav*



*Edition*
First, 2023

*Price*
₹ 500 (Rupees Five Hundred Only)

*Printed at*
Sanjay Printers, Sahibabad

# Author's Note

At the outset, I should clarify that this book has not been written to create a panic situation among the Indian population particularly in view of the forthcoming Kumbh Mela at Prayagraj (previously Allahabad) in the beginning of 2019. This Book was planned three years back and is completed now with extensive research and personal interactions with many people who were involved in this venture, directly or indirectly. I would also like to mention that various scientific reports have stated that this nuclear-powered device is inside a heavy walled outer cladding of Haynes-25 alloy composed of nickel, cobalt, chromium and tungsten. This alloy has high temperature and corrosion resistant properties, and high structural strength. Its melting point is 1330 degree C. It was presumed that its life is around 100 years. By now, 53 years have elapsed, and I assume there is no radioactive danger in Ganga for another four decades. This book is just a wake-up call for the government to take corrective measures to locate the device and eliminate this fear-psychosis for our next generations.

When the author launched his first book "Mission R&AW" in July 2014, the then R&AW Chief Alok Joshi tried to scuttle ceremony of the book by various sordid means. I failed to understand why he was so concerned about this book. One of the chief guests informed me later that a senior cabinet minister requested him not to attend the launching ceremony. This witch-hunting was obvious because the author has made numerous complaints to the prime ministers against the corrupt practices of Alok Joshi. None of the governments took cognizance of this corrupt man. However, the coward Alok Joshi did not dare to file any case against the author under the Officials Secret Act despite the fact that many secrets of R&AW were revealed in the book. Most of these so-called 'secrets' are related to corruption by various R&AW officers. Had he done so, there was every chance of him getting booked for prosecution. Now, the past is past, and the author has no ill-will with his successors in R&AW.

The recent book was planned with the sole objective to draw the attention of the government and other activists who are vociferously raking the cause of cleaning the sacred Ganga. My experience on this issue indicates that majority of the politicians, bureaucrats, media-persons and even these activists are unaware of a nuclear-powered device lying beneath Nanda Devi glacier for the last 53 yrs. I contacted all those who have any sort of knowledge about this unknown danger to millions of Indians, because if this device is broken and radioactive Uranium (Pu-238) contaminates the water of the Ganga, what tragedy it could cause to whosoever touch this poisonous material? I have tried to examine various hazardous aspects of this radioactive device, on the basis of relevant documents available on the subject. I hope that the Indian Government would take serious note of this lurking danger, and take all possible steps to locate it and remove this danger for the future generations of this country.

I am grateful to Captain M.S. Kohli, who was the leader of the expedition team which was sent to install this device on Nanda Devi Mountain, to reply to some of the queries related to this mission. I also extend my gratitude to some former officers of R&AW who provided valuable inputs for this book. They did not want to be associated individually to be named in the book which is a quite obvious trend of this hidden community of Indian Intelligence. I have no regrets to accept this prevalent tradition.

***– R.K. Yadav***

# Contents

# 1

# Holy Ganga

The Sacred Ganga, considered as a Goddess, is the lifeline of every Hindu living in India or abroad. In English it is called the Ganges. This amalgamation to English derived from ancient Greek modes related to various wars which Alexander the Great fought in this region.

## Vedic Version

Historically, it is believed that the ancient Harappan period approximately from 1900 to 1300 BC stretched eastward of the Indus River basin to the Ganges-Yamuna doab but could not cross the Ganges to settle towards its eastern side. In the second millennium BC, the Harappan civilization disintegrated. Thereafter, the hub of the Indian civilization shifted from the Indus basin to the Ganges basin. This is considered the Vedic period and the archaeological culture known as "Cemetery H" linked with Indo-Aryan people. During the first phase of Vedic age, (period of the Rigveda), the Indus and the Saraswati were considered as sacred rivers rather than the Ganges. Subsequently, in the period of the remaining three Vedas, the Ganges was believed to be more sacred and the Gangetic Plain became the centre of power of most of the Empires starting from the Maurya to the Mughal. Magasthenes was the first European traveller who gave a vivid description of the Ganges in his writings in India during 350-290 BC. This is linked as major corroboration of disintegration of the Harappan civilization in the second millennium BC and mark of mushrooming of the Gangetic Plains which harboured various Empires of Hindus and Muslims.

## Religious Significance

During May-June every year, Hindus celebrate descent of the Ganges from heaven to earth, a belief according to Hindu mythology. In Sanskrit it is known as **Avatarana (Descent).** On the day of **Dashami,** the tenth day of the waxing moon of the Hindu calendar month **Jyeshtha, Ganga Dashahara** is celebrated all along the banks of the Ganges where millions take bath in the holy river, which is supposed to get rid of ten sins. In Sanskrit, **Dashahara** is derived from **Dasha** meaning ten and **hara** meaning destruction; combined, it means destruction of ten sins. Alternatively, if anyone cannot travel to the Ganges, he is considered as blessed by the Ganges of identical purification if he takes bath in any body of water adjacent to his place. In the Vedic period, **Avatarana** was believed to be the handiwork of **Indra,** the **Lord of Swarga** (Heaven). **Indra** is stated to have killed the celestial serpent, **Vritra** which released **Soma,** the nectar of the Gods. This nectar plunged into the Earth water with considerable sustenance.

In another mythology prescribed in **Vaishnav** version, this heavenly water is called a river **Bhagavat-Padi or Vishnupadi (Emanating from the foot of Vishnu).** Lord Vishnu or Vamana, while measuring the universe, crossed the earth, sky and heaven in three strides. When Vishnu reached heaven, he pierced his left toe on the vault of heaven from where Causal Ocean (Divine **Brahm-Water**) was released. Henceforth, it was encircling within the cosmic egg. This divine **Brahm-Water,** after washing the lotus feet of Lord Vishnu which are covered with reddish saffron, acquired a very beautiful pink colour. Once out of the vault, **Vishnupadi** plunged to heaven where she was received by **Dhruva,** the worshipper of Lord Vishnu. Every Hindu still considers **Dhruva**, fixed in the sky as the Polestar, as in heavenly abode. Crossing the sky called the Milky Way, **Vishnupadi** enters the moon and thereafter enters **Brahmaloka or Brahmapura**, the kingdom of Lord Brahma, a divine lotus atop Mount Meru, whose petals form the continents of the earth. Here, the divine water takes different routes and one flowing from one petal, the **Alakananda,** flowing down to the **Bharatvarsha** (India), is called the Ganges. Lord Shiva received the Ganges on his head to prevent destruction of **Bhumi Devi** (Mother Earth) and thereafter it is released from his hair. In other descriptions, Himvan is stated to have fathered both **Parvati** and Ganga.

There is another version with regard to descending of the Ganges on earth. A king named **Sagara** magically got sixty thousand sons. He wanted to perform a religious ceremony for the welfare of his kingdom wherein a horse was its essential performer. Lord **Indra** was jealous of this ritual and he stole this horse and took it to the netherworld. He deliberately kept it in the **Ashram** of a sage **Kapila** who was meditating for several years. This was a ploy of **Indra.** While searching the horse in the netherworld, sons of Sagara hurled insulting words to sage **Kapila** which disturbed his penance. When **Kapila** opened his eyes in rage on them, all sixty thousand were burnt to death. It is believed that souls of these sons of **Sagara** became ghosts because their last rites after death were not performed according to Hindu sacraments. Only the Ganges water, then in heaven, could bring these dead sons their salvation or **Moksha**. King **Bhagiratha,** the grand-son of one of the nephews of king **Sagara** undertook rigorous penance to **Lord Brahma** to bring the Ganges on earth and then to netherworld to cleanse the souls of his ancestors, the sixty thousand sons of **Sagara.** When **Brahma** asked the Ganges to go to earth, she felt insulted and decided to sweep the whole earth after the descent from heaven. King **Bhagiratha** was aware of the turbulent velocity of the Ganges which could have destroyed the earth. He requested Lord **Shiva** who was on Mount **Kailash** to receive **Ganga** in the coils of his tangled hair to control her fall on earth. Though **Ganga** fell arrogantly on the head of Lord **Shiva,** the touch of the Lord further sanctified her. **Ganga** emerged in small streams and arrived in Himalayas where she was received by King **Bhagiratha.** He took her to the plains at Haridwar, then to the confluence with the Yamuna at Prayag and later to Varanasi. Eventually, she came to the **Ganga Sagar**, where she entered the ocean to reach netherworld to save the sons of King **Sagara.** On earth, **Ganga** maintained a different stream to purify other unfortunate souls which is still continuing. The Ganges in the Himalayas is known as **Bhagirathi** in honour of King **Bhagiratha's** pivotal role in the **Avatarana.**

In Hindu mythology, **Ganga** is considered as the vehicle from earth to heaven meaning thereby that last ritual of a Hindu in her water would pave his way to the heaven. She is the only river to descend through all the three worlds - **Swarga,** the heaven; **Prithvi,** the earth and **Patala**, the netherworld or hell. That is why in Sanskrit **Ganga** is described as **Triloka-patha-gamini** (**triloka** - the three worlds, **patha** - road, **gamini** - one who travels). This circle for Hindus is known as **Tirtha**, the crossing points of all beings, the living as well as dead. Due to this background of **Avatarana,** the Ganges water is used in Vedic rituals for the **Shraddha** (last rites) ceremonies of the deceased in Hinduism. It is the popular belief of every Hindu that he should breathe his last in the Ganges water to attain **Moksha**, the abode of heaven. Hinduism without the Ganges is just like a body without soul. Her water is considered not only pure but purifying. Hindus firmly believe that the Ganges not only purifies physically but also wipes away the sins not for the present but for one's lifetime.

There is another story wherefrom name of the Ganges is derived as Jahanvi. It is believed that after descending to earth, when the Ganges was on her way to **Bhagiratha,** her gushing speed created havoc and destroyed normal life. One sage called **Jahnu** was deeply involved in his spiritual practice when this turbulence disturbed him. He was so agitated on this disturbance that he swallowed all the Ganges waters to punish her. When all the Gods requested the sage **Jahnu** to pardon **Ganga** so that she could proceed for the mission for which she descended from heaven, he released **Ganga** from his ears. Due to this reason, the Ganges is also known as **Jahanvi,** the daughter of **Jahnu.**

It is a strong belief in Hindu mythology that the Ganges would dry up at the end of **Kali Yug** i.e. the era of darkness which is currently in progress just like the Saraswati River and that would be the end of this era. Thereafter, **Satya Yug** (meaning the Era of Truth) would begin again.

## Consort, Power & Mother

In Hindu mythology, Ganga is a consort to all three major male deities of Hinduism. She is companion of Brahma and always remains with him in the form of water in his Kamandalu (water-pot). In Avatarana, she emerged from the foot of Lord Vishnu and is titled Vishnupadi. She is his co-wife along with Saraswati and Lakshmi. In one myth, it is mentioned that during one absence of Lord Vishnu, the three wives quarrelled to outwit one another. Ganga and Saraswati heaped tribulations on each other despite Lakshmi's mediation and efforts to calm them down. They cursed each other to become rivers to carry within them the sins of their human worshippers, by washing. On his return, Vishnu calmed them down and ordered Saraswati to become wife of Brahma, Ganga to become wife of Shiva and the conciliator Lakshmi to remain his own wife. Ganga and Saraswati wailed loudly on this judgement forcing Vishnu to take back his words. Consequently, in their lives as rivers they are still thought to be with him.

In Ganga mythology, her relationship with Lord Shiva has been enunciated. Her descent, the Avatarana is not a singular event but a continuous process of flow wherein she is forever emanating from heaven to the locks of his hair and calming down thereafter. In Hindu iconography, Lord Shiva is depicted as Gangadhara, the "Bearer of the Ganga" with Ganga shown as a stream of water rising from his hair. The Shiva-Ganga relationship is intimate and perpetual. Shiva is sometimes called **Uma-Ganga-Patiswara** (Husband and Lord of Uma, i.e. Parvati and Ganga) and Parvati is often shown as jealous of Ganga due to this relation.

Ganga is often portrayed as the power or the moving, restless, rolling energy in the form of which the otherwise recluse and unapproachable Shiva appears on earth. In the form of water, this moving energy of Ganga could be felt, tasted and absorbed. The Ganges as Ganga Mata (mother) is worshipped as a culture accepting and forgiving all with no intention of destruction unlike other Goddesses. She is also a mother of other Gods. She absorbs the energy of Fire-God Agni in her waters for the welfare of the world. This union produces Skanda or Kartikeya, the God of war. In Mahabharata, she is the wife of Shantanu and the mother of the heroic warrior-patriarch, Bhishma. When Bhishma is mortally wounded, Ganga comes out of the water in human form and weeps uncontrollably over his body.

The Ganges is the purifying lifeblood of the Hindu tradition, its divinities, holy books and enlightenments. She is the way of life of every Hindu which does not require any usual rites of citation at the beginning and dismissal at the end unlike the worship of other Gods. Her sanctity is everlasting and unquestionable. A sip of its waters with the last breath of a Hindu is considered a guarantee to the soul's passage to heaven. Bathing in its waters means cleansing the sins of the soul.

The Ganges is manifestation of all sacred waters in Hindu mythology. Many other rivers are revered like Ganga in distant parts of India. The Kaveri River of Karnataka and Tamil Nadu, in Southern India, is called the Ganges of the South. The Godavari which was led by the sage Gautama is called the Ganga of Central India. The word 'the Ganges' is invoked whenever water is used in Hindu rituals, and is therefore present in all sacred waters. Ganga water is the lifeline of every Hindu from his birth to his last journey.

## Kumbh Mela

Kumbh Mela is a huge gathering of Hindu pilgrims wherein Hindus from all over India gather at four cities to take a dip in holy water. This gathering is the most sacred of all pilgrimages of the Hindu population. The normal Kumbh Mela is celebrated every three years and the Ardh (half) Kumbh Mela every six years at Haridwar and Prayag (Allahabad) on the banks of the Ganga. The Purna (complete) Kumbh Mela is held every twelve years at four places—Prayag, Haridwar, Ujjain and Nasik. The Maha (great) Kumbh Mela comes after twelve"Purna Kumbh Melas" or 144 years, and is held at Prayag on the banks of the Ganga. Besides the ritual bathing on the banks of the river, many other religious activities like religious discoursing, devotional singing and mass-feeding of gathering take place. So also, religious doctrines are debated and standardized for future generations. Sadhus across the country clad in saffron clothing with ashes powder rubbed on their skins and smoking various Indian tobaccos can be seen descending in groups in these cities for a number of days. Naga Sadhus can be seen naked in these celebrations. These huge celebrations can be a matter of big law and order issue for the respective state governments; hence several departments are deployed months in advance to make it a successful event at regular intervals. The worst after effect of these congregations is pollution which can be gauged from the fact that for months afterwards, the sanitary condition around these areas is so dismal that air and water take months to become normal for the general public residing there.

## Origin and Course

The main course of flow of the Ganges starts at the confluence of the Bhagirathi and Alakananda in the town of Devprayag in the Garhwal division of the Uttarakhand State of India. Alakananda the source stream of this confluence is formed by the snowmelt of peaks Nanda Devi, Nanda Kot, Trisul and Kamet. The Bhagirathi rises at the foot of the Gangotri Glaciers at Gomukh mythologically referred to as residing in the matted locks of Lord Shiva, and symbolically called Tapovan being a meadow of ethereal beauty at the feet of Mount Shivling around 5 km away.

Although, many streams form the headwaters of the Ganges, only the longest six and their five confluences are considered sacred in Hindu mythology. The six headstreams are the Alakananda, Dhauliganga, Nandakini, Pindar, Mandakini and Bhagirathi rivers. The five confluences, known as Panch Prayag, are all along the Alakananda. In downstream order they are Vishnuprayag (where the Dhauliganga joins the Alakananda), Nandprayag (where the Nandakini joins), Karnaprayag (where the Pindar joins), Rudraprayag (where the Mandakini joins) and finally Devprayag where the Bhagirathi joins the Alakananda to form the actual Ganges River. After flowing through the narrow Himalayan Valley for around 250 km, the Ganges emerges from the mountain at Rishikesh. Thereafter, it enters the Gangetic Plain at the holy city of Haridwar. This is the starting point of journey of the Ganges in the plains.

The Ganges flows through two nations of Asia, i.e. India and Bangladesh. Its actual length from the point of emergence to the confluence with the Bay of Bengal is around 2,525 km. It is the third longest river in the world.

In India, the Ganges flows through five states, Uttarakhand, Uttar Pradesh (UP), Bihar, Jharkhand and West Bengal, while in Bangladesh it passes through Rajshahi, Dhaka, Khulna, Barisal and Chittagong. Thereafter it empties into the Bay of Bengal. It crosses the cities of Rishikesh, Haridwar, Kanpur, Allahabad, Varanasi, Patna and Bhagalpur. Many tributaries like Rāmgangā, Gomti, Ghaghara, Gandaki, Koshi, Mahananda, Yamuna, Son, Tamsa and Punpun emerge in the Ganges at various points of its stream. In West Bengal, its first attrition begins with the branching away of its first distributary, the Bhagirathi-Hooghly, which is known as the Hooghly River. It flows through the cities of Murshidabad, Kolkata and Howrah. Hooghly River enters the Bay of Bengal near Sagar Island. In Bangladesh, it is known as the Padma River which is joined by the largest distributary of Brahmaputra, the Jamuna River. Further, the second largest distributary of Brahmaputra, Meghna also merges in it and enters the Meghna Estuary before flowing into the Bay of Bengal. The Ganges Delta formed by the large sediment-laden flows of the Ganges and Brahmaputra rivers is the largest in the world. Its total area is around 59,000 sq km with a stretch of 322 km along the Bay of Bengal. It is believed that prior to Padma becoming the main distributary of the Ganges, Bhagirathi-Hooghly was the main channel of the Ganges but due to increased choking with silt, the main flow of the Ganges shifted to the Padma during the 18th Century.

## Apparent Pollution

The Ganges flows through 29 cities with population over 100,000, 23 cities with population between 50,000 to 100,000 and about 48 towns of smaller population. Thousands of riverside villages are located on its banks in India and Bangladesh. It provides water to more than 40% population of India residing in 11 States. This constitutes around 550 million people which are about 10% of the estimated world population. One-third of the Indian population lives in the Ganga Basin. There is a mythological belief that the Ganga has a self-purifying quality which is sometimes ascribed to sulphur springs or to high levels of natural radioactivity in the Himalayan headwaters or to the presence of bacteriophages viruses that can destroy bacteria. Mughal emperor Akbar was so impressed with its purity that he called it, "The water of immortality" and ordered to serve it at his court. Hindus still consider it nectar (Amrit) and all religious ceremonies are conducted using bottled Ganga water. Indians living abroad can now buy a bottle of Ganga water through Amazon or eBay at a price of $9.99. Plans are afoot to supply bottled water of Ganga all over the country through various modes.

But a pertinent question arising in the mind of the general public is, "Is this water still pure despite so many types of polluting activities of the 550 million people residing around the Ganges?" Certainly, yes. The Ganga is suffering from extreme pollution which is hazardous to the health of the population residing around it. This population is victim of their own deeds or misdeeds and apathy of the perhaps semi-literate politicians of India to this growing danger, has added misery to this volcano of diseases, infectious or otherwise.

It is beyond any doubt that a sizeable proportion of the effluents in the Ganges is caused by the population through domestic uses like bathing, laundry and open defecation. Numerous tanneries, chemical plants, textile mills, distilleries, sugar mills, pulp and paper mills, rice bowls, contaminated agricultural runoff, religious offerings, hospitals and slaughterhouses releasing untreated toxic and non-biodegradable waste into the Ganga, mainly contribute to its pollution. This huge volume of pollutants released in this river every day are causing immense damage to the ecosystem and contributing to significant sanitation problems. It is estimated that around 1.3 billion litres of polluted water flows into the Ganga directly or through its tributaries.

The Govt. of British India through an agreement on 19 December. 1916, agreed that the uninterrupted flow of holy water in the Ganga is the rudimentary right of Hindu believers. Sanctity of this agreement has not been preserved by the Government of India or its states after independence though it is legally valid. The Gangotri glacier which is the largest source of water for Ganga is 30.2 km long and around 0.5 to 2.5 km wide at different locations. Over the last two decades, it has retreated more than 850 meters with a recession of 76 meters from 1996 to 1999 alone. The UN 2007 Climate Change Report has suggested that the glacial flow could completely stop by 2030 at which point the Ganges would be reduced to a seasonal river during the monsoon season. Hence, either the government has dumped the 1916 agreement of Hindu population's right to uninterrupted flow of the holy Ganga water or is deliberately allowing various haphazard activities to interrupt its flow.

Below Gangotri, the path of the Ganga is degrading increasingly due to various hindrances caused by installation of small hydropower stations, diversion tunnels and blasting of solid rocks which have made hundreds of miles of riverbed a dry zone. The large hydroelectric dam at Tehri, becoming operational in 2006, releases either a flood or a trickle or nothing at all, depending on the vagaries of the season and the fluctuating demands of the power grid. The first significant human pollution on the Ganga begins at Uttarkashi itself which is around 120 km from the actual origin of the river. This small town has no proper planning of disposing the garbage of its population of around 20,000, leave aside maintenance of the sanitation facilities. The entire garbage is piled up in an open dump site which, during the rainy season, enters the river. In Haridwar, a dam built in 1854 during the British regime has led to the decay of the Ganga by greatly diminishing its flow of water. This dam is ill-equipped to cope with the pollution and inefficient use of water for irrigation further downstream.

Kanpur which used to be called "the Manchester of India" during the British period, is microcosm of everything that hallmarks the stinking urban India. Erstwhile textile industries have been steadily shut down and replaced by the tanneries, the most polluting industry in the world. Kanpur has around 400 tanneries which discharge more than two-thirds of their waste into the Ganga. Political establishment is the main culprit for this pollution. In 1994, the government opened a central plant to treat the tannery waste wherein the industry owners were asked to contribute a large portion of the cost. Subsequently, the budget of this project was tripled and the contribution of the factory owners was gobbled up by the corrupt politicians and bureaucrats and the plant was never upgraded. This plant treats only one-third of the waste which the tannery industry generates every day. This water contaminated by tannery waste has been dangerously increasing chromium in agricultural products and in milk. According to a survey conducted by UP Jal Nigam and National Mission for Clean Ganga, there are 151 polluted drains which flow into the Ganga carrying garbage and other pollutants.

Varanasi, a city of around one and half million people, where thousands of pilgrims visit every day to take a "holy dip" in the Ganga, releases more than 200 million litres of untreated human sewage into the river every day. In the four mile stretch ghats, the low water at the river's edge is a clotted soup of dead flowers, plastic bags, faeces and human ashes. This conglomeration of human and material waste leads to concentration of faecal coliform bacteria. According to medical science, water safe for bathing should not contain more than 500 faecal coliforms per 100 ml, yet on the up-stream stretch of Varanasi ghats, river water already contains 120 times as much, 60,000 faecal coliform bacteria per 100 ml. According to official sources, only one-third of the sewage generated in Varanasi is treated by the existing pumping stations and the rest goes directly into the river.

After the cremation of the deceased at Varanasi ghats, the bones and ashes are thrown into the Ganga. In the past, thousands of un-cremated bodies were thrown into the Ganga during cholera epidemics thus spreading the disease. Even today, dead bodies of holy men, pregnant women, people with leprosy/ chicken pox, people who had been bitten by snakes, people who had committed suicide, the poor and children under five are not cremated at the ghats but are floated free to decompose in the Ganga. Even half-burnt body parts are thrown into the river. Hence, drinking and bathing in its waters carries high risk of infection.

The practice of throwing ashes into Ganga waters at various places will never stop due to the Hindu rituals. In North India, Haridwar and Garh Mukteshwar are the two places where thousands of pilgrims come to immerse ashes of their deceased relatives from far-flung areas. In Allahabad, immersions done at Triveni, an imaginary point where the Ganga, Yamuna and hidden the Saraswati are stated to confluence is considered as most sacred for every Hindu. This tradition is prevalent in major cities along the Ganga River up to the Bay of Bengal. Government too cannot interfere in this religious belief of Hindus. Every government is aware how dangerous such pollutants are for the living population, but fearing religious repercussions, no one has ever dared to stop such immersion of ashes and dead bodies in all cities situated on the banks of the Ganga. Admittedly, this practice would continue according to the Hindu mythology and should be allowed to prevail. However, some alternative arrangements in all these cities should be made whereby this contaminating immersion can be done through treatment plants.

## Cleaning Efforts

The first concerted scheme to clean the Ganga was launched by Sri Rajiv Gandhi, the then Prime Minister of India on 14 January 1986. This was known as Ganga Action Plan. The main objectives enumerated in this programme were to control pollution, improve the quality of water through interception, diversion and treatment of domestic sewage and prevent toxic and industrial chemical wastes (from identified grossly polluting units) entering the river. Other objectives of this plan were to control the pollution from agricultural lands, human defecation, cattle wallowing and throwing of unburnt and half-burnt human bodies along the entire stretch of the river. It also included the research and development measures to conserve the biotic diversity of the river to increase its productivity. New technology of sewage treatment and thorough afforestation were envisaged for all major entering points of the river. Resource recovery options like production of methane for energy generation and use of aquaculture for revenue generation were demonstrated in the plan. The ultimate objective of this plan was to have an approach of integrated river basin management considering various dynamic interactions between abiotic and biotic ecosystems. This plan generated considerable interest and set the scene for evolving a national approach towards replicating it for other polluted rivers of the country. The government of India proposed to extend this model with need-based modifications to the national level through a National River Action Plan. Thereafter, river basin studies identified various rivers for an action plan for the polluted stretches.

The Ganga Action Plan was not implemented in the right spirit by various states. Thirty-five sewage treatment plants built in some cities were never upgraded in proportion to the increase in population, and thus became non-functional. The Central Government paid for the construction of these plants but the state governments did not adhere to the standard of upkeep. Even the wages and electricity bills were not paid. Thus, the efforts to control the pollution level in the Ganga became abortive after spending Rs. 9,017.10 Million. This plan was shelved on 31 March 2000. Thereafter, in 2009, the Manmohan Singh Government established the National River Ganga Basin Authority (NRGBA) which declared Ganga as the National River of India. In 2011, the World Bank approved $1 Billion in funding for the NRGBA.

## Namami Gange Programme

Namami Gange Programme is a mega project of the Narendra Modi Government to clean the Ganga. Verbatim announcement on this programme by the Prime Minister's Office is reproduced below:

"The River Ganga is important not only for its cultural and spiritual significance but also because it hosts more than 40% of the country's population. .........To translate this vision, the government launched an integrated Ganga conservation mission called 'Namami Gange' to arrest the pollution of the Ganga River and revive the river. The Union Cabinet approved the action plan proposed by the centre to spend Rs.200,000 Million till 2019-2020 on cleaning the river, increasing the budget by four-fold and with 100% central share - a central sector scheme.

Recognizing the multi-sectorial, multi-dimensional and multi-stakeholder nature of the Ganga Rejuvenation challenge, efforts have been made to improve the Interministerial and Centre-State coordination with increased involvement in preparation of action plan and increased monitoring at central and state levels.

The implementation of the programme has been divided into entry-level activities (for immediate visible impact), medium-term activities (to be implemented within 5 years of time frame), and, long-term activities (to be implemented within 10 years).

Entry-level activities include cleaning the surface of the river to address the floating solid wastes; rural sanitation to arrest the pollution (solid and liquid) entering through rural sewage drains and construction of toilets; renovation, modernization and construction of crematoria that prevent the disposal of unburnt/partially burnt bodies in the river; and repair, modernization and construction of ghats to improvise the human-river connection.

Medium-term activities will focus on arresting the municipal and industrial pollution entering into the river. To address the pollution through municipal sewage, additional treatment capacity of 2,500 MLD is to be created in the next 5 years. Major financial reforms are underway to make the program efficient, accountable, and sustainable in the long term. Hybrid Annuity based Public-Private Partnership model for project implementation is currently being considered by the Cabinet. If approved, a Special Purpose Vehicle will manage concessionaires in all major cities, market will be developed for treated water, and sustainability of assets on a long-term basis will be assured.

For managing the industrial pollution, efforts have been initiated to improvise the compliance through better enforcement. Grossly polluting industries located along the Ganga have been directed to reduce the quality and volume of effluentsor implement zero-liquid discharge. Action plans for the implementation of these directions by Pollution Control Boards are already prepared and timelines have been assigned for each category of industry with detailed consultations. All the industries have to install real-time online effluent monitoring stations.

Apart from these activities, biodiversity conservation, afforestation, and water quality monitoring are also being taken up under the programme. Programmes for conservation of key iconic species such as Golden Mahaseer, Dolphins, Ghariyals, Turtles, Otters, etc. have already been initiated. Similarly, under 'Namami Gange', 30,000 hectares of land will be afforested for increased recharge of the aquifers, reduced erosion, and improved health of river ecosystem. The afforestation programme is set to begin in 2016. Also, comprehensive monitoring of the quality of water will be done with installation of 113 real-time stations monitoring the quality of water.

Under the long-term activities, providing adequate flow to the river is envisioned through determination of e-flow, increased water-use efficiency, and improved efficiency of surface irrigation.

It is worth mentioning that cleaning of the Ganga River is extremely complex due to its socio-economic and cultural importance and yet, exploitation for various uses. Never in the world has such a complex programme been implemented and it will require participation across sectors and of each and every citizen of the country. There are various ways in which each one of us can contribute to the cause of cleaning the river Ganga:

- **Contribution of funds:** Restoring the quality of a river with the length and population as large as that of Ganga requires huge investments. Government has already increased the budget by four-fold but it still may not be enough to meet the requirements. A Clean Ganga Fund has been established to provide a platform to all for contributing funds to clean the river Ganga.
- **Reduce, Reuse and Recovery:** The majority of us do not realize that used water and filth of our homes can end up in the rivers if not disposed of properly. Sewerage infrastructure is already being constructed by the government but citizens can reduce the usage of water and generation of waste. Reusing and recovery of used water, organic waste and plastics can greatly benefit the programme.

Let us all join hands to save our national river Ganga which is a symbol of our civilization and is an epitome of our culture and heritage!"

This is the official projection of Prime Minister Office on this dream project to clean the Ganga River. As a part of the programme, the Government of India has ordered the closure of 48 industrial units around the Ganga. Around 1,000 polluting industrial units across five states which are polluting the Ganga with untreated waste are under the radar of the Central Pollution Control Board in the coming future. According to the government, the municipal sewage generation from the 118 towns along the river in five states is about 4,790 Million Litres per Day (MLD). A treatment capacity of only 1017 MLD is available in these towns. Paper and Chemical industries are the worst spoilers.

However, the proposed expenditure during the first two years of the present government under Modi gave baffling results despite the high-decibel campaign by the Prime Minister himself for cleaning the Ganga. Budget allocation of Rs. 21,370 Million during 2014-15 was reduced by Rs. 840 Million to Rs. 20,530 Million. Despite so much hype by the Government, only Rs. 3,260 Million was spent during this period and more than 17,000 Million was left unspent. During 2015-16, budgetary allocation from the Rs. 27,500 Million was slashed to Rs. 16,500 Million out of which Rs. 180 Million remained unspent.

In another revelation, after four and half years of Modi Government, it is informed that out of total 221 projects sanctioned for various activities such as treatment of municipal sewage, treatment of industrial effluent, river surface cleaning etc., only 58 have been completed. Total cost of 22,238.73 Crores has already been spent on these projects. This means that another Rs. 22,238.73 Crores over and above the sanctioned cost has been released with more than one and half year to go. Only one fourth of the sanctioned projects have been completed.

Another worrying situation is that 105 sewerage infrastructures and sewage treatment plant (STP) projects were sanctioned, which would have prevent 3293.68 MLD of untreated sewage discharging directly into Ganga; Out of these 105 projects only a total of 26 projects have been completed till August 2018, which is also one-fourth of the sanctioned projects. In May 2018, Union Water Resources Minister Nitin Gadkari had set March 2019 as the new deadline for cleaning the Ganga and ensuring a "70 to 80 percent" improvement in the water quality. It is strange how this mission can be accomplished when one-fourth of the sanctioned projects were completed in four and half years. How the government would pull off miracles within the next six and seven months to complete this task as claimed by the Minister?

Another strange aspect of this neglect is evident from the fact that Modi himself attended only one meeting of the National Ganga River Basin Authority out of the three scheduled for it during the first two years. On the basis of these data, the situation seems to be murky on the actual outcome of this dream project of the Modi Government. Experts of Centre for Science and Environment have predicted that this snail-pace approach to clean the Ganga would take another 30 years to reach any logical end.

## The Ganga/Yamuna Rivers & Gangotri/Yamunotri Glaciers Declared Living Entities By High Court—Supreme Court Stayed It

In a landmark judgment, the Uttarakhand High Court decreed on 21 March 2017, that the Ganga and Yamuna as well as their tributaries and sister bodies be declared as legal and living entities having the status of a legal person with all corresponding rights, duties and liabilities. The Court observed that it was necessary to ensure preservation and conservation of the two rivers so that the faith and recognition of the society is protected. Subsequently, this Court accorded the same status to the Gangotri and Yamunotri glaciers. Court further emphasized that the rivers, streams, rivulets, lakes, air, meadows, dales, jungles, forests, wetlands, grasslands, springs and waterfalls in Uttarakhand should be given corresponding rights, duties and liabilities of a living person in order to preserve and conserve them. The Court unequivocally stated that the past generations have handed over the "Mother Earth" to us in its pristine glory and we are morally bound to hand over the same "Mother Earth" to the next generations.

Ecuador was the first country which recognized the rights of nature in its constitution in 2007-08. Subsequently, New Zealand Parliament formulated a bill declaring its Wanganui River as a legal entity for Maori natives. Thus, India is the third country to declare two glaciers and two rivers as living entities to save from global warming, climate change and pollution.

This judgment would have limited ramifications on the ecological status of the Ganga and Yamuna because this order is limited to the boundaries of Uttarakhand state only. Confluence of the Yamuna at Allahabad is in UP and prior to that it flows from Himachal Pradesh, Haryana and Delhi also where it is polluted with different types of toxins. Obviously, these states are not covered by this judgment. From Uttar Pradesh, the Ganga crosses into Bihar, Jharkhand and then to West Bengal. Hence, the living entities of Ganga and Yamuna beyond Uttarakhand state would be subject of various litigations surmising various polluting factors vis-à-vis tributaries, industries and religious congregations. Hence, this judgment besides having limited implications, did not hit the bull's eyes in view of the fact that many other water-related activities are prevalent in the Ganga in Uttar Pradesh, Bihar, Jharkhand and West Bengal.

Precisely, the "personhood" of the Ganga is subject to different perceptions in every state wherein it enters. In UP, while passing through Hastinapur plains in complete ferocity, it stumbles at Narora first and then at Kanpur barrages. The

Ganga's living entity is severely intoxicated in this region by sewage, pollutants and effluents. The Ganga would attain its spiritual entity after confluence with the Yamuna at Allahabad and up to Varanasi in view of the clean-up flagship project of Namami Gange at the behest of the Prime Minister. So, this human entity is precisely monitored by the Ministry of Water Resources up to Varanasi to appease the holy community of this region. It is pertinent to know that beyond Varanasi this "Namami Gange" is almost non-existent and the garbage flows to Bihar and Bengal. So, in UP, this human entity, though not declared yet, is getting maximum government attention in view of its passage through Varanasi, the Lok Sabha constituency of the Prime Minister.

In Bihar, it regains its vigour when four tributaries, the Ghaghra-Sarju, Gandak, Bodhi-Gandak and Kosi accelerate its flow almost 50 percent more. But here the Ministry of Water Resources is taken over by the Ministry of Shipping and Transport in view of the fact that the Ganga was declared the "National Waterway No. 1" in 1982. This part of the personhood is thus ruled by Mafias carrying out various types of nefarious activities on the flow of the Ganga. Under the 2016 National Waterway Act, the Ganga beyond Varanasi-Allahabad upstream is being developed as National Waterway to carry coal and cargo to various destinations which is in the hands of these Mafia groups. Despite a stay imposed by the National Green Tribunal, dredging in the Ganga is a menace beyond Varanasi which covers an area of around 500 km. It is estimated that around 28 ships would pass simultaneously along its bank by 2020 if the projected capacity and infrastructure is built in the proposed proportions. In order to create the cargo-carrying facilities, dredging is rampant to build more barrages and navigation locks to artificially increase and level out water depths for the ships to journey smoothly in this region of the Ganga. Although, waterways transportation is touted cheaper by this modus, given the dredging counter-effects, it would demand serious exposure to maintenance when implemented in full strength. The worst implication of dredging and ship movement would be on dolphins, otters and even on the livelihood of fishing communities who are already making lot of hue and cry for their survival. Hence, the living entity of Ganga should be unequivocally extended up to the borders of Bangladesh in West Bengal so that beyond cleaning, other measures should be put in force to do away with inhuman activities in various parts of Bihar and Bengal.

In a rare and unwonted judicial diktat, the Uttarakhand High Court issued notice on 27 April 2017 to 'human' Ganga seeking explanation from her as to why its land was allotted for the construction of a trenching ground. A Division Bench of the Court issued notice on a petition filed by a private person against the decision of a proposed Solid Waste Management Plant on 10 acres of land near the Ganga. Custodians of the river, the Chief Secretary, the Advocate General and the Director of Namami Gange project would respond on behalf of the Ganga. It would be the first legal wrangling on its stature after the Ganga was accorded the status of living entity by the Uttarakhand High Court. If this waste management plant is abandoned, it would have far reaching consequences on all such future projects particularly those meant to dilute pollution around the river. Such legal protection beyond Uttarakhand territory is still a far cry for this human entity because of the existence of many industrial units spread along the banks of the Ganga/Yamuna in other states. Delhi, situated on the Yamuna River, could face numerous legal issues in view of the worst polluted water flowing into the Yamuna through various entries carrying huge sewage wastes of the City Municipal Corporation. However, the Uttarakhand Government challenged this High Court order in the Supreme Court quoting various legal questions and administrative issues. This High Court order has put the state government in a quandary. Since, the river flows through many states, only the

Central Government can formulate rules for its management. Two major reasons cited by Uttarakhand Government were whether the victim of a flood in the rivers can sue the state for damages and also whether the state and its officers would be liable for action in case of pollution in the rivers in another state through which it flows. This legality would ultimately be decided by the Central Government taking into consideration various issues related to pollution, management and diversity of public opinion. The Supreme Court ultimately stayed this High Court order for various administrative and judicial reasons. However, the Supreme Court has issued notice to the concerned person also who had filed the Public Interest Litigation in this matter.

## Potential Danger

Aforesaid details are ample proof to indicate as to how water of the sacred Ganges has been regularly polluted through various means causing numerous diseases to the bulk of population living on both sides of the river. These pollutions cause many diseases like dysentery, cholera, hepatitis A, severe diarrhoea, typhoid, acute gastrointestinal illness and in many cases, cancer in different forms. The situation is very alarming and increasing day by day despite the lukewarm responses both from the Central Government and all respective state governments.

However, beginning with the Ganga Action Plan of Rajiv Gandhi in 1986 and now the proposed Rs.200,000 Million mega plan of "Namami Gange" of Prime Minister Modi, efforts are afoot to clean the water of the Ganges in one way or another. But is any government starting from 1980 with Prime Minister Indira Gandhi at the helm and now Narendra Modi in 2014-19, ever aware of the real radiation danger posed to the life of this approximately 550 Million population, which is around 10% of the world? Apparently not, in the least. Given below are some devastating facts and figures which are eye-openers to indicate that the existing pollution in the Ganges constitutes only a very small proportion of danger in comparison to the hidden huge danger posed to the life and survival of this population.

The CIA and Intelligence Bureau (IB) launched a secret operation during October 1965 to install a nuclear device on the Nanda Devi Mountain after the Chinese nuclear explosion of 1964. This device was meant to monitor the future Chinese atomic plans across the Himalayas. However, due to some unforeseen circumstances, this device was lost in the glaciers of Nanda Devi after the plan of installation was abandoned due to adverse weather conditions in October 1965. There are conflicting media reports and disclosures by Government of India that around 5 kg of PU-238 or 239 (a purified form of Uranium) was placed in this device. Initially, efforts were made by IB to locate this device, which proved futile. It should be pertinent to mention here that during the Second World War, the US dropped atomic bombs on Nagasaki and Hiroshima in Japan killing more than 200,000 of Japanese. Half of the deaths occurred on the day the bombs were dropped there. This form of Uranium (PU-238 & 239) was stated to be the component of those bombs which were dropped by the US on the Japanese territories. The Government of India has never assessed as to how much danger this lost nuclear device is posing to the population living around the Ganges if the contents kept in the device are exposed to the holy Ganga water, thereby contaminating it. This is the reason to highlight the ancient history of Ganga and how it is the lifeline of billions of Indians, its present pollution condition and government efforts to clean the existing pollution. But, has government ever examined the extreme hidden danger lying somewhere in the Ganga water which could bring devastating misery to the living population of around 550 Million? This is the sum and substance of writing this book. Apparent danger of low intensity is expressed in this chapter which is based on the available information and data released by the government and other sources. Actual perception of threat could not be elaborated because the estimate of actual weight and type of uranium placed in the device is not known either to the Government of India or to any other institution. These details are in the cupboard of the CIA which are neither revealed to Indian Government nor declassified even after fifty years of this fiasco. This chapter on the Holy Ganga is reminiscent of the fact that there is no purpose to declare it a living entity until the worst contaminated material lying in its stomach is operated upon and removed, if it has to live like a real person.

❑

# 2

# Dragon Nuclear Threat

## Chinese Hegemony in the Sixties

Belligerent China was a matter of deep concern for the neighbouring countries of Asia in general and the United States of America in particular, after the overthrow of Chiang Kai-shek by the communist forces in December 1949. India too was on its radar. Hapless India had to swallow the plundering of Tibet by Chinese Communist forces in December 1950 owing to its weak military propositions due to the partition that took place after British rule. Thereafter, the Sino-Indian agreement "Panchsheel" of April 1954 was a self-saving formula of Nehru's diplomacy; else, India's frontier with China was parlous in the absence of a single security person there. Nehru pursued friendly approach and ties with China in its foreign policy in bitter anguish, knowing that if India could not save Tibet, it could at least secure its own frontiers, albeit temporarily. Although the McMahon Line continued to be a disputed issue even at the height of Indo-China friendship around this period, their amity remained unaffected, which Nehru assiduously sought to foster under the banner of Panchsheel, the Bandung spirit, Non-Alignment and Asian solidarity. 'Hindi-Chini, Bhai-Bhai' spirit was flaunted as a face-saving formula to the Indian public through Panchsheel. Nehru further broadened his China-contain diplomacy and chaperoned the Chinese Premier Chou En-lai to his brainchild, the Non-Aligned Conference in Bandung, Indonesia, in April 1955. He introduced Chou En-lai to the delegates of many Afro-Asian countries whose locations were not even in his knowledge. This inanity of Nehru proved fatal there itself when Chou En-lai tried to dominate that conference in Bandung by emulating emergence of China from foreign dominance. Nehru became a victim of his own conviction by fostering the henceforth non-entity China at such an International Conference, which was not even there on the agenda of the conference. Further, the repressions of Tibetans in Tibet and granting of asylum to the Dalai Lama along with millions of his countrymen inside India deteriorated its relations with China precipitously which still exists, and glares up time and again on various issues.

Some Sinologists, while evaluating Nehru's China policy in 1959, questioned the intention of some Chinese comrades in attacking Nehru so uncompromisingly in the garb of 'cohesion and struggle'. According to them, Mao Zedong, the Chinese Supremo, while unmasking Nehru, perceived him as a "double-dealer", "half a man, half a devil", "half a gentleman, half a hooligan", etc., and in doing this they allegedly "forced" him to strengthen India's friendship with China during this period. Such polemics while amusing, even comical, were a gross distortion of history even though conceived by a hypocrite like Mao. Had it been so, Nehru could have desisted from granting asylum to the Dalai Lama and its subsequent repercussions which he then dared the Chinese to swallow. Mao should have cavilled off his assumption while underlying this incident. Such misconception of Mao about Nehru's intentions stemmed from a paranoid dictator's isolation from the outside world. He was surrounded by sycophants and stooges of weird conduct. Their assumptions were hypothetical and creation of a psychoanalytical ploy like leaning on feeble linguistic crutches in the absence of real analytical legs for ambulation which could be effective for obfuscation but not as an explanatory tool.

The Korean War of 1950-53 marked the Cold War tensions between the superpowers wherein China was a late entrant. Although the Russian aided Communist attack was thwarted under the garb of US International Peace Keeping Force, in reality it was dominated by US and other anti-communists allies of NATO. Gen. MacArthur, the brave US Commander behind the conquest of the northernmost provinces of North Korea, made China worried of a strong American presence in its neighbourhood. The Chinese Army secretly attacked the UN forces to contain them across the "38 parallel" so that its territories are secured in any future combat with Americans. In the ensuring peace negotiations, India played a very significant role. India was designated as Chairman of the Neutral Nations' Repatriation Committee for the repatriation of war prisoners captured by the two sides of Korea. Krishna Menon, the then Indian Defence Minister, visited Beijing and secured the release of many American soldiers who were taken prisoners in this war. Though India stepped in with honest bargaining in this exchange of POWs, it was accused of siding with the Americans by the Chinese. Trusting anyone was a far cry among the Chinese at every stage.

China too made a reappraisal of the rapidly changing international situation around 1960-61 to realign its compulsions and designs towards its neighbouring countries. China was passing through a lean phase economically due to draught and other internal factors. Around this period, the Soviet Union withdrew its technical know-how from China and discontinued the economic aid due to strained relations. In Laos, China was helping the communists of Pathet Lao faction who were confronted by American aided Phoumi group; this was snowballing into an international crisis wherein China was not finding any ally. The Vietnam War had not escalated to its peak during this period. On the other hand, China was apprehending invasion by Chiang Kai-shek with the assistance of the USA through Korea and Vietnam. Simultaneously, the same proposition was explored in the south where India could attack its territory through Tibet with American help. China was not excepting to get any direct Soviet assistance on these two contingencies. This apprehension by the Chinese was a fear-psychosis without any proper assessment of the ground situation because there was no question of any such collaboration among these countries at that time or even later.

When hostility with India was emerging on its future agenda, China hastily concluded border treaties with Nepal and Myanmar (then Burma). In a flurry of events, it recognized the de-facto existence of the McMahon Line bordering Tibet which is remnant beyond the North-East States of India. Actually, it was recognition of McMahon Line as international border which China recognized with Myanmar but disputed with India. China established diplomatic relations with thirty countries without any obstruction by Americans. It also concluded friendship treaties with Cambodia and Afghanistan. In another neighbourly appeasement to outwit India, Chinese made a special exception in the case of its borders with Nepal. They proposed that there would be no Chinese post within 25 kilometres of its border from Nepal. They were extremely apprehensive to avoid clashes with the army of Nepal and also with the Tibetan guerrillas who were close to Nepal to avoid any ill-will in that country. This was a calculated measure by China to isolate India by ostentations friendliness to India's acquiescent neighbours.

China was adopting a policy of peaceful co-existence towards Asian, African and other countries of the world whilst maintaining resolute opposition to the USA. China postured to the world community that the American might is challengeable only by its communist ideology and even without it entering the UN forum, it could dictate its terms to the world fraternity. However, China apprehended a possible invasion by the American Army which was numerically inferior but vastly superior in arms. They defined it as two types of warfare, long-range and short-range. Long-range implied war through bombing, artillery, missiles, nuclear and biological attacks wherein it was weak and there was no way to make up this deficiency in the near future. Obviously, China had to concentrate on the conventional short-range fighting without which long-range fighting was impossible to consolidate the gains. In the short-range fighting, weapon power could easily be matched by the human element; and, if America had the largest fire-power, China had larger man-power; and it had exhibited in Korea that it could swamp the United States' fire-power by its man-power. Moreover, it was the man behind the machine who were counted in the ultimate end; and in close fighting the bayonet, rifle and mortar were all that would count and greater fire-power will fell to secondary importance, because it could not be applied. Acting according to these directions, China trained its army to improve the efficiency in close fighting tactics; and it was this close fighting tactic which was adopted in the 1962 war with India in which the training and motivation of the Chinese troops did ultimately prevail.

In this pursuit, the first salvoes of what the Chinese characterized as "Counterattack in Self-Defence on the China-India Border" were fired in October 1962, in the remote north western (Aksai Chin) and north-eastern (NEFA) border areas of India. After a total of 10 days of active fighting, the Chinese campaign came to an end on November 20, with the enigmatic unilateral Chinese declaration of ceasefire and withdrawal of its forces from territories more than 100 miles inside India. Nehru sought US military assistance when he found himself embroiled in quagmire of militant public opinion, parliamentary intransigence, factional politics, misguidance from the Historical Division of the Ministry of External Affairs and the trauma of the impending military catastrophe in the eastern sector. While justifying this attack, Mao later told a Nepalese delegation that the war with India was not about the border issue but with Nehru and his government's belief that Tibet belong to India. But on another occasion, he bragged before the Ceylonese Foreign Minister that Beijing wanted to demolish India's illusion of grandeur in order to establish China's pre-eminence in Asia. Such misconceptions of Mao had different yardsticks while negotiating the Taiwanese presence in its neighbourhood where the Chinese People's Liberation Army (PLA) could not dare a single foray fearing American outrage beaming even on the existence of their own survival. Taiwan's unification to the mainland was a top priority of Mao's Neighbourhood Foreign Policy which seemed nondescript in a real sense of American fear and might. Taiwan continued to be member of Security Council at that time and Chinese locus standi was questionable before the world community.

The Sino-Indian border conflict, a relatively limited military engagement and basically a frivolous melee with virtually no ground war, was apparently an "unfought war". However, political ramifications of this debacle were far more significant than military rout because it defenestrated Krishna Menon, Nehru's Non-Alignment Policy was discredited, popularity of Congress party declined and arms lobbies hibernated fostering India's military assistance towards Washington and London. This war demolished the "Nehruvian consensus" and option for nuclear deterrence emerged on the Indian political arena which was opposed by Nehru himself earlier as a drain on the Indian economy. Strangely, the loyalty of the Indian Communists was in utmost questionable form in these pride-hurting Indian sentiments wherein they never criticized China for this unprovoked invasion and rather raised questions on "Forward Policy" of Nehru. Still that schizophrenia is prevalent and incurable in the mind and body of this clan in India.

American war phobia made Chinese apprehension more intricate in view of the nuclear superiority of the former. The US possessed all the nuclear weapons and China had none. Bereft of Russian support, China would have to fight the United States' nuclear attack literally with bare hands. This position of inferiority was not soluble in the near future. China was thus averse to any direct confrontation with the US due to this deficiency. But China in view of its expansionist policy, though shirking from a nuclear war, was not hesitant to local wars, particularly on the border areas, if these could be quickly ended and did not bring in American reprisal in a very big way. Actually, there might be situations on the border in which China might find it profitable to indulge in a quick war to forestall massive American intervention. It was literally experienced by them in 1962 war when despite considerable intrusions inside Indian territories, China unilaterally declared ceasefire and returned to its pre-war positions without any world diktat. It was out of fear of anti-communist forces of the world which were determined to surround China, had it not vacated Indian territories.

## Indo-US Thaw

Historically, though the US and India established contacts prior to the American Revolution through soldiers and seamen who had lived both in the US colonies and in India, it practically materialized only during British regime in the late eighteenth century. In 1794, Indo-US trade was legally authorized by Jay's Treaty by the British and an American, Benjamin Jay, was appointed the American Consul. Later missionaries, tourists, intellectuals and Indian freedom fighters enhanced mutual contacts. US Missionaries established schools, distributed religious literature and did humanitarian work among the poor Indian masses. The number of missionaries rose from 139 in 1885 to 2,478 in 1922. Later in 1893, two Indian preachers,

P.C.Majumdar of Brahmo Samaj and Swami Vivekananda earned fame at the World Parliament of Religions in Chicago particularly when Vivekananda addressed the participants as "Sisters and Brothers of America". Harvard University offered him the Chair of Oriental Philosophy and University of Columbia the Chair of Sanskrit.

Lala Lajpat Rai was the first Indian political leader to visit the US in 1905. He professed for the importance of Indian independence before the US people. In 1906, some Indian political leaders were exiled from the USA. Among them, Lala Hardayal formed the Hindustan Ghadar Party at California to garner US support for Indian independence. These leaders started a weekly newspaper called the Ghadar in USA. Many Indians and Americans established various organizations for the Indian cause like India Home Rule League of America, National Committee for India's Freedom, India League of America, Society for the Advancement of India and Friends of Freedom for India. Many leading American politicians, intellectuals, jurists, scientists and writers emphatically pleaded for the Indian cause of freedom when these Indian freedom fighters vouched for it there. Though the American people were sympathetic to the Indian demand for independence, the US Government cold-shouldered it owing to their good relations with the British regime. Katherine Mayo's book "Mother India" depicting the Indian society as deprived, squalid and without redeeming virtues became very popular, but it rang the death-knell to the British. However, US media later appreciated the unique way of fighting of Mahatma Gandhi to attain independence through Non-Violence and Satyagraha.

During the Second World War, the US was oblivious of Indian assistance in its fight against Japan. In that pursuit, the Roosevelt Administration exchanged diplomatic personnel with India and Britain. Thomas H. Wilson was appointed the first US Commissioner in New Delhi and Sir Girja Shankar Bajpai was appointed as India's Agent General in Washington and was placed under the supervision of the British Embassy. The US and India exchanged goods on reciprocal basis with one another under the aid programme. Americans participated in construction of roads, airports, industries, etc. American troops were stationed in India in substantial numbers. President Roosevelt wrote to Churchill suggesting formation of an Indian Government comprising various section of the society. His representative Colonel Johnson was the official US mediator during the Cripps Mission in 1942. So, overtly USA was pursuing the Indian cause of freedom with the British during the Second World War obviously to sustain its own strategic presence in this region. Though the Cripps Mission failed to achieve the desired results, it heralded a new era in the US-India political relations.

Pre second World War relations between India and the United States have no strategic relevance because India was all along ruled by foreign plunderers by then and as such there was no role of its own in any foreign-related incidents. However, in the wake of the Indian freedom movement, the US gave very strong support, much to the discomfiture of the British Empire. During the Second World War, thousands of American troops were stationed in India when India was made a base to thwart Japan on China-Burma-India frontiers. Thereafter, the American President Roosevelt raised the bogey of Indian independence which was vehemently rejected by the British Prime Minister Winston Churchill. The American proposition was based on its opposition to colonialism, desist war-like situation and its future role to dominate the post-colonial era. Years later the USA was preoccupied to contain the communist menace in Asia and was deliberately oblivious of the horrific division of British India. But Nehru had a soft corner for the Soviet Union even prior to Indian independence. He wrote a letter to his sister Mrs Vijaylaxmi Pandit, who was representing India in the inaugural session of the United Nations in 1946, cautioning her to be on friendly terms with both Russia and America but to side with the former for the present, but not always.

After Indian independence, the US think-tank was wary of the adaptation of Fabian socialism by the first Indian Prime Minister Jawaharlal Nehru because of his influence on this thought due to his exposure to the same during his student days in Britain. Nehru was influenced by George Bernard Shaw and Bertrand Russell who were staunch propagators of reformist means in a gradual manner through attritional warfare. Although Nehru was a socialist inspired by Fabian views, he was a non-believer in strong socialist measures. However, he enforced land reforms, privatization and entrepreneurship. His concept of Mahalanobis socialism was Nehru's way of implementing Fabian thought. This policy of Nehru was viewed by Americans as a ploy to dither away from the democratic values which these two countries cherished after colonial rule. But these divergences were obvious in view of the long independence cherished by Americans and the experimental economic development of newly independent India and Nehru was not to be blamed from experimenting new ideology.

After the accession of Jammu and Kashmir in the Indian Union and Pakistan's invasion of large part of it, India brought this matter in the Security Council in the UN on 1 January 1948. However, the USA and Britain's connivance managed to divert the matter of Pakistan's aggression on India as an India-Pakistan dispute, which was never existent. Mysteriously, the US was silent on the Indian point of view and instead of declaring Pakistan an aggressor, the US delegate emphasized to hold plebiscite in Kashmir much to the embarrassment of the Indian delegation. The inner voice of US in all such deliberations was hidden towards favouritism to the Pakistani cause. The USA had its own agenda of establishing its military bases in this region and in this mission none other than Pakistan was the soft target. In this pursuit, the US proposed military aid to Pakistan which queered the pitch of any settlement of the Kashmir issue because this aid emboldened the makers of Pakistan's foreign policy to be of equal footing with India in so far as military strength was concerned. Taking the excuse of "India Hides Behind Russia's Veto", the US coloured the Kashmir issue as communist and non-communist imbroglio since Russia was backing India in the Security Council. Hence, US-India relations at that time were measured with parameters of Russian influence on Indian side and not on any logical conclusion. Underlying the estrangement was a sense of mutual disappointment led by unrealistic apprehensions. Democratic and secular India was hopeful of US support on Kashmir issue while the US desired Indian backing on the general thrust of US policy in dealing with the communist menace. The US was thus cautious of Indian attitude of western democratic and communist totalitarian camps especially after the US entanglement in Korea. Thus, Indo-US relations were off to mutual distrust after the Indian independence.

Wary of Nehru's Non-Alignment Policy after independence, the American Ambassador in India, Henry P. Grady, told him that the United States did not consider neutrality as an acceptable position. He informed the State Department that he had informed Nehru that India cannot be straddled and should get on the democratic side immediately. The first state visit of Nehru to US in 1949 was disastrous. Nehru spent three weeks there to explain his foreign policy to the general public. However, President Truman cold-shouldered him diplomatically and refused economic or food aid. The US could not afford to accept the Indian stand negating the alignment with democratic forces. Truman was irked at neutral India's suggestion to recognize Communist China and have cordial relations with the Soviets. Nehru was averse to the American policy which he found too disdainful on the Cold War and callous to the cause of colonial countries. Nehru never warranted US domination on his foreign policy even at the embryonic stage of its formation. He was miffed at the US attitude of being ignored in this visit but at the same time Pakistan Prime Minister was accorded better comfort in political parley by the USA. He sardonically attributed his remark that, "Nobody should visit America for the first time" when he found the Pakistani PM's terms with the USA equivalent to his.

Despite the initial hiccup to match the broad vision of Nehru by the USA, in 1950 he played a very positive role during the North Korean aggression. He supported the United Nations resolution condemning North Korea's action in that war. How Nehru secured the release of American POWs was explained earlier in this chapter. However, in his second visit to USA in 1956, Nehru was accorded a very warm welcome by the President Dwight D. Eisenhower. Nehru had 14 hours of discussion with him at his Gettysburg farm. The Nehru-Eisenhower bonhomie heralded a new era of friendship in US-India relations. This positive chemistry was unacceptable to a certain section of US administration and John Foster Dulles was one of them who summed up his foreign policy doctrine as "those who are not with us are against us". Despite such a self-professed policy, in the next few years, the USA enhanced economic aid to India to $822 million and approved the PL480 programme. This author cannot forget to remember how as a child he ate the reddish coloured wheat breads made from PL480 Aid Wheat which took more than double the time of ordinary bread to chew. It continued for several years till India was able to produce enough grain after the evolution of the Green Revolution which fructified in late sixties and early seventies. Significantly, Indo-US Technological cooperation commenced during this period especially in the high technology sectors like heavy industry and nuclear power.

Eisenhower reciprocated by visiting India in 1959. He was the first US President to visit India which strengthened the sagging Indo-US relations. It was perceived that India got discreet guarantee against any Chinese aggression during this visit of Eisenhower. Although the US Arms for Pakistan remained a main concern for India during this visit but there was also satisfaction about the warming trend in relations in form of US economic aid which was forthcoming in increasing measures then. India's Non-Alignment Policy no longer seemed an anathema to the USA. Nehru was able to dilute some acrimonious issues with Eisenhower while further continued during Kennedy regime.

John F. Kennedy was an important friend of India in the US Senate. Unlike Eisenhower, he was not averse to Nehru's Non-Alignment policy. As a Senator in 1958, he sponsored the senate resolution to increase economic aid for India and criticized the Republican policy of relying on military pacts like with Pakistan to meet the communist threat in the Third World War. He was more sympathetic to the aspiration of developing nations and less antagonistic towards non-alignment. Much to the Indian benefit was the presence of another Indian friend, former Ambassador Chester Bowles as the foreign policy advisor of Kennedy during campaign for Presidential election in 1960. Kennedy viewed China as the most serious threat to Asian stability. In his opinion, prosperity of India was the only alternative to counter China. After becoming President, Kennedy, unlike his predecessor, pursued a different policy towards India. He appointed Indian experts in key foreign policy appointments. These experts played a pivotal role in establishing some intelligence/security outfits in India during and after the Chinese conflict with India.

Nehru visited US in 1961 but it was disappointing for Kennedy who found him too tired to keep the spirit of negotiation in congenial atmosphere. Despite this hiccup, Kennedy held Nehru in high esteem and increased economic aid to India. It was not Nehru's intention but his advisors were to be blamed for such a misconception. They were so amateurish that they emphasized more on insignificant engagements than to focus comprehensively on vital matters in the Nehru-Kennedy summit. Kennedy described this meeting as the worst state visit ever by any high dignitary. Time magazine mocked that Nehru's schedule was so crowded that it barely left him time to change the perennial red rose on his tunic. Such bureaucratic misdemeanour can have far-reaching consequences on foreign-policy strategies of any country and Nehru was made a scapegoat by Foreign Ministry of India. Such "Babudom" could not achieve anything significant from this high profile visit wherein the Americans were out of the way to render many more concessions to Nehru and his contingent.

However, the Kennedy era was the turning point in strengthening Indo-US friendship which was on rocky ground since the cold war imbroglio. Kennedy gave out all support to India during 1962 conflict with China. The US Air Force brought arms, ammunitions and clothing for the Indian troops. Kennedy ordered the Navy USS Kitty Hawk aircraft carrier to proceed from the Pacific Ocean to help India in case the war became a long feature. The US administration even formulated a contingency plan that could be implemented in the event of another attack by China on India. Defence Secretary Robert McNamara and General Maxwell Taylor advised President Kennedy to use nuclear weapons in case American intervention was necessary in such a situation. Kennedy administration openly declared, "We should defend India and therefore we will defend India." In New Delhi, US Ambassador John Kenneth Galbraith, the noted Economist was a close friend of India. He helped India to open one of the first Indian computer science departments at the Indian Institute of Technology in Kanpur, Uttar Pradesh. During his period, the largest ever US foreign aid programme to India was implemented. During the third week of November 1962, a high level delegation led by senior Statesman Averell Harriman accompanied by top Pentagon and CIA officials visited New Delhi to discuss various areas of support to India. In addition to these military and economic aids, the US contributed immensely to strengthen Indian Intelligence on Chinese borders. CIA contingent and top IB brasses hashed out joint covert programmes to counter China. New departments under the Intelligence Bureau (IB) of India were devised and formally given a kick-start on emergency basis. These departments were:

## Establishment-22 (Now Special Frontier Force)

One politician who helped Indian Intelligence to get wings and teeth beyond Nehru Cabinet was Biju Patnaik, father of Naveen Patnaik, the present Chief Minister of Odisha. Biju Patnaik paid a secret visit to USA as representative of Nehru to seek details about the blue-print of a guerrilla force for the cross-border operations in Tibet. Two days after the formation of the Indo-Tibetan Border Police (ITBP), during the ongoing conflict with China, Establishment-22, a secret Guerrilla security force was given approval by Nehru on 26 October 1962. This force recruited the Tibetans who entered India after Chinese invasion of Tibet and asylum of Dalai Lama in India. Its main objective was to carry out special assignments inside Tibet. Around 80,000 Tibetans of all classes and ages migrated to India and considerable numbers to Nepal and Bhutan along with Dalai Lama. Chinese ruthlessly trampled not only on Tibet's political autonomy but also deprived Dalai Lama his status and demeaned the autonomy of the monasteries and respect for the religion.

One of the major advantages of recruiting Tibetans into the Establishment-22 was to overcome the language problem. The Tibetan language is as different from Chinese as Sanskrit is from Chinese. In fact, the Tibetan language was derived from Pali which was one of the early forms of Sanskrit. Like Sanskrit and Pali, Tibetan has alphabets whereas the Chinese script is based on ideography. From the seventh century when the Tibetan script was borrowed from India, it has shown no changes and the form of letters and its orthography is virtually the same as at the time of its inception. Therefore, on the score of language if any country can claim close affinity with Tibet, that would be India, whereas China would be the farthest from it.

Tibetans had been working for the British Indian Army as spies, intelligence agents and even covert militia in northern India and Tibet during the period of "The Great Game". This period is known as one of mistrust and one-upmanship between the British and Russian Empire when both empires were apprehending constant threat of war in and around the Central Asia. Due to this reason, the British overlooked the northern region of India and this isolation was responsible for its non-development. In post-cold war era, CIA and IB established Mustang Base in Nepal where Tibetans were trained in Guerrilla warfare for infiltration inside Tibet. The Mustang rebels were responsible for bringing Dalai Lama to India during the 1959 Tibetan Rebellion.

Establishment-22 was formally set-up on 26 October 1962 and Chakrata near to the hills of Dehradun was selected as its headquarters. The Gorkha Regiment, which was earlier stationed here, had moved out. So, plenty of unutilized infrastructure facilities were available there. On the advice of Lt. Gen. B.N. Kaul, Defence Minister Krishna Menon recommended the name of Brigadier S.S. Uban to head this force. Nehru approved the appointment and Uban took charge of this new assignment in the first week of November 1962. Uban was from the Twenty Second Regiment of Artillery. Hence, the Establishment-22 was named in honour of his earlier posting with this army unit. He was an outstanding Sikh officer with great courage and aggressiveness which was suited for this job. Uban was a Military Cross holder and a legendary officer in the during British Indian Army World War II. In December 1966, Establishment-22 was given a new, equally ambiguous cover designation, the Special Frontier Force (SFF).

Formation of this force was tough and hazardous for Brig. Uban in view of the fact that this unit was to be raised without invoking Army Act meaning thereby a guerrilla outfit trained like army or paramilitary force with civilian discipline. It was like taming tigers softly because Tibetans were physically tough, fearless and believing death as the gateway to the rebirth to a better life in future. This instinct made them a tough stuff for the Guerrilla warfare. They have enormous lung capacity which clubbed with their extraordinary physical stamina was ideal for fighting in high altitudes. Chushi Gangdruk, leaders of Tibetan origin, were deployed for recruitment of Khampas, the warrior Tibetans, into Establishment-22. Initially around 5,000 Tibetans, mostly Khampas, were recruited at the Mountain Training Facility at Chakrata under Uban. Some of them were imparted extensive tradecraft training at a CIA base in Colorado in the USA.

Tibetans were considered totally of independent nature with considerable manly pride which made them less amenable to enforced discipline. So, it was decided that if they were brought under the Army or the Police Act, their very qualities of independent initiative and decision-making, so vital in a patriotic guerrilla would not have desired results. It was, therefore, decided to organize this volunteer force as a civilian force working under the administrative control of the IB. Their training and deployment in peace and war were to be entrusted to an army officer. Initially, there were conflicts of opinion regarding training and placement of this outfit with the army authorities because it was to function in close support of the Indian Army in the formations manning the borders. However, the diktat of Uban prevailed and he imparted training to these guerrillas on his own skill and measures. Ultimately, when General Sam Manekshaw visited Chakrata and appreciated the skill, strength and motivation of this force, the army authorities mended their attitude towards this outfit. Intelligence agencies of US and India too worked hard to raise this outfit with Uban. US provided most of the weapons to SFF which consisted of mainly M-1, M-2 and M-3 machine guns. Heavy weapons were not provided due to the difficulty of the hilly terrain. By 1968, SFF (then renamed) with the help of ARC in airlift facility, became fully airborne-qualified and a dedicated mountain and forest warfare unit was operational on the Tibet border.

It would be pertinent to mention here that Jawaharlal Nehru and Dalai Lama visited Chakrata separately to boost the morale of the Tibetan commandos. Nehru promised full support for their cause from his government.

Around this period, the Indian Government also created the Ladakh Scouts and Nubra Guards paramilitary force on similar parameters. As explained above, due to the intra-services rivalry, criticism of this unit by the army became an issue of debate among the government agencies. In order to counter this criticism, Uban sent 120 commandos of SFF for a field exercise, codenamed Garuda, with the army counterparts. The SFF commandos proved their mettle and outwitted army men in this exercise which forced the army bosses to mend their ways and stop criticism. Uban conducted airborne exercises at Agra Air base and later at Sarsawa. By the late sixties, the SFF was organized into six battalions for administrative purposes. Each battalion, consisting of six companies, was commanded by a Tibetan who had a rank equivalent to a Lieutenant Colonel in the army. A Tibetan Major or Captain commanded each company, which was the primary unit used in operations. Cross-border reconnaissance operations were conducted during this period.

Uban played a very important role not only inside the Tibet but also in the Bangladesh war where a large number of SFF men were deployed prior to and during the war. Chakrata was the principal training centre of the Mukti Bahini freedom fighters. Thousands were trained here in the guerrilla warfare. General Manekshaw deployed SFF in the most difficult terrain of Chittagong Tract during this war. This tract of trackless forests and hills surrounded on all sides by water was the most challenging job for the SFF to fight the enemy. This operation codenamed 'Eagle' was conducted by SFF commandos with

AK-47 and US carbines. SFF was given various mission plans in this war which included destruction of Kaptai Dam and other bridges. SFF countered the Pak Army of 97 Independent Brigade and 2 Commando Battalion in the Chittagong Hill Tracts. SFF sealed the only escape route of the Pakistan Army across Arakan Road into Burma (now Myanmar) during the war. It blocked all chances of the Pakistan Army to run for safety when they were awaiting the arrival of the Seventh Fleet of US Navy in the Bay of Bengal. Uban called SFF "Phantoms of Chittagong" and Manekshaw called it "The Fifth Army" after liberation of Bangladesh. In this war 56 SFF commandos lost their lives and 190 were wounded. 580 SFF members were awarded various incentives by the Indian Government for their bravery in this battle. Uban was decorated with the highest award in India, the Param Vishisht Seva Medal (PVSM) for his role in liberation of Bangladesh. Later, Sheikh Mujibur Rahman, the President of Bangladesh, requested the Indian Prime Minister, Mrs Indira Gandhi to send Uban as his Personal Advisor which he did for a brief period.

Prior to the National Security Guard (NSG) which was created by R.N. Kao in 1984 during the wake of militancy in Punjab, SFF was the only crack commando force under R&AW. SFF played a heroic role in the Siachen operation also.

## Aviation Research Centre (ARC)

The Aviation Research Centre (ARC) was a joint venture of India and USA created in 1963 for air intelligence after the 1962 war. It was again the brain-child of the articulate Biju Patnaik, the then Chief Minister of Orissa (now Odisha)and the mercurial confident of Jawaharlal Nehru. Patnaik himself was running the Kalinga Airlines. He was a brilliant and pioneering aviator. His father was imprisoned for around ten years for his fight of Indian independence. Such activism and adventurism were imbibed in him due to this family background. As a teenager, he cycled across the subcontinent, in a remarkable feat, despite the poor road conditions of those days. Patnaik joined the Royal Air Force during World War II and was trained as a pilot. He was honoured by the British for evacuating several British families stranded in Burma (Now Myanmar). He piloted some wartime flights to the Soviet Union and Iran during this war. Despite this background, he too spent several years in prison prior to the independence of India fighting British regime. After his release, Patnaik transformed his flying experience into the aviation business and floated Kalinga Airways, his private enterprise. His initial assignment was to drop food to isolated Indian outposts in the NEFA areas. In a daring operation, he smuggled out an Indonesian leader Muhammad Hutta from Jakarta for an Asian tour when the Dutch were ruling Indonesia. Hutta later became Vice-President of Indonesia. ARC was meant for air support to the SFF commandos during their cross-border operations. It was also assigned the task of training SFF men in para-jumping, dropping supplies in Tibet, electronic intelligence and covert air operations across border. In practicality, it was a system of support to the SFF for espionage activities inside the Tibetan region. R.N. Kao was the obvious choice to head this wing of IB. Kao selected a team of brilliant police and air-force officers for this new outfit. Some scientists too were selected for ARC keeping in view the scientific aspect while conducting some sensitive operations.

Besides Palam Airport, five other small airports were reserved for the secret operations. Of these, the major airbase was set up at Charbatia, 14 Km from Cuttack in Orissa. This was used by Biju Patnaik for the operations of Kalinga Airways. Patnaik provided two sets of crews to ARC at the initial stage. The US provided a team of around a dozen pilots who were stationed at Charbatia. Among them, Jim Ryne was an eminent espionage pilot who besides providing training and coordinating with Indian pilots, carried extensive secret flights over Tibet.

Dumduma beyond Dibrugarh in the north-eastern state of Arunachal Pradesh was another airport used for cross-border operations around eastern Tibet. Sarsawa near Saharanpur was set up for operations in the north-western region. An airfield at Kalsi between Chakrata and Dehradun was mostly used for the SFF operations. The most strategic operational base opened by ARC is Farkhor Air Base in Tajikistan near Pakistan border. It became operational in 2005 with Russian help. This base is within striking distance of a few minutes inside Pakistan. There was lot of hue and cry by Pakistan on its existence but Tajikistan Government did not heed to the protests.

The USA lent full support to establish ARC as an elite air intelligence wing along the Chinese border. ARC was soon equipped with some of the best planes of the time. This included vertical short take-off and landing aircrafts (STOL). Half a dozen C46 commando aircrafts provided by the USA were used for para-drops and transportation purposes. Around 7-10 tonnes of cargo used to be transported by these planes. One of the commando planes, DSA, was fitted with all surveillance equipment. This plane was extensively used around 10-12 hours daily for surveillance flying over 10,000 feet over the Tibet territory. Once a US pilot Jim Ryne landed this plane at Charbatia in almost zero visibility in an area the size of a football ground. This espionage aircraft could land at night and take off at the speed of a car i.e. around 35 miles per hour. These aircrafts were designed by America for the Korean War. These heroics were rare since the secret operations were in an experimental stage at that time. ARC also had two single engine Helios and four twin engine Helios which could fly to a height of over 25,000 feet inside Tibet. Besides these aircrafts, ARC was provided about half a dozen MI-4 and a couple of ME-8s. Another aircraft Huskies H-43 given to ARC was always piloted by Americans. CIA operative Col Culligham was coordinating all these operations from the New Delhi Embassy of USA.

Initially, USA imparted training to the ARC officers in Washington. A six week training programme for the pilots and scientists was conducted for the covert air operations. A team comprising T.A. Subramaniam and L.S. Grewal attended this training. These two were the pivotal force in making the ARC a commendable organization. At a later stage, Subramaniam became head of ARC when Kao was the R&AW Chief.

During the 1971 Bangladesh liberation war, ARC was instrumental in transporting not only the war material for SFF but also carried the guerrillas of Mukti Bahini to far-flung areas of East Pakistan. ARC worked neck-to-neck with the Indian Air Force which decimated the Pakistani air strength in the beginning of the war, and made it non-functional in only in two to three days. The Indian Air Force's supremacy was unchallengeable all over East Pakistan in the liberation war and the ARC was part and parcel of all operational and espionage activities. So, in a span of around 8 years, ARC became one of the best air intelligence organizations of the world. Credit for such ascendancy of this department goes to none other than the legendary R.N. Kao.

In the 1999 Kargil intrusion by Pakistani, ARC was again pivotal in locating the hideouts of these infiltrators. R.S. Bedi, the brilliant Sikh head of ARC, was initially not approached by the army bosses to locate those infiltrators. At that time, ARC planes were stationed on the Chinese border. After request from the army and orders from the Prime Minister Office, ARC planes conducted reconnaissance of the entire Kargil area and provided pictures of almost each and every infiltrator at various locations. This belated exercise conducted by the army authorities remains a matter of mystery and subject matter of investigation. Due to the inept handling of initial operations by army commanders including this delay, many brilliant commandos of the Indian Army lost their lives. When ARC provided actual locations to the army and Air Force, the whole Kargil region was evacuated by their commandos with the help of raids by the Air Force.

After the war, both army and air chiefs highly commended the ARC for providing the exact locations of the infiltrators. They observed that, "The electronic and optical information provided by the ARC before and during the actual operations was of immense value to the conduct of air strikes." The K. Subramaniam committee report on the Kargil war also observed that, "No intelligence failures have been attributed on account of functioning of R&AW and ARC. However, certain equipment inadequacies were highlighted such as satellite imagery and UAVs." These UAVs were not the operational subject of R&AW or ARC to be more precise.

There were media reports during 2015 that the ARC is being bifurcated between the Air Force and National Technical Research Organization (NTRO). This move was floated by the then NTRO Chief Alok Joshi. This officer was mired in a corruption controversy while working as R&AW Secretary. ARC is functioning under R&AW since its inception and proved its worth on every occasion and the latest was the Kargil intrusion by Pakistani infiltrators. Its functioning is co-related with the analytical data of R&AW substantiated with deep research by its operatives on every border location around India. NTRO is not designed to work on the pattern of R&AW. Hence, it would be a suicidal attempt, if ARC is ever divested of R&AW at any period of time.

In addition to these two outwardly different but totally new experiments in the IB, the Special Service Bureau(SSB) and Frontier Rifles (Indo-Tibetan Border Police) too were established with the US and UK collaboration. SSB was created in March 1963. It was envisioned by B.N. Mullick and Patnaik as a motivated and empowered border populace that would offer stiff opposition in very village on every hill bordering China in case of any future intrusion by the Chinese. SSB employed local residents of this hilly terrain in various civic projects such as building roads, schools, hospitals etc. Officials were designated as divisional officers and area organizers to supervise these activities. Rudimentary weapons and guerrilla warfare techniques were also imparted as training to the local population. A Frontier Officers Administrative Training Centre was established for senior SSB officers in the forested hills near Mumbai wherein a six-week training in resistance operations, map reading, demolitions, airdrop techniques and booby-traps was given to them. Weapons from the US, China and the Soviet Union were displayed to the trainees. Initially, for two years the British Military Advisers assisted IB in this venture. Two British Officers, Terrance Kitcat, from SAS and John Edwards of the Royal Maritime Commandos were involved in these training programs with the IB.

ITBP (initially Frontier Rifles) was raised on 24 October 1962 to patrol the world's highest border along China. This name was changed to bar the restriction of deploying military units close to the Tibetan frontiers. Since, the ITBP was to operate in the most rugged and difficult terrains on the borders of China, its members were trained in special skills such as skating, survival in cold-weather and mountaineering. Balbir Singh, another important IB officer was the prime architect of ITBP formulation. Eight battalions were initially sanctioned by the Government for the ITBP. Tenzing Norgay, the famed Sherpa who accompanied Sir Edmond Hillary on the first ascent to the Mount Everest and Captain M.S. Kohli selected some confident Sherpas to train the SSB cadre in mountaineering and snow-craft activities. The ITBP has now 54 battalions deploying around 90,000 personnel.

Following the assassination of John Kennedy on 22 November 1963, the Indo-US relations nosedived gradually. A dilemmatic Johnson administration desired to maintain relations with India as maintained by his predecessor Kennedy to counter the Chinese influence but at the same time sought to strengthen ties with Pakistan with an intention to ease tensions with China. This double-digestion was not acceptable to the Indian policy makers. Johnson being feasted by Ayub Khan with grand honour on his visit to Karachi in May 1961, was sceptical about the favoured position which Kennedy initiated with India in the US South Asia policy. As President, the first senior Indian politician Johnson met was Indira Gandhi. She visited the US in April, 1964. She carried a letter from her ailing father Nehru for Johnson wherein Nehru appreciated the US economic and military assistance during and after the Chinese conflict of 1962. In this meeting, though Johnson indicated US neutrality to the Kashmir dispute between India and Pakistan he mysteriously did not discuss the United States' military assistance to Pakistan which was most important item then on the agenda of both Indian and the American Governments. At that time, the USA was entangled in the Vietnam conflict where 500,000 US soldiers were fighting to save South Vietnam from a communist onslaught from the North Vietnam border. The US policy makers thought pouring millions of dollars on economic aid to India a waste, especially as little development was indicated from it and India remained at odds with much of the US foreign policy. Further, the 1965 India-Pakistan war was perceived by the US as an indication that the two countries were more worried about each other than any other external threat. The USA then considered India an insignificant strategic partner being a big country full of poverty and bad economic conditions.

## Chinese Nuclear Quest

After the formation of People's Republic of China (PRC) in 1949 by the communist forces, the People's Liberation Army (PLA) defeated the Nationalist Kuomintang (KMT) Army of its erstwhile ruler Chiang Kai-shek which was the historical upheaval in Asia much to the chagrin of the US policy makers. At that stage, PLA though victorious over KMT, could not dare to capture Taiwan which was enjoying the US patronage in its vicinity.

Chinese economy too was in shambles at this massive political change-over. More so, China needed an ally for economic, scientific and technical development which could have been none other than its half-brother, the Soviet Union. Soon after the revolution, Mao Zedong, Chairman of the Communist Party of China (CPC) visited Moscow in December 1949 and signed the Sino-Soviet Treaty of Friendship, Alliance and Mutual Assistance with Stalin, the Premier of Soviet Union despite inherent suspicion with which both were viewing each other at that time. Since its inception, Stalin was sceptical of the revolutionary potential of the minuscule Chinese proletariat against the mighty KMT which was bent upon their extinction. Indeed, the Soviets were cooperating with the KMT until 1949. In the concluding civil war with KMT, Soviets favoured partition of territory between two factions which CPC declined. During the last stages of civil war, Soviet Union hastily concluded agreements with KMT forces for special mining rights in Sinkiang and with the Chinese North-East People's Government for trade. Therefore, mistrust was apparent but Mao considered these actions of little significance in comparison to other Soviet sacrifices.

Stalin and Mao, although underneath various pros and cons against each other for past misdemeanour, had common antagonism towards the might of US which underwrote all other considerations in nurturing the alliance. Although, this Sino-Soviet cooperation was not particularly favourable to China, it promised China a Soviet "nuclear umbrella" against any such threat from US or Japan. Both China and the Soviet Union were apprehensive, as such, that the US was asserting in Asia through rearmament of Japan.

The Soviet Union imposed some severe terms and conditions in this first phase of Sino-Soviet military cooperation. First phase of a $300 million loan was to be repaid by China with exports of raw materials thus tying Chinese extractive industries to Soviet processing facilities and Soviet markets and deepening China's economic dependence on the Soviet Union. An even more exploitative action was the Joint-Stock Rare Minerals Corporation set up in the Sinkiang Province. Soviet domination of this venture resulted in the whole of the uranium production of China returning to the USSR.

However, the intervention of USA in the Korean conflict redefined the new Sino-Soviet military relationship and China got the latest war planes including Mig-15s but Soviets never allowed any assistance in defence production including nuclear armaments. A strong challenge to the credibility of the Soviet deterrent to a US attack on China was imminent when in 1953 President Eisenhower threatened PRC of nuclear invasion if a truce was not reached immediately in Korea. Soon thereafter, Chinese nuclear scientists rushed to Moscow with the main objective of transfer of nuclear weapons and delivery systems on priority basis to China. Obviously, the Soviet Union offered China all possible support in this regard. Thereafter by 1953 the Chinese, under the guise of peaceful use of nuclear energy, had initiated research leading to the development of nuclear weapons. Thus, a technology transfer agreement was initiated with the Soviet Union to produce nuclear weapons and ballistic missile-delivery systems.

After Stalin's death, his successors were not so eloquent to support China and risk a nuclear confrontation with the USA over Korea or even Taiwan issue. As a result of this non-cooperation of the Soviet Government, China was forced to sign an agreement with the United Nations on Korea war wherein more than 200,000 soldiers were lost including the POWs in addition to bearing the expenses of the war. China thus suffered again from its dependence on the Soviet Union during the Korean conflict.

In 1955, Nikita Khrushchev, the successor of Stalin, provided scientific and technical assistance to China for the development of atomic energy for peaceful purposes. A chemical separation plant was set up in Sinkiang and an Institute for Physics and Atomic Energy was established in Beijing with Soviet aid. Further, a gaseous diffusion uranium enrichment plant was established in Lanzhou to produce weapon-grade uranium. Later, the Soviet Union signed another agreement providing China with a reactor, cyclotron, fissionable material and the required technical assistance. Experimental heavy water reactor too was supplied. Soon thereafter, approximately 260 Chinese scientists and technicians were trained at the Dubna Non-Military Research Centre near Moscow. Around the same number of scientists from counterparts of the Soviet Union visited China to work in its nuclear industry. Later, China sent uranium to USSR in exchange for two R-2 ballistic missiles. Khrushchev was however having some ideological and strategic disagreements with Mao which made him suspicious of the Chinese around this period. Events during 1956 began to manifest the stress in Sino-Soviet relations.

In 1957, the Soviet Union reviewed its foreign policy towards USA and emphasized "peaceful co-existence" as the general principle for all practical purposes. This Soviet dictum sent a hidden message to China's aspiration of liberating Taiwan and other offshore islands and did not wish to become involved in conflicts with the USA over China's ambitious plans such as taking over Taiwan which was protected by the American fleet. There was no better way to prevent China from becoming too ambitious than slowing down Soviet military aid to it, especially cooperation in nuclear development. It was targeted against China to control its increasingly militant and untenable assertions strategically against USA and its other neighbours. It was apparent that China would not risk attacking Taiwan without the Soviet nuclear backing.

Chairman Mao was always apprehensive of the Soviet leadership to make China an independent entity in nuclear capability. He was however, desirous to get whatever assistance the Soviet Union could provide without compromising the

Chinese independence. However, Mao was ambitious to acquire nuclear technology at any cost to make China a world power. So, China had no option but to depend on the Soviet nuclear umbrella as well as Soviet aid to its own nuclear production. On 15 October 1957, an agreement on "new technology for national defence" was finally concluded between the USSR and the PRC. The precise terms of this agreement are still unknown to the world community but it was likely, as some experts on Sino-Soviet relations observed, that they were vague and general. China's disclosure in 1963 of this agreement did not specify its content but stated that in June 1959, the Soviet Government unilaterally disbanded this agreement and refused to provide China with a sample of an atomic bomb and technical data concerning its manufacture which was earlier agreed to.

There were some pertinent compulsions for Khrushchev while withholding this nuclear aid to China in view of its dominance over the entire communist community of the world. The Soviets were not having any political control or military presence over China which they had on other East Europe allies. More so, as there is no evidence that the Soviets ever contemplated sharing nuclear weapons with any of their East European allies, there was no reason for them to provide such strategic weaponry and technology to China when there was no control over its eventual end use.

At that point of time Khrushchev too was engaged in power struggle in his own country. He was anxious to seek CPC support of its elements so that the Chinese could be convinced that his supremacy would be in their own interest. Khrushchev was aware that China would go nuclear, with or without his assistance. In that case, it was in Soviet interest to entangle in Chinese nuclear program so that presence of their technicians would ensure inside information on what the Chinese were doing and some degree of control over the evolution of the

Chinese weapons development programme. More so, in the guise of this aid, Khrushchev ensured tacit Chinese acceptance of Nuclear Test Ban Treaty which he was negotiating with the US and Britain. In this backdrop, the Soviets used the nuclear aid as leverage in 1958 to exert military control over China and to influence their foreign policy. China refused to yield to this agenda of the Soviet Union. Thus, the Chinese put some harsh conditions in the bargaining for the nuclear aid in order to test Soviet reliability. Once the Chinese were convinced that they could not get what they had expected, they continued on their own course contrary to Soviet policies with the West. The Sino-Soviet treaty ultimately boomeranged and China defied the Nuclear Test Ban Treaty when it did not get Soviet nuclear aid.

Three major events during 1957-58 were the genesis of mutual distrust between the Soviets and the Chinese. In May, 1958, China officially launched the "Great Leap Forward" philosophy wherein the need to make China economically strong was emphasized so that a support base is available for military and nuclear development. The theme that men were more important than weapons and weapons alone could not decide the outcome of war was though propagated but a nuclear arsenal too was linked with this ideology. Khrushchev was against the "Leap Forward" movement of China. In view of this Chinese open dictum of independent desire to become a nuclear power, the Soviet Union was forced to rethink its policy to provide nuclear aid to China. Khrushchev did not want to increase the risk of any sort of conflict with the west on this count. He had probably imagined that a China with atomic weapons would be more reckless and could become dangerous to the Soviet Union in future. Secondly, in 1958, China attacked two disputed islands Quemoy and Matsu in its quest to ultimately capture Taiwan to which the US retaliated and threatened a nuclear attack on mainland China. No Soviet support came forward in this Taiwan

Strait crisis at that time. In a face-saving scenario, China relented and the Chinese Premier Zhou En-Lai offered to renew ambassadorial level talks with the US to resolve the crisis. Status quo was maintained. Thirdly, the Soviets maintained neutrality on Sino-Indian border clashes in 1959.

By this time it was evident that no substance was left in any sort of Sino-Soviet alliance for nuclear cooperation. In 1959, the Soviet Union unilaterally abrogated the 1957 secret agreement and withdrew all Soviet experts and technicians from China by 1960. This decision of abrupt Soviet disruption of all nuclear cooperation slowed down the development of nuclear weapons in China. The Chinese were then convinced that the Soviets could not be trusted as an ally henceforth in the future. In retrospect, the Sino-Soviet secret agreement of 1957 was doomed to failure. Thereafter, from 1960 onwards, the Chinese proceeded with the development of their nuclear capability on the basis of self-reliance. This Sino-Soviet split on nuclear cooperation was irreversible, even though the full extent of it was revealed only three years later.

Khrushchev justified his policy toward China by over-emphasizing China's military, economic and political vulnerability. He apparently believed that China was totally dependent on the Soviet Union for its nuclear deterrent and this split would be fatal to China which would have to come around to the Soviet policies sooner or later. More so, Khrushchev had a strong disliking of Mao whom he considered as chauvinistic, arrogant and bloodthirsty. Unfortunately, the Chinese were more than willing to compete with Khrushchev in risk-taking.

When the Nuclear Test Ban Treaty (NTBT) was formulated by the USA, Britain and the USSR, China declared them gangsters for trying to exert pressure on China not to go nuclear. Officials statements subsequently issued by Beijing and Moscow also served to confirm China's intent to develop its own nuclear weapons and Moscow's reluctance to see Beijing acquire an independent nuclear capability. Around this period, China was on the threshold of completing the development of an atomic weapon. Chinese criticism of NTBT was obvious in view of its own competence to go nuclear. Hence, its assessment of a post-nuclear test-blast hostility among the World Community made it employ a deceitful move wherein China made an appeal for immediate and complete prohibition and destruction of nuclear weapons through a summit conference of all nations in the World which was a ploy to save its own skin.

China was aware that no country would yield to its self-proclaimed peace initiative which was devised to unfold its own intention in the near future. Failing in the acceptance of this appeal, China continued its own program of nuclear development and on 16 October, 1964 exploded its first nuclear weapon at Lop Nor in Gobi desert of Xinjiang province, Western China, close to the ancient Silk Route. By sheer co-incidence, it was the time Khrushchev was falling from power. So, China became the fifth nuclear power along with the USA, Britain, France and the Soviet Union. In this operation code-named 59-6, an implosion type device was mounted on the top of a steel tower, producing a yield of 22 kilotons, comparable to the atomic bomb dropped on Nagasaki in the Second World War. Incidentally, the code-name 59-6 was a titular in-your-face reply to the Russians derived from 1959 and June when the USSR declined to give China a prototype nuclear weapon.

The US Govt. was caught unaware on the possibility of China's capability to acquire such nuclear capacity wherein enrichment of U-235 isotopes could have taken place and that too, without Soviet help. This Chinese test came about two years after the Cuban Missile Crisis, three years after the 1961 Bay of Pig invasion wherein the CIA failed to oust Castro from power and at a time when the US was deepening its commitments in South Vietnam. In other terms, this test was conducted during a period wherein unprecedented tension had mounted between the US and the Communist Bloc particularly in Vietnam. More so, a regional challenge to the allies of USA was seen in the offing by some experts. China attained a boost of its morale in the success of this test which could heighten its profile as a major Asian power, militarily and otherwise. Taiwan, then holding a permanent seat in the UN Security Council, desired to attack China with the US support, which was not considered feasible by the US authorities in view of other compulsions like its deep involvement in the on-going Vietnam War.

Subsequently, declassified documents from various agencies/ departments of the US Government during Kennedy and Johnson administration revealed that the CIA was monitoring the Chinese nuclear program through various channels. The CIA deployed U-2 flights by Taiwanese pilots for satellite photographing but failed to provide any proof about the gaseous diffusion plant of China at Lop Nor. The CIA earlier made secret use of Peshawar Airport in Pakistan to monitor Xinjiang region of China but it was abandoned when U-2 launched from here was shot down over the Soviet Union and subsequent diplomatic wrangling erupted among the major powers.

India too was concerned about its own safety after the Chinese nuclear blast in its vicinity, Xinjiang being on the northern border of India. More so, India was keen to know the status of China's nuclear program. ARC was established with the help of CIA. Charbatia, one of its air bases was selected by the CIA for air facility of its U-2 plane for surveillance prior to the Chinese blast. In May 1964, a CIA team reached Charbatia with an unidentified spy plane. This plane was sent over Xinjiang for air surveillance. When it returned and landed there, its brake failed and it crossed the end of the runway. The plane was taken to the hangar by ARC officials. Thereafter, the CIA and US air-force officials came to Charbatia, made necessary repairs of the plane and discreetly flew it to some unknown destination.

Thereafter, no such attempt was made from any Indian base by the US administration.

Some US experts suggested direct action against the Chinese nuclear facilities to eliminate its capability. This suggestion was abandoned because majority of their think-tank was unsure whether such action would fully eliminate China's capability and in any case, China could reconstruct its facility again. Suggestions to enforce a test-ban on China with Soviet support were considered as out of reach. Policy Planning Council of the State Department mooted a proposal to reduce the political impact of this blast to make India a nuclear power because it was in their mind that the Non-Communist India would be a countering force to the Communist China in this region. Although India was cautioned by a visiting Japanese parliamentary delegation in 1963 of Chinese nuclear designs, it was not given any credence in view of lack of concrete evidence. US, India and even Taiwan in combined efforts could not form some reliable intelligence network in the mainland China to keep a tab on its nuclear advancement.

China's nuclear mission sent the US Government in general and intelligence community in particular into a state of extreme tizzy. The US Air Force Technical Applications Centre, which was responsible to operate a global network of nuclear-event detection sensors to monitor nuclear program, was the most concerned agency in this regard. From a total of thirteen of its worldwide electromagnetic pulse stations, eleven of it along with seven of its acoustic stations accumulated data on the timing and yield estimate of this Chinese explosion. Special Jet aircrafts were flown from Japan and Alaska to collect traces of nuclear debris. It was concluded on the basis of these data that this Chinese bomb had been of small capacity of about twenty-five kilotons and was not suitable for delivery by missile.

In the aftermath of this explosion, Washington was apprehending further high-priority objectives of China to conduct a sophisticated thermonuclear test in the near future. the US experts had indicated prior to this test that China could develop a nuclear-tipped missile of medium range which can target any Asian country. Monitoring of China's missile technology was more difficult than its nuclear tests because unlike bombs, rockets do not have acoustic or electromagnetic signatures which could be detected from a long distance. They also do not release any debris which could be collected to measure the intensity. Missile tests, however, had some other flaws when conducted. During such tests, rockets are rigged to radio data so that the scientists and engineers could determine pressure, temperature, direction and fuel consumption of all sorts. Overall, the telemetry would provide a blueprint on the capabilities of the delivery system. More so, these transmissions were vulnerable to eavesdropping.

The USA had discreetly launched its first Ferret satellite in June 1962. This satellite was capable of tapping telephone conversations and missile telemetry. It was further supplemented with a number of ground-based dishes operated by the US Air Force which focused mainly on recording remote telemetry signals. However, there were some drawbacks in both of these eavesdropping systems. The USA did not possess the number of Ferrets satellites required in such operations. Positioning of any of such satellites over the target during the missile launch was extremely dim. The ground-based dishes were operating from the soil of USA wherefrom it was extremely difficult to monitor China's likely missile test on Xinjiang or any other island. The USA had monitored such USSR launches from Badaber in Pakistan during 1959 but existing mountains and the curvature of earth were deterrent to monitor such Chinese tests.

Despite all such pros and cons measured by the US administration, Chinese nuclear blast was a flashpoint on the agenda of the CIA. Now, whatever happened was a matter of discussion only and what should be done to monitor the future dimensions of such blasts became the priority for the CIA and none other than India was chosen as the partner in this venture of unpredictable consequences.

❑

# 3

# Device On Nanda Devi

Neither the US administration nor the Indian Government has disclosed as to how the idea to plant a remote nuclear sensor high in the Himalayas got momentum after the October 1964 nuclear explosion of China. The only reliable details available about this dangerous and discreet operation are in the book "Spies in the Himalayas" written by an American Kenneth Conboy and Manmohan Singh Kohli, the Indian Mountaineer. Kohli was head of the expedition of this mission. Conboy has probably contributed the US version of various events in this book whereas Kohli has revealed his participation in this mission under the direction of the then IB hierarchy who got this operation conducted, who were none other than the mercurial IB Director B.N. Mullik and the then head of ARC, R.N. Kao. In the book "Mission R&AW" written by the author, hundreds of pages have been written exclusively about the legendary R.N. Kao. Hence, it would be futile to repeat those details here to describe Kao's heroics as an Intelligence Icon of India. Kohli too has disclosed the real story of this operation after a revelation of this mystery which surfaced on 17 April 1978, when Howard Kohn wrote a detailed article in the US magazine "Outside".A lot of hue and cry was sounded not only in the Indian Parliament on that day but also in the print media across India.

Curtis Emerson LeMay, the US Air Force General during 1961-65, conceived the idea of planting a nuclear device on the Mount Everest after the first successful American expedition to this summit with a small team of Sherpa guides. This idea was dropped because the Mount Everest was found vulnerable to being discovered by a potential Chinese summit attempt. LeMay was qualified to take such dangerous and controversial decisions in view of his dubious past misdemeanours. His own theory on the use of nuclear weapons must have spiced up his dangerous imaginations. He was a hardcore opponent of communism and did not hesitate to use any weapon, be the conventional or nuclear. In 1949, when the Soviet Union detonated their first A-Bomb, he proposed dropping the entire US stockpile of atomic bombs in a single massive attack meaning thereby to drop 133 atomic bombs on 70 cities of the Soviet Union in just 30 days. During the Cuban Missile crisis he clashed with President Kennedy and Defence Secretary Robert McNamara desiring to bomb the nuclear missile sites in Cuba and to defy the naval blockade imposed by the USA. Even after the crisis was over, he suggested bombing Cuba which was not accepted by Kennedy. During the Second World War, LeMay while directing the bombing campaign against Japan, was responsible for the killing of around 500,000 Japanese civilians and left five million homeless. Around 40% of the built-up areas of 66 cities of Japan were destroyed including much of Japan's war industry.

During the summer of 1964, LeMay was convinced by an American mountaineer Barry Bishop, who climbed the Mount Everest in 1963, to plant this nuclear device at Kanchenjunga Mountain facing China's Xinjiang province. LeMay was responsible to track and monitor the nuclear testing program of various countries. So the Bishop idea was practically acceptable to LeMay who ventured it with the US authorities including CIA, which attained warm relations with India's IB after the 1962 debacle of China. Barry Bishop was also a staff photographer with National Geographic Society where LeMay was a trustee. Bishop was also scientific adviser to the US Rear Admiral Richard Byrd prior to his death in 1957. In view of his proximity with these top US defence hierarchy, Bishop was acclaimed as a resourceful and dynamic personality whose words carried weight. Therefore, LeMay acknowledged his proposal as a possible attempt to monitor the Chinese nuclear devices.

According to M.S. Kohli, it was intriguing that Bishop came to India and met him on 20 February, 1965. Obviously, Bishop was on this CIA assignment after a decision was taken by both India and USA to plant this device in a mountain in India. Kohli, knew Bishop, but had met him only once in a brief meeting when an American mission was heading for the Mount Everest in 1963. Bishop also did not perform the mandatory requirement of informing the Indian Mountaineering Authorities prior to his arrival. He asked Kohli to accompany him on a scouting trip to the Zemu Glacier at the base of Kanchenjunga Mountain. Kohli refused because he was preoccupied with his expedition to the Mount Everest along with his other team members. Apprehensive of the sudden arrival of Bishop and his insistence to accompany him to Kanchenjunga, Kohli sent a brief note to B.N. Mullik, Director of IB, to monitor the motives of Bishop in India. Kohli revealed that Bishop was actually sent by Mullik to him. It is intriguing that instead of roping in Bishop to gauge Kohli's desire to participate in any such operation, Mullik was too powerful to call all and sundry including Kohli, who was his subordinate in ITBP, to discuss the plan of planting the nuclear device with CIA. Such titbits revealed by Kohli throw poor light on the personality of the indomitable Mullik. Apparently, it was uncalled and inconceivable.

Initially, the CIA broached this program with R.N. Kao who was the then Director of the ARC the air intelligence wing of

IB newly conceptualized with the help of CIA. Kao discussed this plan with Mullik and agreed in principle subject to political approval. Lal Bahadur Shastri, the then Prime Minister of India, gave his consent to Mullik for this placement. There is no reference anywhere whether consent of the Indian Prime Minister Shastri was taken or not. This was confirmed to this author by the late R.N. Kao during a course of routine discussion with him. Hence, all apprehension that B.N.Mullik was the final authority for approving this expedition is absurd and intentional in view of his dominating personality. Although, Mullik had retired as the Director of IB, he was holding charge of ARC, SFF and SSB which were at embryonic stage at that time. An agreement to this operation was duly signed by the IB and CIA for a joint Indo-US climbing operation to install the device at some suitable mountain facing Xinjiang in China. It would be pertinent to mention here that the CIA did not disclose the components of this nuclear device in this agreement. Surprisingly, the IB authorities particularly Mullik did not take cognizance of this fact either out of the urgency of this matter of national security or sheer dominance of the CIA on various security aspects in India. It is intriguing that none of the Atomic Energy scientists were brought in the loop to monitor the components of this nuclear device. Probably, the dominance of the CIA was so obtrusive that IB did not feel it proper to go into deep details about such inside secrets which were CIA's brainchild. The ultimate danger was not the concern of the intelligence community of both the countries. An adventure gone awry?

Once, the Indian authorities consented, the CIA retained Barry as the coordinator of this programme. His selection was based on geo-political consideration as well as on his past foray in this region where the device was to be placed. Bishop had to select a place where the Chinese overreach was a far cry and the Indian jurisdiction was paramount. Hence, the mountains in Nepal and Bhutan bordering China were discounted for this purpose. In order to have an uninterrupted approach towards

Xinjiang, Bishop found Kanchenjunga as the mountain suitable for this mission. It was quite tall and shared border with Sikkim, which was then a protectorate of India and was not on Tibet border. The CIA approved this proposal of Bishop. A joint team of US and Indian climbers was also made, the concern of Bishop which made him visit Kohli at New Delhi in February 1965. Most of the prominent Indian climbers at that time were busy for an expedition to the Mount Everest under the command of Kohli. In the meantime, Bishop was asked by the CIA to assemble the other paraphernalia of this mission.

China conducted another nuclear test on 14 May 1965 by dropping it from an aircraft. It was estimated to be a thermonuclear material and double the size of the first one. So, a missile test could be the next explosion of China nonetheless. In view of this frequency attained by China, the US was keen to place the monitoring apparatus as early as possible on the proposed mountain. Since winter was few months away, Bishop on his side started identifying the private US climbers for this mission assuming the CIA would not provide this facility to him. According to Kohli, a monthly salary of $1000 per month was assigned by the CIA to these climbers. Bishop sought the help of an another climber James McCarthy who was a practicing lawyer in the USA.

However, a Japanese author Pete Takeda in his book "AN EYE AT THE TOP OF THE WORLD" disclosed that these private climbers were paid huge sums of money rather than the paltry $1,000 per month claimed by Kohli. They were also stated to have sworn to secrecy on penalty of death. This could be an acceptable disclosure in view of the secrecy of this mission. But a real absurdity mentioned by Takeda was that the plutonium-powered device was stolen from the fissile material in a secret Pakistani nuke. This weird assumption could perhaps be a by-product of fairy tale mongers living on the US soils. Takeda too visited India while exploring details of this mission. But in

India there was no chance of floating any such felonious theory because participants in this mission were die-hard nationalist serving officers on an oath of secrecy. Takeda was either grossly misled by some US element or he deliberately mentioned to sensitize it for the sale of his book. It seems an absolutely worthless and stupid statement without having any historical or political knowledge of this region.

After consultation with McCarthy, Bishop selected Luther Jerstad, Gil Blinn, Tom Frost and Harthon Sandy Bill, all private citizens of USA for this assignment. Jerstad had accompanied Bishop on the 1963 Everest expedition. He was a young mountaineer who had climbed many mountains in the USA. He was a speech instructor and held a doctoral degree in theatre. Jerstad selected Gil Blinn who was a fellow trail guide from Mount Rainier. He had a brief stint in the army also. McCarthy proposed Tom Frost, a pioneer climber of USA of that period. He was an aerospace engineer who was designing mountaineering equipment as his business venture. McCarthy's next choice was Sandy Bill who had considerable mountaineering experience in Europe and Pacific Northwest. Bishop proposed to the CIA a medical doctor and climber Robert Schaller for this mission who was undergoing surgical residency in his profession. Schaller had undertaken many known climbs and was well conversant with high-altitude medicines. The CIA directly approached Schaller who agreed to participate in this cloak-and-dagger mission.

This team of climbers assembled in May 1965, in USA to study the technical aspects of the expedition. Bishop was coordinating every aspect of this mission with the CIA help. Bishop, on his own, finalized Kanchenjunga which was a horrendous climb. These climbers were expected to take heavy and delicate equipment which were required to be assembled at an extreme altitude. This had to be accomplished with India's help which was not decided by then. So, a trial run prior to this expedition was proposed in Alaska at Mount McKinley.

While the US climbers retreated from this trial at Mount McKinley due to the frequent avalanching which could be fatal at times, Kohli's Mount Everest mission was a monumental success of mountain history. Under his stewardship, Indian mountaineers had climbed the Mount Everest four times in ten days which is a record even today. India became the fourth country to scale the peak after Britain, Switzerland and the USA. Kohli and his team were accorded a rousing welcome at the New Delhi Airport by a gathering of thousands of people. Most of the political dignitaries were also present on the tarmac to greet Kohli and his team of 19 members. Kohli was acclaimed a National Hero by the Indian media.

Just after his arrival from the Mount Everest mission, Kao called Kohli to his R.K. Puram office and asked him to prepare to go to the USA along with a team of his climbers for a specialized training. Kao revealed to Kohli that an Indian team would be trained in the United States to install a monitoring device on a major mountain peak. Kao informed Kohli that he would be the leader of the joint Indo-US team. Kohli was asked to select his team of mountaineers along with a doctor. Kohli sought a fortnight's time to complete all these formalities to which Kao readily agreed in view of Kohli's pre-occupation after the Mount Everest victory celebrations by the government and civil society.

Unlike the USA, India did not recruit private climbers for this mission because a number of the IB officials were trained in mountain climbing after the 1962 war with China. So, Kohli had the best climbers at his disposal, and most of them were his good friends. Kohli selected the following four mountaineers from the available lot. Some of these legends are no more now. Readers may be anxious to know their past life and present status. So, small descriptions about these luminaries would be a best tribute to them.

## Harish C.S. Rawat

The first and foremost choice of Kohli for this mission was none other than H.C.S. Rawat, a highly acclaimed mountaineer of that era. Harish Rawat was born in the family of the famous Pandit Brothers who surveyed Tibet. His grandfather Kisan Singh and his cousin were pioneering employees of the Survey of India. In order to rebuff the xenophobic myth of the Tibetan Buddhists, they disguised themselves as monks and carried a hidden equipment to survey distance and locations in these difficult terrains. Once when Kisan Singh went to Tibet and did not return for more than four years, he was assumed as dead. He returned with the most accurate cartographic sketches of Tibet made at that time. Harish Rawat was born in this brave family in 1934. He was a devout Hindu, devoted mountaineer and above all, a selfless man of rare qualities. Rawat's mettle was beyond reproach. Kohli remembered one incident when he fell more than 3,000 feet when he was swept off his feet by an avalanche during the 1964 expedition of Trishuli. After a perfunctory check for broken bones, Rawat spent no time scrambling back to regain the lost altitude. Such an instinct for the natural climbing was imbibed in this genius of his trade. Beside this mission, Rawat participated in a number of expeditions including Kanglacha, Hathi Parbat, Trishuli, Rathong, Nandakhat and Nun Kun. In 1965, he climbed Mount Everest. During this expedition, Rawat alone walked through the death zone to join the advance party of H.P.S. Ahluwalia and Phu Dorji on the summit. He is the only person in the world to achieve this rare feat. This was a world record also because never before had three members reached the top of Mount Everest together. Rawat was a member of the Silk Route Expedition which followed Marco Polo's route to China. He could identify some of the areas visited by his grandfather, in Tibet as well as in Central Asia. This author had the privilege to meet him while he was serving on a desk in R&AW. Rawat had served in the Indian embassies in Nepal and Bhutan. Rawat was decorated by the Govt. of India with various awards including the Arjuna Award, Padma Shree, Police Medal and IMF Silver Medal. He had served the Indian Mountaineering Foundation for over two decades and was instrumental in taking it to the international level. After his retirement from R&AW, he was involved in greening of the high-altitude areas and took active interest in empowerment of women of his birth place. This climber of par excellence passed away on 20 January 2008. Such a distinctive mountaineer was in the team that was selected by Kohli for this US training program.

## Sonam Wangyal

The Second choice of Kohli was Sonam Wangyal, an IB official who had climbed the Mount Everest in 1965 at the tender age of 23. Hailing from Ladakh, Wangyal was a born climber. In addition to his mountaineering feat, Wangyal had a distinctive past when he almost lost his life for this nation. He is the sole survivor of the encounter that took place between the Indian CRPF patrol and Chinese forces on October 21 1959 under the leadership of Karam Singh, the valiant IB officer, at Hot Springs on the Indo-China border in Ladakh. Ten CRPF soldiers were killed by heavily outnumbering Chinese forces. Nine others including Karam Singh were taken as prisoners by the Chinese forces. The remaining personnel, most of whom suffered serious injuries in the heavy firing by the Chinese forces, retreated. Among them was the wounded Sonam Wangyal. October 21 is commemorated as the Police Day all over the country by the police forces in memory of the 10 CRPF officials who had laid down their lives at Hot Springs. Young Wangyal had several outstanding qualities which Kohli referred to. He was found thoroughly trustworthy, utterly selfless and impossible to anger. He was an outstanding team man. He was far away from any ego even after accomplishing a rare feat at an early age. He had superlative physical power due to his upbringing on the mountains. He possessed a seemingly inexhaustible supply of energy. Kohli recalls that during a famous episode, he had been blown into an impossibly deep crevasse, a predicament that would have killed most men. But Wangyal, totally freezing, injured and without proper equipment, somehow managed to work his way out of the chimney like a spider. Such was the power dominance of this great mountaineer. He was awarded the Padma Shree by the government and later he earned the Arjuna Award. He was the Principal of the Sonam Mountaineering Institute in Gangtok, Sikkim, from 1976 to 1990. He retired as an Assistant Director from the ITBF in 1993. He settled down in Leh to look after a hotel - The Mentokling Hotel - which he opened on a piece of land gifted by the Jammu and Kashmir Government in 1968. His expertise of high altitudes is often utilized by the ITBF to guide the young recruits on healthcare at high altitudes. His knowledge of the hills and mountains is mind-boggling. He is acclaimed as a"Hero" in Leh for his rare past achievements. This son of the soil was the second choice of Kohli for the mission ahead.

## Gurcharan Singh Bhangu

Gurcharan Singh Bhangu, a turbaned Sikh like Kohli, was working with the Punjab Police prior to joining the IB in 1961. He started climbing while serving in police. He was a technical officer handling wireless communication work. His expertise was immensely useful for the climbing operations wherein he was an important link to the base and summit expeditions. During the 1965 Everest mission, he was responsible for handling the radio transmission and did his job marvellously. This veteran mountaineer is leading a healthy retired life in Mohali in Punjab after his retirement from the IB. Kohli's selection of Bhangu for the US sojourn was quite appropriate.

## Sonam Gyatso

Sonam Gyatso was the first person from Sikkim to scale the Mount Everest. He was the oldest person to do so in mountaineering history then. He set a world record by spending 50 minutes without oxygen supply on this highest peak of the world. Gyatso as a young man was a travelling cigarette salesman and would trek upto 15,000 feet every month to keep himself fit. Subsequently, he joined the Frontier Constabulary Force of Indian Air Force in 1949 before the IB recruited him for a mountaineering career. In 1957 he climbed the Nanda Devi and missed it by ending up 500 feet apart. Gyasto's first major achievement was his successful expedition of Cho Oyu peak in Nepal during 1958. This was the first successful Indian expedition to one of the Himalayan super peaks which Gyatso scaled without bottled oxygen. This success was followed by several successful climbs like Annapurna III in 1961, Kanchengyao in 1961, Hathi Parbat in 1963, Rathong peak and Langpo Chug in 1964. He was selected by the government to run a new Mountaineering Institute in 1963 in his native state for the IB. The prime objective of this institute was to train IB personnel to perform duties at difficult terrains in the high Himalayas. He and Kohli were part of the 1960 and 1962 Everest teams wherein in one mission they both spent six nights in the death-zone without bottled oxygen. Government of India awarded him the Padma Shree in 1962 and later with the higher award of Padma Bhushan in January 1965. Sikkim Government too awarded him with their highest civilian award of Pema Dorji the same year. He was also given Arjuna Award by the Govt. of India. Gyatso also received the Gold Medal from Indian Mountaineering Foundation in 1960 after his first attempt of Mount Everest. Sikkim Government named the Old Tibet Road as Sonam Gyatso Road in his honour after his death. The Mountaineering Institute at Rathong, Sikkim where he served as the founder Principal was renamed in his memory as Sonam Gyatso Mountaineering Institute since 1968, the year he died. Hence, Gyatso was the natural choice for the forthcoming mission of Indian mountaineers. Besides Gyatso's stamina, fortitude and formidable climbing experience, Kohli wanted him due to his extreme enthusiasm. Kohli revealed his love for drinking when he took several glasses of beer prior to a reception with the Indian Prime Minister Nehru. He was a prolific narrator of events and had close rapport with the Sherpas and porters due to his extraordinary quality of humour. Kohli found in him the perfect expedition companion for the forthcoming mission.

Despite these four experienced climbers, Mullik included two more persons in this training program. One was Devi Singh Sisodia, a Delhi Police official working with the IB. He was a try-out for the Everest climb but could not succeed in the final cut. The second was Pedro Tripathi, a practicing physician serving with the SSB. They both were the confidante of Mullik.

On 19 July 1965, Kohli and his six teammates were discreetly boarded in an Air India flight without frisking of any sort. It was a covert operation probably directed by the CIA to IB keeping future ramifications in view. After a brief stopover at Heathrow Airport, London for refuelling, they landed at New York. The CIA received them and whisked them away without any immigration formalities. After some obligatory sightseeing in New York and Washington, the CIA officials took the Indian contingent in a plane for their next destination at Elmendorf Air Force base in Alaska. They were joined there by their American counterparts for finalizing further action on the proposed training program. Bad weather delayed the climb on McKinley.

However, the CIA technician Gordon Sleeper (could be a pseudo identity) displayed the mock-up of the monitoring device to the Indian trainees. He began the training to familiarize them with the hardware. According to Kohli there were four major components to the sensor duly connected by streams of wires and cables. Two of the pieces were little more than metal boxes placed atop posts to keep them off the snow and ice. These were the transceivers marked or labelled B1 and B2 which would relay the collated missile information to the base station on the Indian soil. The third component was the collection antenna which would catch and transmit the telemetry data from the Chinese nuclear explosions. The six feet tall antenna was similar to the standard television aerial found atop the American homes. The last component described as SNAP 19C, abbreviated from System for Nuclear Auxiliary Power, was a thermoelectric generator capable of forty watts of continuous output for two years. It was informed that the SNAP would derive its power from the heat generated by the radioactive decay. It was stated to be meant for use in devices placed at remote and unattended locations for extended periods. The Indian team was informed that it was incorporated into a mountaintop sensor for the first time. It was also disclosed that various classes of this system had already been integrated into the US Government meteorological stations successfully as lights on buoys and also in satellites. The SNAP resembled a metallic mushroom from some distance. The heart of the system was a hexagonal block of graphite. Seven small rods, termed fuel capsules, went into holes drilled around the block, with one hole along the axis and six around it. According to the US operative, these seven capsules contained 1,734 grams of plutonium, mainly the PU-238 isotope. The block was sheathed in a squat, cylindrical aluminium container. Forty-five aluminium fins were arrayed around it to dissipate heat more effectively. The SNAP was then mounted on a single post, forming the "stem" of the mushroom. The climbers had inspected the entire device but without functional fuel rods. During the next few days, the Indian team practiced unpacking the components, fixing posts and stabilizing wires to the ground and connecting cables. They also did drills on aligning the antenna and doing a system check of the receivers. The Indian team thus became conversant with the mock system of the SNAP and its installation procedure.

When weather conditions improved on 27 July, both Indian and the US climbers were taken to a large snowfield near McKinley where they practiced assembling the device in natural conditions. They were also trained to use explosive, if required, to blast out a shelf to secure the sensor atop Kanchenjunga. However, at no point of time it was discussed neither by the CIA or IB nor the trainees as to what were the chances of losing the sensor in case of any accident or natural calamity. Moreover, it was certain that SNAP 19C was not a nuclear bomb as it did not have a trigger to explode but it was foolhardy not to assess that it was powered by radioactivity and could be toxic to the humankind if encountered anywhere. The plutonium radiation in addition to many health hazards could cripple the bones and even makes plants radioactive. This dangerous proposition eluded the entire think-tank intelligence community of both the US and India.

According to Kohli, after this initial training he realized the practical aspect of this expedition on Kanchenjunga. Named after Five Treasures of the Snow because of its five distinct summits, the highest of which was 28,169 feet, this was one of the most massive and complex mountains in the world. It was considered more difficult to climb than the Everest. Kohli analysed that the combined 125 pounds of sensor gear would require at least four climbers to haul at high altitude. More so, it took about two hours to properly assemble the device on a level snowfield. He realized that in normal circumstances, Kanchenjunga, a monstrous mount, was difficult to climb even without any luggage. It was not possible to sustain for more than 40 minutes if it is scaled, leave aside the two hours' time required for assembling the sensor. In the back of his mind, Kohli developed the inkling that it would be a futile exercise by the CIA and IB to install this device on Kanchenjunga which would be unassailable given the type of training his team underwent in USA. However, it was not imperative on his part to discuss this proposition with his CIA counterparts because it was the prerogative of the IB bosses to decide the particular mountain depending upon various considerations including the one which Kohli developed after the full drill.

After returning to India on 13 August, Kohli met Kao and handed him a note detailing the training drill and further assessment about this expedition on Kanchenjunga. According to Kohli Kanchenjunga was a horrendous climb. It was the third highest after the Everest and K2 of Pakistan. It was considered the world's most hazardous peak in view of avalanches due to the worst monsoon conditions. It was never attempted after the failed British summit of 1955. Kohli informed Kao that the idea of this mission on Kanchenjunga was unsound because it was an extremely difficult mountain and with the equipment to climb, chances of success in climbing were one in four. Kohli further informed Kao that the leaders of Sikkim were extremely sensitive to any climbs on Kanchenjunga due to its perceived sacred status. If it was publicly revealed that they had installed equipment on top, major political ramifications would erupt. In view of these hindrances, according to Kohli, Kao was stunned at his outright rejection of Kanchenjunga as it was the choice of the Americans. However, Kao asked Kohli for other options in place of Kanchenjunga. Kohli suggested three alternatives—Trishul, Nanda Kot and Kamet. After three days, Kao informed Kohli that after consulting the CIA, Kanchenjunga had been discounted. However, Kohli's suggestions were also not agreed to, because the American technicians thought that these three mountains were not tall enough and would be eclipsed by neighbouring peaks. Finally, both the CIA and IB agreed to place the device on Nanda Devi.

Kohli later revealed that he was not aware why the CIA selected Nanda Devi after his rejection of Kanchenjunga and also why the height requirement for this objective was reduced. These details are in the CIA's cupboard. He said that eventually the CIA, continuing to lessen their altitude restrictions, approved elevations for sensor placement as low as 20,000 feet. The odds of placement of sensors on Nanda Devi were better than Kanchenjunga but only barely so. Despite seven international attempts on it, only six climbers from three expeditions had stood on Nanda Devi's summit while three lives were lost. It was perceived that the transceivers placed atop Nanda Devi would intercept radio telemetry signals transmitted between the Chinese missiles and ground control. This device, powered by a plutonium battery pack, would then beam the information to the listening station at the ground level. These data could be analysed to get insight about the range, speed and payload of the Chinese missile.

However, it was surprising that while the Mount McKinley expedition was a failure as a climbing exercise for the joint US-Indo expedition, how a much larger mount, the Nanda Devi, was abruptly agreed by the spying agencies of both the countries to be climbed on the eve of the winter season. Perhaps, phobia of a Chinese missile blast was looming large in the minds of CIA and IB, the two most powerful spying agencies of the world because their own credibility was at stake after the first Chinese nuclear explosion, which occurred undetected by both. Such urgency was echoing in the walls of their headquarters because Mullik was a hard-nut to digest any unfulfilled tasks. However, the McKinley training unveiled the prototype of the device which was to be placed atop Nanda Devi. But that presence of Uranium claimed as PU-238 or PU-239 in the sensor was disclosed to the Indian participant is intriguing because had it been so, the IB would have certainly referred to the Atomic Energy authorities to gaze into its perilous aspects. This mystery was discussed by the author with those honchos who had seen the terms of agreement of the two spying agencies which was signed prior to this expedition. Nowhere was the existence of such Uranium disclosed by the CIA to the IB in the terms and conditions of this agreement. However, the Government of India now has no option but to reveal this fact for the safety and security of billions of Indians.

❑

# 4

# US Sophomoric

Nanda Devi like Kanchenjunga, a two-peaked massif, is not a mountain in itself for the millions of Hindu devotees but regarded as the Mother of the Universe. It is venerated as the creator of life and controller of miseries, thus ruler of the death and birth of a Hindu. From her high abode, Nanda Devi is revered as the bridge between earth and heaven, both physical and spiritual. Mythological beliefs consider it as a transitory link in the process where water from land goes to the sky as cloud vapour to pure snow and revert to earth into the glacier before entering a stream to become the Ganges. Hence, Nanda Devi is the main source of water for the holy Ganges. According to Hindu mythology, Rishi-Ganga emanating from the Nanda Devi glacier is described as the earthly home of the Sapt-Rishis (Seven Rishis), seven sages of Hindus represented as seven stars of the constellation i.e. Ursa Major, where they meditated peacefully. The Constellation of Ursa Major has been seen as a Bear, usually a female, by many distinct civilizations for the last 13,000 years. In Hindu Mythology, the seven central stars of Ursa Major that form the cup shape are referred to as Sapt-Rishis. The seven Rishis are Vashistha, Bhardwaja, Jamadagni,

Gautama, Atri, Vishvamitra and Agastya. These seven Rishis are often mentioned in later works as typical representatives of the character and spirit of the pre-historic or mythical period. The Nanda Devi glacier was the living place of these Rishis according to Hindu mythology.

Surrounded by over a dozen almost identical-sized mountains, Nanda Devi is located in Uttarakhand state of India between the Rishi-Ganga valley on the west and the Goriganga valley on the east. The peak, Nanda Devi, meaning as "Bliss-Giving Goddess" is regarded as the patron of Goddess of the Uttarakhand Himalaya. Nanda Devi is the second highest mountain in India after Kanchenjunga bordering Nepal. Prior to the computations in the year 1808, it was considered the highest mountain in the world. Nanda Devi is the crown jewel of a mythic dominion whereupon the sun never sets and as such it is considered the most beautiful mountain in the world. It is a natural buffer zone between the frigid winds waving from Tibet via Himalayan Plateau and the fertile Gangetic Plains, thus benefitting the farmers residing in this region. Around seventy miles of natural fortress of these dozen peaks is its mysterious isolation where entry to the centre of the ring is limited through a single, steep gorge from the west. Rishi-Ganga flows through this narrow portion in around 250 square miles of snow and ice of four glaciers inside this circumference and then becomes part of the sacred Ganges. In order to navigate Rishi-Ganga, expedition of stretches of downward-sloping rock slabs followed by a narrow natural staircase of stones is obviously a very hazardous exercise for climbers. After traversing this difficult terrain, the navigators could go to the foot-steps of the sacred Nanda Devi. Utmost vigilance has to be exercised while reaching this place; else, tragedy is waiting to happen any time in this transit before these foot-steps of Nanda Devi.

Although the US proposition to select Nanda Devi after Kanchenjunga was unimaginative and unrealistic, their diktat prevailed and the IB had to agree for this option. Kohli proposed Nanda Devi Kot as an ideal suggestion but he was informed by Kao that Americans felt it was too low and unworkable. So, Nanda Devi was chosen against the wishes of Kohli and he had no option but to compromise on this proposal rather than to the ridiculous one of the Kanchenjunga. Most of the Indian Mountains are wrapped with different stories related to the ancient Hindu Mythology unlike the Americans where their Mountains are considered none other than conglomeration of different kind of soils and stones without any religious entity. So, Kohli was aware of this distinction about Nanda Devi also but he did not dare to flout again the IB honchos like he did for Kanchenjunga. Kohli was asked to make preparation for this expedition. The first and foremost task before him was to select the Sherpas and Gurkhas to assist his team.

The Sherpas, unlike the Gurkhas, are a famous ethnic group in Nepal living in the remote north-east region of the country. Their existence came into prominence in the international arena after the first Everest reconnaissance in 1921 and thereafter they remained an important part of all the high-altitude mountaineering expeditions. Thereafter, they started residing across Himalayas in the early Sixties expecting employment opportunity during the expeditions. The majority of this population was residing around Darjeeling. Kohli was aware of most of them from their past idiosyncrasies and achievements. Kohli had got some of the Sherpas recruited in the regular pay rolls of SSB and ARC so that they could be available as Government officials for any expedition of, or sponsored by, the Indian Government. Nineteen of such Sherpas were selected by Kohli for this mission. Thirty-three Bhotia porters from Lata and Reini villages, the last two inhabitated villages from the sanctuary, were also employed for this expedition for carrying various items.

The Nanda Devi operation was basically a project conceptualized by ARC, so the ARC fleet was easily available to Kohli. Since, the route of reaching the Sanctuary vide Rishi-Ganga was arduous, aerial options were the only expeditious mode of supplying various essential commodities to the mountaineering team. Kao placed the relevant ARC choppers at the disposal of the team members under the command of Kohli.

This expedition was planned by Kohli with seven stages of camps starting from the sanctuary to the base camp and then on five camps along the summit before the final placement on the top of the mountain. On August 28 1965, Kohli dispatched first batch of climbers consisting of nine Sherpas and two IB officials to the Nanda Devi Sanctuary vide the Rishi-Ganga gorge. These IB officials, Gautam and Sinha were trained mountaineers. This team was given the task of locating and marking a suitable helipad within the Sanctuary for subsequent ARC shuttles. They were further asked to recruit local porters near the sanctuary who could carry the supplies from the helipad to the base of Nanda Devi. This team arrived at Joshimath on 1 September and made necessary purchases of various items essential in this expedition. Joshimath was the last inhabitated town prior to the Sanctuary's gorge entry. The thirty-three porters employed by these IB officials took the expedition items on their back and departed on September 3 along with the other team members.

In the meantime, India-Pakistan war of 1965 started on the western border. Kohli was thus apprehensive about the commencement of the Nanda Devi expedition in view of this border situation where Indian forces were engaged in fierce battle with the Pakistan Army. The IB echelons were fully entangled in this war. Since winter season was also not far away, Kohli was certain that this mission would be postponed for next year. However, he did not get any information from the IB bosses to stop the preparations for the expedition despite this war certifying how important this mission was after the Chinese nuclear explosion of October 1964. Kohli continued his plans according to his itinerary. On 8 September, he dispatched his second batch of mountaineers comprising of Bhangu, Sisodia and seven Sherpas along with the supplies. This contingent was to reach Gaucher, a place above Srinagar in Uttarakhand where an airstrip abandoned in World War II was renovated particularly for this mission.

On 12 September, ARC pilots loaded the first supply items in a Mi-4 chopper from Gaucher and reached the Sanctuary where the first party of two IB officials and nine Sherpas had already arrived from the Rishi-Ganga gorge along with the local porters. ARC officials air-dropped the load to the awaiting members of the first batch. Thereafter, the IB officials and Sherpas prepared a rudimentary helipad for landing the chopper. Subsequent sorties of choppers landed at this temporary helipad and brought all essentials items for the expedition team. A temporary base camp was developed near this place where tents were pitched and kitchen facility was made functional. Bhangu set up his radio set and established wire links with Gaucher airstrip. Soon, both Sonam Wangyals and Sonam Gyasto who were the most experienced mountaineers previously worked with Kohli also joined the team at the base camp.

The US contingent of expedition arrived at Palam airport in New Delhi on 17 September 1965 on a flight stated to be meant for Embassy support, disguised so for security reasons. Sensitive Sensor equipments were also brought in this flight. The IB and CIA officials of US Embassy in New Delhi whisked away them from the tarmac without necessary immigrations and custom formalities. The secret cargo too was discreetly taken from the side gate of the airport. On 18 September Kohli, who was leader of this joint CIA and ARC team, met the US colleagues and arranged a formal gathering at his residence and discussed the future plans with them. For security precautions, the Indians were to cryptically refer to the Americans as “Friends” and the Indian climbers were designated as “Members”. This was probably an initiative instructed by the IB.

Of late, this pseudo-nomenclature is a strange part of anonymity which I have found an essential part of Indian

Intelligence system. Although it is an essential feature of all sensitive covert operations, during our early period of service it became a routine exercise to adopt pseudo-names for security reasons. In our early career we found that even when posted abroad for a normal posting, names in the missions were changed on official records including passports. It was subsequently observed that many officers faced difficulties while getting admissions for their kids in India with their original names because on official records, the names were different or differing in some alphabets. Although official influence resolved such hiccups, it was unwarranted observing the present day working system. Except for some covert operations, names of intelligence officers are now found mentioned on internet in the official portals of all the Embassies and High Commissions. Nowadays, the working culture of the Intelligence Community has undergone a sea-change compared to the past hush-hush. So adoption of "Friends" and "Members" codes was not surprising in this mission in view of the utmost security maintained at that time by IB and CIA.

According to Kohli, the US team comprised of four private mountaineers - Lute Jerstad, Tom Frost, Sandy Bill and Rob Schaller. Besides these, Bill McKniff was the CIA Case Officer in charge of the US in this mission. Another CIA technician Gordon Sleeper was part of the team that was assigned the task of establishing a relay station code-named as the Field Research Unit. Four Indian technicians trained in the United States were deputed to assist Sleeper in this assignment. A small ridge near a small town Sandev about thirty-one miles south of the Sanctuary was selected to establish this Field Research Unit which would receive signals from the sensor after it was installed on mountaintop. This data would then be retransmitted to New Delhi and Washington offices of IB and CIA respectively. The climbers were informed that readouts received from the sensor would be transmitted within three minutes from the time of inception. Another American mentioned as Jim joined the team later. He was stated to be from the US Atomic Energy Commission and was assigned the task of fuelling of the generator at the last moment before they scaled Nanda Devi. Pete Takeda described him as Jim McCarthy, the Undersecretary of US Naval Intelligence. This intriguing US team member later made some controversial statements about this mission. Kohli ridiculed him when questioned about these statements.

Kohli, accompanied by three US climbers – Lute, Tom and Jim departed from New Delhi on 19 September for Gaucher and took a chopper from Kalsi, an airbase of ARC located between Dehradun and Chakrata. Next day, they reached the Sanctuary on a Mi-4 shuttle from Gaucher. After protracting parleys, Kohli and Lute decided to establish a series of four camps above the base camp which was already functional. The team members and the Sherpas would take supplies from these camps stage-by-stage to the highest site. Thereafter, the sensor would be fuelled and passed upward from the Base Camp. Finally, it would be carried to the final camp and placed on the summit and activated. In the meantime, the full contingent of US and Indian mountaineers assembled at the helipad and base camp.

As planned, this expedition team established the first camp on 24 September at a height of 19,000 foot level. Camp two was pitched at 20,200 foot-level on 26 September with extreme difficulties. Subsequently, when camp three was properly made functional at 21,200 foot-level on 2 October Kohli was anxious to scale the next two heights of Camp Four and Five and to summit because the weather conditions were deteriorating day by day. 4 October being Dussehra, all porters and Sherpas celebrated it with food and drinks, the only fanfare available at such heights. However, by this time Camp Three was reinforced with a four-man tent for the final assault upward. Camp Four was planned at 23,750 foot level prior to the Fifth and the summit.

On 7 October, at base camp Jim broke open the safety seal of the large olive-drab box with radiation warnings written on all sides. Inside the box, seven radioactive fuel rods were nestled in individual glass cradles. Jim took out all the cradles with prefect proficiency and inserted them into the generator. Everyone present at that place was watching this mechanism from some distance with extreme silence and anxiety. Just after this installation, everyone present there could feel the heat emanating from the sides of the generator even five feet away. The Sherpas started warming their hands and faces. Though Jim assured that the chance of dangerous radiation was minimal, the "Friends" and "Members" were not interested to join the Sherpas. However, when the Sherpas carried the warming generator towards Camp One, Jim gave each of them a white badge to be pinned to the front of their parkas. According to him, in the unlikely event of excessive radiation leakage, the badge would change colour. As an added precaution Kohli instructed the Sherpas not to carry the load for more than four hours at a stretch before handing it over to another colleague. This was probably done to avoid excessive heat emanating from the sides of the generator which Kohli and his team noticed at the initial stage of assembling of sensor. Everyone was anxious to take these equipments to the summit as early as possible because news of bad weather from Camp Three was reported by the advance party. However, on 8 October, Lute and Bhangu accompanied the sensor and generator at Camp Two with the help of available Sherpas.

The Indian team examining this heating process starting at such cold weather and at this height of expedition, never doubted the assertion of Jim when he claimed that the chances of dangerous radiation was minimal. No Indian nuclear expert was present there to counter-question this possible emanation of radiation which Jim claimed to be minimal. But possibility of radiation was indicated at this initial stage by Jim, the so-called nuclear expert of the USA. He was not a CIA man but a private person hired for this job. The second reason of suspicion which Indian mountaineer did not take into stride was why a white badge was pinned on the frontier of the parkas of the Sherpas claiming to be changing colours in the unlikely event of excessive radiation leakage. These two unusual warnings of Jim were indicative of the fact that these fuel rods contained something abnormal for the fuelling and heating purpose, on which the Indian mountaineers did not question Jim. Hence, there was lack of proper coordination on the part of IB with CIA about the examination of hidden uranium which was placed inside the fuel rods, and as to what the intensity of this dangerous uranium product was. This was not the subject matter of the mountaineers because their preliminary assignment was just to take this equipment for installation at the summit. Hence, they cannot be blamed for the future fiasco which was looming hereinafter. The CIA and IB, both did not venture to examine any so-called danger from this sensor in case it was exposed to some man-made or natural calamity.

On 10 October, Lute and Bhangu along with three Sherpas carried the components of sensor and generator and joined the other team members at Camp Three. Prior to this, two Sherpas climbed Camp Four at 23,750 foot-level and pitched a pair of tents at the place previously used for expeditions to the peak by some other climbers. Hence, Kohli was confident that in the moderate weather, his team would surge to Camp five and to the top after two Sherpas reached Camp Four. On 12 October, Sonam and his party of four Sherpas reached Camp Three thus marking the presence of fourteen climbers on this small site for the final assault to summit. On 13 October, the inclement weather conditions brought the upward and downward movements almost to a standstill. The three Americans at Camp Three made futile attempts to scale Camp Four on that day. By then Kohli was convinced that if the weather did not improve the following day, he would not take unnecessary risks with the lives of the climbers and would retrieve this expedition for next year.

Fortunately, weather conditions improved on 14 October and thirteen of the fourteen climbers at Camp Three started their expedition for the next destination. By the early afternoon, all the climbers reached the two tents that were pitched earlier by the Sherpas at Camp Four. Bhangu and six Sherpas along with Dawa Norbu, who climbed Nanda Devi the previous year, remained there with the equipment in boxes and the generator while the remaining climbers retreated to the Camp Three. Weather conditions next day made further upward movement stymied. Bhangu and his party at Camp Four were in extremely critical conditions. At 23,750 foot-level their health condition deteriorated due to deficiency of food and medicines in the worst weather conditions. Kohli's original plan of replacing Bhangu and party by Sonam and other Sherpas to carry the equipments to Camp Five from Camp Four and place it near the summit, was thrown in disarray. He had decided to depute Bhangu, Wangyal, Lute and Sandy to further assemble and activate the device there. If that task would take more than three hours, Rawat and a reserve team of Sherpas would move up to finish the job. Hence, it was decided that in the event of bad weather next day, those at Camp Four would be permitted to go down to Camp Two but not lower to that.

Next climbing was possible only based on the weather conditions of 16 October morning. Kohli was informed that morning of a blizzard at Camp Four. Although, calling off this mission was the appropriate decision, Kohli himself could not take it without the consent of CIA man Bill present with him there. Lute was at Camp Three wherefrom radio link was patchy. Lute climbed back to Camp Two and informed Kohli that snow was continuing and it had reached the point where the lives of the men were in definite jeopardy. Lute informed Kohli that everyone on the mountain should return to the Base Camp in this deteriorating condition. Kohli had no option but to agree to Lute's suggestion to which Bill was also in agreement. Kohli relayed this decision to Lute and then he and Bill immediately sent radio messages to their respective seniors at New Delhi to abandon this mission for the present. Delhi honchos left the decisions to the judgment of Kohli and Bill. So, the mission was abruptly stopped fearing the lives of the mountaineers. Lute passed the message to Camp Three which further informed the Camp Four climbers.

Since the sensor and generators were hauled up to Camp Four with extreme difficulties in adverse weather conditions, it was considered not to repeat this feat the following year. More so, the components were stated to be built to withstand the calamity of the mountain because the generator was reportedly fully resistant to rust and corrosion. Also, nobody in future would be scaling the peak without the approval of the government. So, it seemed an intelligent idea to safely secure the equipment at Camp Four to place further on the peak next year. Kohli gave his consent and informed the IB bosses in New Delhi accordingly who left the decision on the mountaineers meaning Kohli, Bill and Lute.

Bhangu searched for a suitable place at Camp Four to secure the equipment at a safe place. There were five loads in all: four cardboard boxes containing elements of sensor and one for the generator. He found a suitable cavity near the Camp Four tents and got those boxes wrapped with nylon ropes and secured them to the rock using pitons and carabiners with the help of Sherpas. The generator was anchored by extra rope to be on safer side. About a third of the load was sheltered inside the cavity. After completion of this exercise, these seven team members vacated Camp Four and returned to Camp Three. Bhangu relayed the message to Kohli about the steps taken to secure the generator at Camp Four which he passed on to the IB at New Delhi.

Pete Takeda in his book "AN EYE ON TOP OF THE WORLD" has mentioned that Jim McCarthy who was one of the CIA climbers in this mission said that he did not have a high opinion about the Indian climbers. According to him, the climbers were not tech-savvy enough to adequately secure the device at Camp Four. Takeda also claimed that he denounced in strong words the dumping of the device to Kohli and asked him to bring it back to the Base Camp. McKniff the CIA staffer did not intervene on the pretext that it was their country and whatever was their decision, would prevail. According to Takeda, Dr.Schaller, the co-mountaineer admitted that, "I wasn't present when that confrontation happened. I know that Jim was appalled by the idea and said as much as he's apt to do. Things were intense in the Base Camp and leaving the generator was a bad mistake." According to Kohli, McCarthy was not with him on the mountain and what Takeda wrote in the book about his diatribe was all absurd. McCarthy's version about Indian climbers was also refuted by Kohli as "Nonsense". The CIA Case Officer Bill McKniff and Lute Jestard consented to the suggestion of Kohli to secure the device and equipments at Camp Four. According to Kohli, even the Americans were unaware about the contents of the boxes at that time. Had everyone known of the implications which everyone is mouthing in Takeda's book, there would have been no reason for securing the device at Camp Four except to retrieve it safely to the base camp. Nor any apprehension was raised by the CIA officials at New Delhi who were duly informed about the decision prior to securing the device at Camp four. These false claims in Takeda's book were baseless and conjectures according to Kohli.

On 17 October, every mountaineer was back at the Base Camp. Kohli informed Kao that all the climbers were safe but the weather was still extremely bad. He further informed that the climbing season was over that year and it was impossible to even think about tracking Nanda Devi in that calendar year. Kao consented to the decision of Kohli.

In the next two days, all friends, members, Sherpas and porters packed up the available supplies for transportation. By 19 October, the Base Camp was not in the sight anywhere. Next morning, the Americans were flown back in three choppers with their personal equipments to Gaucher. On 21 October, the remaining supplies and climbers were evacuated by the ARC and IAF choppers. IAF was introduced only after the Americans had departed to maintain the secrecy of this joint IB and CIA operation. The porters were accompanied up to Joshimath by six mountaineers so that they should not develop a feeling that they were abandoned at the Sanctuary after this expedition because their service would be required the following year.

The implications of securing of sensor and other equipments in extra-ordinary circumstances due to bad weather conditions at Camp Four was reviewed in many meetings by the IB and CIA senior officers at New Delhi. Kohli was present in all those meetings. After protracted deliberations over a month period, both sides agreed that the decision to leave the sensor and generator at Camp Four was correct. However, it was decided to scale Nanda Devi again in May 1966, when land route from Joshimath to the Sanctuary would be easy to negotiate.

In an interview to a magazine at a much later period, Kohli disclosed that, "The Americans were very upset about the generator. How they made it, how the capsules were loaded, all these were top-secret things. They didn't expect to lose it. The Indians were worried by the first response from the American scientists, who told Mullik that millions of Indians would die if it reached the Ganges." According to Kohli it could have been a deliberate exaggeration by the Americans to scare the Indians of any complacency in the search efforts that year. However, the phlegmatic Mullik was obviously concerned with the unforeseen nuclear catastrophe in the holy river, the Ganges.

In early 1966, the CIA conveyed to Mullik that a decision has been taken to place this device on a lower peak. Such placement would not affect the interception ability of the sensor according to the US experts. Hence, it was decided that senor would be retrieved from Nanda Devi and placed on another peak with easier access where it would not require periodical repair unlike at Nanda Devi. The next year mission of May was thus assigned to retrieve the sensor from Nanda Devi for subsequent installation at an alternative location. This decision too was unilateral by the the US authorities and Indian intelligence had no inkling about the modus-operandi of recalculation about the height of the mountain. Such domination by the the CIA was questionable but the Indian authorities bore the brunt in view of the threat of nuclear capability designs of China looming on their border. However, it was a good news for the Indian mountaineers because placing it on Nanda Devi was still a ticklish task to carry further from Camp Four to the peak. In the meantime, China conducted its third nuclear test on 9 May 1966. Its strength was estimated as five times the kilotons of the previous test; it was assumed to contain some thermonuclear material.

## Retrieval of Sensor

Once the retrieval plan were approved by the IB, Kohli decided to deploy much lower number of mountaineers in comparison to the previous year's venture of taking the load up to Camp Four. Kohli estimated that four Indian climbers, six Sherpas and a cook along with a complement of low-altitude porters to carry the supplies into the Sanctuary would be sufficient folk to carry out this mission. The US participation in this operation was ruled out by Kohli. However, the ARC was asked to conduct a reconnaissance flight to estimate the weather conditions of Nanda Devi peak. On 26 April, an ARC chopper was sent which found the top of the peak free from snow which encouraged Kohli to start his mission early.

As usual, Kohli hinged on his trusted past colleagues with Rawat as team leader and Bhangu, Wangyal II and Sisodia his other partners in this operation. Six sturdy Sherpas who participated in the previous expedition were also selected by Kohli. One IB man Sinha meant for radio messaging was also included but was replaced by Dayalu later due to his ailment. At the last moment another IB man Mohinder Singh was unceremoniously added in the fray by the IB honchos without consulting Kohli. Dr. Tripathi joined this team later at Rishikesh. American involvement was restricted to a nuclear expert who would fly into the sanctuary to remove the fuel rods after the generator was removed to the Base Camp. Kohli was asked to monitor this operation from New Delhi from logistical point of view.

The team started from New Delhi on 1 May 1966 and after procuring essential commodities at Joshimath faced the problem of hiring porters to carry up to the Sanctuary. Ultimately, this contingent was hired from Nepal. On 15 May, the team arrived at the Sanctuary. Rawat and his party had already reached the Base Camp. On 24 May, the full contingent assembled with Rawat there to receive them. The retrieval expedition started on 25 May morning.

Although the mission started on a positive note, there were some health problems to the mountaineers in between which further aggravated due to adverse weather conditions. Rawat stationed himself on Camp Two and Bhangu along with four Sherpas pushed up to Camp Three on 31 May. While pursuing the last leg of this expedition to Camp Four, Bhangu found that most of the fixed safety ropes left behind in October last year were snapped and buried along most of the route. In the final pursuit, Bhangu and his Sherpas struggled a lot to overcome the sudden snow pelting and wing whipping. In this blizzard these daredevil mountaineers were nearing the last phase of their journey.

According to Kohli, what happened after Bhangu crossed a last rock :

"Bhangu stood atop the cramped platform that had held Camp Four, his chest heaving with the effort. He let his eyes run across a collapsed but intact tent. There was a butane canister nearby, as well as some utensils and dehydrated food rations strewn among rubble. He then looked to his left toward the shelf where he had secured the sensor eight months earlier. Bhangu's breath caught in his throat, as his brain began to register the sight before him. The rock shelf where he had left the boxes was completely gone, as if a massive knife had surgically severed that one corner of the slope. A minute later, Bhangu's Sherpa partners arrived at his side. Moving closer, they identified the crushed remains of a single cardboard box holding one of the receivers. The other boxes and the generator were missing. Frantic, Bhangu peered over the edge where the shelf had apparently been swept. One hundred feet down, he saw what looked like a cluster of twisted wire. In between the slope, was a precarious heap of jagged boulders set at a near-vertical angle."

The Generator along with the sensor was wiped away by an avalanche. Undaunted, Bhangu descended the cliff to a considerable distance to trace the lost items but did not get any trace except broken pieces of wire which he collected as proof. This was a death-fighting effort by brave Bhangu. All the available items left in the last year expedition were collected by them. Bhangu repeatedly tried to contact Rawat over his walkie-talkie in his futile attempts. However, Bhangu was certain that on the basis of the missing rock shelf and the wires recovered by him on the slope, the device had been carried in the direction toward the glacier below. In view of the snow limiting the visibility and with the descent of sheer rock wall made especially dangerous in the desiccated air, Bhangu decided to postpone a more thorough search until consulting Rawat.

Descending to Camp Two on June 2, Bhangu got walkie-talkie link with Rawat and informed him of the disaster. New Delhi was immediately informed by Rawat. Obviously, this news created grave panic among the Indian and US officials who were minutely monitoring this mission. An emergency meeting was convened wherein Mullik, Kao and the CIA officials from US

Embassy were present to discuss its repercussions and future course of action. Lal Bahadur Shastri, the then Prime Minister who died in January 1966, had been duly briefed by Mullik about the device secured by mountaineers in previous October at Camp Four. However, Mullik was certain that he would be made accountable on the decision to leave the generator on Nanda Devi over the last winter. Hence, its recovery was the priority for all and sundry involved in this operation and Mullik was nonetheless the prime target. At the initiative of newly appointed CIA operative Tucker Gougelmann, the CIA headquarters immediately rushed a team of experts with technical recovery equipments to India to help the Indian counterparts.

On 3 June, Kao ordered the expedition team stationed at Base Camp to launch search operation of the Camp Four vicinity. Despite some unrest among the Sherpas, Rawat and Wangyal II reached Camp Four and took photographs for the New Delhi and Washington officials. They concluded that according to the existing geological evidence, the generator had been carried off the left side of the ridge on south-western face either by a rock slide brought on by seismic catastrophe or by an avalanche caused by melting snow. The south-western side extended all the way to the glacier at the base but they found a slightly levelled snowy field at about the 18,000 foot-level. They concluded that further searches should be focused in that lower area.

On directions from New Delhi, Rawat got some samples collected from each of the camps and removed all traces of this operation with the help of the Sherpas and porters. In this intervening period, Bhangu and Tashi scaled the Nanda Devi summit without the knowledge of other team members. It was a remarkable feat in this desperate and gloomy situation. Rawat asked them to keep this accomplishment as secret because the emergent task was to locate the device. So, from 9 June onwards, this mission was more of a geological investigation than a mountaineering expedition. Rawat hiked to around one mile near Camp One on the likely fall of the device from Camp Four without any success.

During the search operation, Rawat and his team concluded that from Camp Four up to 18,000 feet, there were no rocky protrusions where the generator could hang in between. They were certain that the device could have gotten stuck in the snow line and it depended on the momentum from the fall when it had slipped further. The team further concluded that between 18,000 to 15,000 feet, there were two steep gullies or small drains, known locally as nallahs, which flew downward. If the momentum after falling down at 18,000 feet was of high velocity and it tumbled past the snow line, then it would have certainly flown down in one of these gullies or drains. These gullies emptied onto a glacier abutting the western side of Nanda Devi. The search party was optimistic that if the device had somehow stuck in the snow line around 18,000 feet, the chances of it remaining exposed were slim. If the device had rolled into one of these gullies, it would have hidden anywhere along the steep and rocky bed. Further, if the generator had reached the glacial moraine level, it might have been camouflaged under the thick layer of alluvial sediment deposited over the previous weather conditions.

However, Rawat and his team made all possible efforts to locate the generator at various points to survey the terrain for signs of man-made debris but all those proved a futile exercise. In the end, they collected gravel samples and filled a can tin with melt water before reaching the Base Camp. To their surprise, they found Gordon Sleeper, the CIA technician who set up the relay station at Sandev, waiting for them with a black box in his hand. His body language was indicative of the fact that some serious encounter was in the offing. He halted all the team members on the tracks, played some dials on the alpha counter and passed the black box over the hands and feet of all the team members. Sleeper was accompanied with two other Americans who were experts from the Atomic Energy Commission who examined the gravel, water sample and a steel ring found on the way, for emissions of alpha particles with the equipments they brought with them. Out of curiosity, Bhangu asked Sleeper what was going on. Sleeper replied that they were checking for radioactivity. He said that he had already swept the stones from the four camps, as well as water from the Rishi-Ganga which gave normal readings. When Bhangu further queried as to what could have happened if there were abnormal amounts of radioactivity, Sleeper responded that the water to Calcutta would become poisonous and millions of Hindus taking baths in the holy Ganges would be affected. This abrupt disclosure was the beginning point of awareness of the enormity of this grave disaster which was hidden in the Nanda Devi glacier, and which is still elusive.

In New Delhi, the US and Indian officials assessed the on-going search operation and decided on 11 June to regroup later in the summer after a more structured recovery program was devised by the experts. Prime Minister Indira Gandhi was duly briefed on the progress of this operation. However, the team members were ordered to remove the equipments from the Base Camp to the helipad for evacuation. An ARC chopper carried away whole of the paraphernalia to Gaucher. Three Americans too travelled with the equipments. Remaining party of Indian climbers went to Joshimath for road journey to New Delhi. Mullik grilled the mission team which demoralized them because this expedition had already brought a sense of failure to a big cause and all were emotionally wrecked.

After the mountaineers were allowed some time off, a series of high-powered meetings between the US and Indian Intelligence officials were held in New Delhi to evaluate the hazard conditions of the lost nuclear device. Obviously, they had to conduct the post-mortem of all events and the likely positioning vis-à-vis the danger perception of the nuclear device in case it was bared open in such a hazardous accidental situation. In one of such meetings on 5 July, Kohli, CIA operative Tucker Gougelmann and ARC number-two T Subramanian participated to discuss the types of evaluation of the hazard. They discussed three main categories of credible accident conditions and two other categories of less likely accident conditions. According to Kohli, these conditions were categorized as under:

"The first category of credible accident conditions focused on the packing material inside the generator. Sandwiched between the graphite core and aluminium housing was some low-density material. As the device rolled to the snow line or below it, it was possible that the contents of the generator got crushed and compacted inside the housing due to the poor protection offered by the low-density packing. In this crushed but intact state, it might have reached the glacier, where it could be buried under soil or carried into a stream.

The second credible accident condition hypothesized that the device was trapped in the snow line at 18,000 feet. Buried in snow during winter and exposed during summer, it could remain static for years. No major structural damage was assumed in this case.

The last credible accident condition presupposed that the bottom lid of the generator's aluminium casing had been damaged by hard impact on rock. This resulted in the fuel capsules coming free. Although this did not necessarily mean that the fuel capsules were damaged, this condition was deemed a significant hazard.

As for the two less likely accident scenarios, the first involved the device getting swept into a stream that carried it far down the Rishi-Ganga. The second involved the fuel capsules hitting hard rock at extremely high velocity, shattering their shells and exposing the tantalum cladding. If the cladding was also ripped off, the active alloy would come into contact with air and instantaneously burn due to its pyrophoric nature, giving off a puff of radioactive smoke.

Most of the accident conditions were contingent on when the device had fallen. If it had taken place during the early snowfall period—within the first few months after it had been left in October–the glacier and the foot of the south-western face would have been covered with soft snow, which would have provided a good cushioning effect. Structural damage might not be great and with the melting of the snow in the spring, the generator might have been carried down-stream intact.

If the device had fallen down form the mountain in the late winter or early spring, the snow on the slope would have been hard. Objects sliding down such hard, icy surfaces tend to bounce. Repeated bouncing would shatter the device, especially as it picked up speed during the fall. If the generator came apart and reached the surface of the glacier, the pieces could have gotten buried in soft soil or rock. Alternatively, the hot capsules could have come in direct contact with the glacier ice and sunk into its interior. Theoretically, they could have been carried in subterranean water flowing inside the glacier.

When all these eventualities were focused in these deliberations, Kohli was obviously concerned to face the worst-case scenario if the radioactive material was released into the environment due to loss of device in the glacier. The CIA man Gougelmann promised to provide all logical support in this expedition of recovery including air assets, technical equipments and mountaineers. Kohli geared up for another mission as early as possible but an impatient Mullik did not want to waste a single more day in this endeavour.

Kohli along with Sisodia, Wangyal, Sonam Bhangu and ten Sherpas assembled at the same Base Camp on 15 July 1966. B.N. Mattoo, an SSF officer of DIG rank too joined this team. Mullik got a company of ITBP deployed to ferry the supplies in the Sanctuary from the land route. An exhaustive search was conducted by this team in two directions of the south-western face of Nanda Devi. On his return to the Base Camp,

Bhangu duly checked the availability of radioactivity with the alpha counter in which he was trained earlier. Nothing adverse was found recorded. Kohli returned New Delhi on 21 July to coordinate search operation with his US counterparts. Gordon Sleeper joined the search team on the same day. Mullik and Goungelmann went to Base Camp to acquaint themselves of the ground realities of this mission. Mullik then realized his mea culpa for launching this operation with haste and without proper planning. Kohli chronicled the shortcomings in this operation through a letter to Mullik which he circulated to those who were involved in this mission.

This search operation continued for more than a week in a very haphazard manner and without proper planning. Duplicity and lack of identification of future targets brought adverse effect on the mental and physical health of the team. Four Americans Tom Frost, Rob Schaller, Dr. Bill Brewer, a nuclear expert and a doctor David Dingman later joined the Indian contingent. By 15 August the climbers completed their initial operation at the glacier near the two drains. No trace of any debris or unusual radioactivity was found in this long futile search. This mission was too unorganized with no sense of how far they had progressed and how much more and where to search for the lost device. This dilemma brought a sense of defeated approach among the Indian climbers but Americans were determined to continue it till some results were attained to locate equipments.

In a last ditch effort to find the possible place of fall of device, on 16 August, the American Nuclear Ezpert Brewer dropped a dozen butane canisters from Camp Four riding an ARC chopper. Although ten of these canisters were never found by the search team,the two found near the drain number one were indicative of a possible path of the fall. Some areas near this location were excavated but no trace of the device was found by the team. Although search operation continued for almost four months, not even the faintest trace of the sensor was found by the locating team. However, 271 samples were taken from the drains and glacier to examine the contamination, if at all happened.

On 27 October 1966, China conducted another nuclear test in Xinjiang desert. A twenty-kiloton bomb was detonated according to the monitoring stations of various countries. It was one-tenth the size of the device detonated in May that year. This bomb was fixed atop a single-stage intermediate-range missile which was the main cause of concern for New Delhi and Washington. Named as Deng Feng 2 (East Wind), this rocket had an approximate range of 1,643 miles which brought most of the cities in the subcontinent and north-eastern Asia within the range of nuclear strike of China. Two months later, China conducted another encore detonation of 300 kilotons, fifty percent larger than the May explosion, on a platform. These explosions sent a stern message to the US and Indian policy makers because of their increasing intensity and diversification of mode and range of these nuclear detonations. The Nanda Devi monitoring mission had totally collapsed into an unforeseen catastrophe which was another cause of concern for the Indian Intelligence in particular because it was a closely-guarded secret till then. The only politician aware of this misdemeanour was the Indian Prime Minister Mrs. Indira Gandhi and some selected officers of the IB.

❑

# 5

# Double Jeopardy

Although search for the nuclear device proved futile, the continuation of nuclear tests by China was a source of extreme anxiety among the Americans in particular and Indians in general. Representatives of Intelligence of both countries had many rounds of discussion about the future course of action after the loss of device. Some American conspirators in the CIA floated a theory that the device and the generators were removed by the Indian Intelligence in June 1966 itself. They propelled the theory that the nuclear fuel in the device has been stolen for the nuclear weapon programme of the Indian Government. Captain Kohli who was the team leader during the whole of this operation when Bhangu and his companions discovered the disappearance of the rock where the device was packed in October 1965, has emphatically denied this allegation. He confronted such a rumour that no such action was taken and he had never heard a word about this conspiracy. Who else could be the best judge to comment on such false assumptions of the US conspirators except him? It was all humbug as per Kohli's version and assertion.

While all such breast-beating was going between the US and Indian experts, China one-upped their nuclear capability and on

26 October 1966 launched their Deng Feng-2A missile which was copy of a Russian design. Deng Feng means East Wind. This eighteen-wheeler metal tube was filled with volatile liquid oxygen as a propellant which was sported a dangerous cargo. Deng Feng was tipped with a 2.838 pound atomic bomb with a 12-kiloton yield. It should be pertinent to know that a kiloton is the explosive yield of a thousand metric tons of the high explosive TNT. This Chinese warhead was identical to the explosive force of the Hiroshima bomb. Although it was too small compared with cutting-edge arsenal of the Soviet and US bombs which were already measured in million or mega-tons, it still flew 500 miles to Lop Nor where the device successfully detonated. Its implications were worrying because Japan, an American ally, was now in the firing range of a nuclear attack from the Chinese soil.

After prolonged discussions by the experts of both US and India after this Chinese demonstration of nuclear capability, it was decided that the impending danger of fast-developing nuclear program of China was of more concern and should be monitored on priority basis. Hence, on 15 March 1967, they formally approved to send an expedition to another mountain to install the same device to monitor the impending Chinese nuclear program. It was already decided to place this device at a lower height with easier access where periodical repair of sensors could be conducted regularly.

In this pursuit, Kohli was the only expert whose opinion of placing the device on 22,510 foot high Nanda Kot Mountain was approved by the CIA and IB officers. Kohli weighed many merits while selecting Nanda Devi Kot. It was located along the outer region of the sanctuary and as such was directly accessible from the outer regions without hiking up the Rishi-Ganga gorge and into the sanctuary itself. In this approach, the large logistic support systems could easily be driven to the proposed expedition. According to Kohli, this mountain had less technical challenges than Nanda Devi. It was 3,000 feet shorter and its slope was less steep and there were few complicating overhangs or knife ridges. Moreover, Kohli had already climbed Nanda Devi Kot and was aware of its idiosyncrasies including a gentle bulging incline of glassy ice, nicknamed the Dome near 22,000 feet level. The CIA found this place the most suitable height to place the sensor thereon. Hence, both the US and Indian officials agreed to postpone the search of the original generator to a later stage and to push forward the new decision in the earliest possible time. Once again, Kohli was selected as the joint team leader.

However, there are some pertinent questions as to how and why this operation was allowed to be carried further when the hazardous nuclear device and other boxes lost in the Sanctuary in 1965 mission were untraceable. When in June 1966, Bhangu discovered that the shelf, where the generator and other boxes were placed was hit by an avalanche, he had encountered three US climbers at the base. Two of them were experts from the Atomic Energy Commission and the third, Gordon Sleeper was a CIA operative. These Americans checked the hands and feet of Bhangu and his companions with the alpha counter black box to find the presence of alpha particles. When Bhangu asked Sleeper what he was doing, Sleeper replied that he was checking for radioactivity. Sleeper confirmed that he had already checked radioactivity in the stones and waters of Rishi-Ganga and found nothing abnormal. When Bhangu further queried as to what would happen if there were abnormal amount of radioactivity, Sleeper replied painfully that the water to Calcutta would become poisonous. Millions of Hindus taking baths in the holy Ganges would be affected by this hazardous contamination.

Search for this lost nuclear device in the Sanctuary yielded no results and the apparent danger was the view of the Americans who devised this nuclear device. Even then, the Indian Government in general, and B.N. Mullik in particular, agreed to plant a similar type of device atop the

Nanda Kot knowing well the hidden danger to around half of the population of India. Such unimaginative, intriguing and mysterious adventure was not only questionable but was also probe-worthy then. Arguably, Mullik was dominative in all his decisions but if a single thought is unknowingly abrasive enough to cause enormous danger to humanity, others at the helm or in a supportive role were equally responsible for this unforeseen catastrophe. The American expert's warning was ample testimony of the impending tragedy to the Hindu population, if the nuclear device was dismantled due to any natural or man-made circumstances. Even then, another expedition was planned on American suggestion and allowed to enter into the same game-plan. The phobia of Chinese nuclear acquisition was looming large in the heads and souls of both the US and Indian policy makers. Such was the post-cold war one-upmanship and competitiveness prevalent between the non-communist and communist blocks around this period.

Kohli selected his old foxes of the trade, Rawat, Bhangu, Wangyal II, Sisodia and Sonam for this mission on Nanda Kot. One Captain B.S. Shetty of the Indian Army as the physician and Gyan Singh, radio officer, from the ITBP were the new faces. Besides, there were a dozen of Sherpas to assist this team. The IB assigned the SFF to this expedition team for logistical support. The SFF was asked to provide porters from its ranks as well as beasts of burden. Their commandos were presented ponies for this expedition. The Indian contingent assembled at Tejam, a dusty hill town at the terminus of the road leading north towards Nanda Kot. The relay station of the previous Nanda Devi mission was established atop a ridge of the nearby town of Samdev adjoining Tejam. The SFF also had a field camp here. The entire complement of Indian climbers huddled at Tejam to discuss the strategy. They decided that the SFF porters would ferry loads to the Advance Base Camp at approximately 15,000 foot-level on the side of Nanda Kot. After stocking that locale, only six of the Tibetans would be required for porter work. It was also decided to establish three camps up the slope to reach the Dome. On 5 May 1967, the entire team reached a position at the 13,000 foot-level where Kohli decided to make the Base Camp. Tents and kitchen were pitched there. A helipad was also made functional near the Base Camp for bringing regular supplies of fresh vegetables and other perishables from Haldwani, the major town near to this expedition place.

The CIA was asked to select their team of participants. Bill McKniff, the CIA case officer, was replaced probably due to the failure of mission on Nanda Devi and subsequent inability to trace the missing devices in 1966. Sam Currie was the new participant in this operation. Unlike the Indian climbers who were all government employees, this time also the CIA was searching for civilians on temporary contracts. Surprisingly, due to their sheer patriotism and passion for mountaineering, some Americans took leave from their lucrative jobs and volunteered to work for the paltry monthly stipend of $1,000 per month. Two doctors, Rob Schaller and David Dingman were such professionals who forfeited their better paid jobs as medical professionals for this cause previously. In this team, old heads, Tom Frost and Rob Schaller agreed to participate. New faces were Barry Pather, nicknamed "Balu", an aeronautical engineer who worked previously on the movement of ice during the Everest expedition of 1963. The second such climber was James "Berry", Corbet of a previous Everest expedition.

Currie took these four climbers to the Harvey Point peninsula near Elizabeth City, North Carolina where the CIA had a highly classified base reserved for the paramilitary combat exercises. At this place, the CIA had extensive and isolated facilities for a variety of weapons and demolitions courses. In the previous mission of Nanda Devi, the climbers including Tom were given a primer in the use of explosives in case they required to blast a shelf for the device. This exercise could not take place at that time. So, in case a platform was required to be made on Nanda Kot, the CIA instructors at Harvey Point gave them pointers on detonating a range of charges. They were also introduced to the sensor, minus the nuclear generator and were trained in assembling the component parts.

All the US climbers reached Palam Airport on 6 May on a Pan Am flight. The Indian authorities made arrangements for Tucker Gougelmann, the CIA operative, at New Delhi Embassy, to receive them at the tarmac. Currie was given a pseudo identity for a Seattle-based front company called Inter-Ocean Aviation because he was not under the diplomatic cover. The Indian Intelligence insisted that he use a fake identity for strange reasons. The CIA too made arrangements for verification of his bona-fides with a lawyer to answer an overseas telephone number at Seattle. Strange were the intelligence intrigues particularly when the governments of both USA and India were involved in this operation.

The US climbers were taken to the Base Camp where Kohli received them. Tom and Rob were old friends from the previous expedition. The Indian climbers had already selected a site for the Advance Base Camp at 15,000 feet. Aware of their previous experience on the potential difficulties with the walkie-talkies, they had laid a telephone wire between the Base Camp and Advance Base Camp. The expedition started on 14 May. Amid some life-threatening avalanches, this expedition team reached Camp three at 20,000 foot-level known as the Saddle on 19 May 1967. Dome, the last destination was barely 1000 feet away for installation of the device. In the meantime, A.K. Dave took over from Kao as the Director of ARC. Kohli briefed Dave of the progress of this mission who informed the arrival of two US nuclear experts from the Atomic Energy Commission later that day.

Kao was replaced by Dave due to a particular decision of Prime Minister Indira Gandhi to form an external intelligence outfit for India. She picked up Kao for this new assignment.

When the Indian Cabinet decided to bifurcate the IB, Kao was asked to prepare a blueprint of the new agency. During 1959-60, Kao had been instrumental in forming an Intelligence Agency of Ghana when President Kwame Nkrumah requested Indian Prime Minister Jawaharlal Nehru to help his country in this regard. Kao successfully created Intelligence Department for Ghana after studying the colonial background and prevalent political compulsion of that African region. It was a remarkable achievement.

Indira Gandhi briefed Kao to not replicate the IB structure in the new agency. Kao studied and analysed the structural working of major Intelligence wings of all democratic and other major countries. He gathered a deep insight into the CIA of the USA, Mossad of Israel, MI6 of the UK, KGB of USSR and the French, Japanese and German Intelligence Agencies. Kao focused on creating an Intelligence Agency with a modernized and flexible-outlook based on the latest multi-national developments all over the world. Kao prepared a pilot scheme for the new outfit wherein some modern wings like Satellite Monitoring, Science & Technology, Economic, Technical Laboratory, Foreign Languages, etc. were newly entered in external intelligence. Based on this new and modern concept, Research & Analysis Wing (R&AW), the new External Intelligence Agency of India came into being on 21 Sept. 1968. Kao was 50 years old at that time. He continued to be at its helm upto 1978 when Morarji Desai, the first non-Congress Prime Minister of India did not extend his tenure. This unsung hero had many remarkable successes during the ten years of his unobstructed continuance as R&AW Chief. His pivotal role in the liberation of Bangladesh is unparalleled in the history of any Intelligence Wing in the world. The bloodless merger of 2,500 square mile territory of Sikkim was another feather in his cap. In his second tenure, when Indira Gandhi again became PM in 1980, he became her Senior Advisor. He got Siachen captured from Pakistan, created LTTE for Tamil cause in Sri Lanka and formed the elite commando force, the National Security Guard, in the wake of Sikh militancy in Punjab.

This Nanda Kot mission was of paramount importance for Kohli in view of the Nanda Devi failure. A second failure would be the biggest catastrophe not only for Kohli personally, but for the IB also. So Kohli was personally supervising this expedition along with his team at Nanda Kot, though Mullik was still helming this operation despite relinquishing his post of Director General of Security in the middle of 1966. Dave had replaced Kao as the Director of ARC. Around this period, the Indian and US bilateral relation started deteriorating due to geopolitical happenings wherein the American policy in Vietnam was the major factor.

The Intelligence bonhomie attained during the Chinese aggression on Indian borders in 1962 between India and the USA started waning. the SFF was fully functional by that time and CIA's indulgence was negligible at that time. In February 1967, The New York Times and The Washington Post published a report as 'Ramparts Scandal' wherein the CIA was accused of funding some organizations including media agencies in the 1967 general election in India. Although, the then Ambassador in New Delhi, Chester Bowles tried to contain the damaging effects, the statement of the previous Ambassador John K Galbraith added insult to the injury. Galbraith lamented about the CIA and warned it to rein its activities in India. Exasperated by Galbraith's indiscretion, the CIA's Director, Richard Helms curtly informed the former ambassador that he had raised unshirted hell in India for an acrimonious debate in the Indian Parliament. On 23 March 1967, the Indian Minister for Foreign Affairs, M.C. Chagla bowed to the mounting pressure for government action and announced that a thorough official inquiry would be conducted to ascertain whether the CIA had interfered in Indian politics. He assured that no foreign agency would be allowed to dictate what sort of a government India required and what sort of people should be elected. He further asserted that the government would unearth any activity that was objectionable or against the national interests. Indian Communists too raised a hue and cry blaming the CIA for the dismissal of their elected government in Kerala State in the late fifties.

In addition to such anti-US tirade, the Soviet Union was increasing its presence in India to eclipse the American inroads. When it was evident that the US was not scheduling further aircrafts to ARC, the Soviets entered the fray and provided the An-12 transport aircrafts to the ARC fleet. In this acrimonious background, the US diplomats in India and the CIA in general were pariah to the Indian Government. Tucker Gougelmann, the CIA's paramilitary adviser had no major role with the Indian authorities except to this covert Nanda Kot expedition. Its success was of primary importance because the reputation of both the CIA and IB was at stake in view of the previous disaster at Nanda Devi.

After strenuous efforts of both the Indian and US contingents, they reached the Dome on 23 May 1967. The sensor was to be installed there. A site chosen for this placement was excavated and levelled by noon that day. The previous day, Rawat and Bhangu along with two sturdy Sherpas were sent by Kohli to take receipt of the sensor and bring it to the Dome. This team reached the Dome in the afternoon along with the sensor and other equipments. In comparison to the last mission on Nanda Devi, the climbers were readily provided fresh food and other requirements by the ARC choppers on a daily basis. These supplies kept the whole team in good health and spirit.

When the sensor and other equipments were loaded at the Dome, Kohli asked for an inventory of the implements required to secure the device into the ground. Surprisingly, no one answered. Since the planning of the mission in April, everyone was fully aware of the thick snow and ice capping the Dome. For that reason, they had intended to use extra tent pegs and rope to keep the antenna and transmitters upright and properly aligned. Bhangu had assured Kohli that a load of pegs, carabiners and safety lines had been procured for this purpose and dispatched from New Delhi with the rest of their gear. Nobody had a clue why that load was missing. Some top US and Indian mountaineers were standing haplessly and helplessly atop the final assault on a major Himalayan peak with a nuclear-powered spy sensor but were missing basic items necessary for its installation. All intelligent folks were looking foolishly at one another. What a real comedy or tragedy! Only it was a comedy of errors.

When the leadership team was brainstorming on a way of securing the device without pegs or ropes, the weather started deteriorating. As the snow and wind reached blizzard conditions, everyone thought it imperative to descend the slope. Since there was only a single tent at Camp Three, the team members retrieved towards Camp Two. They had not forgotten the fate of leaving the generator on Nanda Devi. So, the sensor device and other equipments were carried back with the team. Around nightfall, they safely reached Camp Two. On 24 May, when the weather further worsened, Kohli took the inventory of their stock and calculated that they had less than two days of rations on hand. Calculating all risks including weather condition, food reserve and health concern of members under frigid condition, Kohli decided to err on the side of caution to return to Base Camp to wait out the storm. While returning, Kohli was swept by an avalanche and was fortunate not to meet an end of his life journey forever.

Till 27 May, there was no way to move out of the Base Camp due to the excessive rain and snowstorm. Obviously, New Delhi was worried about the situation. When the blizzard entered fifth day, Kohli was apprehensive that the monsoon season was in full swing which could extend to four months. Because any further attempt would be futile in such conditions, he figured out to wait a couple of days more; and to defer the mission if there was no silver lining. Just like Nanda Devi, their goal was too near, yet too far, only to be frustrated at the last possible moment. What an identical fate at Nanda Kot too!

However, on 28 May the rain stopped and weather conditions improved miraculously. Although they got a second chance for the expedition, the opportunity was for an extremely limited period. Taking advantage of the situation, six climbers—Rob, Tom, Barry, Rawat, Bhangu and Sisodia along with eight Sherpas and six Tibetan commandos restarted the gruelling climb with the disassembled sensor. The missing equipments needed to secure the device was nowhere to be found. It was assumed that it could either have been pilfered en route from New Delhi or perished with one of the ponies that plunged to its death on the way. After much brainstorming, they arrived at a primitive yet practical solution with no other alternative. It was decided that water would be heated to a sufficient temperature to use for boring four holes deep into the snow-cap. Posts of the main components of the sensor would be inserted into each hole. Cold water would be poured around these posts which would quickly harden these spots into icy cement. This basic physics appeared practical though they did not have a chance to field-test this theory. So, a butane stove was carried by the team for this exercise to install the sensor.

In view of the blizzard during the previous week, progress in the new expedition was rather very slow. They reached the Camp Two that evening. If all things remained normal the following day, success was within their reach. On 30 May, Sisodia and one Sherpa stayed behind to manage requirements of food and the remaining five climbers and three Sherpas departed for the Saddle at 05.30 hours. Heroics of these climbers paid dividends and after three hours of gruelling scaling, they were across the upper lip of Saddle, from that point, it was a comparatively easy hike past the barely visible tent at Camp Three and onto the Dome. At Base Camp, Sam and Kohli were catching sporadic glimpses of them through a set of high-powered binoculars.

After reaching the Dome, the team members initiated the primitive exercise of boiling snow to hot water by the butane burner and pouring the hot water into the pointed spots of snow-capping. Antenna and transmitter were positioned by that afternoon and the instrument was made functional. After checking the system Sam and Kohli transmitted the message to Samdev where the US technician Gordon Sleeper was supervising the relay station along with the US-trained Indian technicians. After cross-checking the functions of the antenna and transmitters, Gordon confirmed to Kohli that everything was in position perfectly. When this confirmation was conveyed to the team at Dome, the team members safely returned to the base camp in the evening. Mullik congratulated Kohli and his team members for this rare achievement. That evening was celebrated with much fanfare after two years of continuous frustration of the team members. Next day, Mullik and Dave personally came to congratulate the expedition team. Soon thereafter, the Sherpas and SFF commandos disassembled the upper camps and the whole gear was transported to New Delhi through helicopter. Sam, the American tem member had removed and burnt all the remains which were left there. Nanda Kot and the rest of the mountain in and around the Sanctuary were declared out of bonds to climbing expeditions by the Government soon thereafter.

In August 1967, H.C.S. Rawat was again assigned the job to search for the missing device. Kohli was out of India at that time. Rawat was assisted by a team of 18 officials including the IB men, physician, radiomen, scientists and ten Sherpas. Apart from Rawat and Sherpas, the others were newcomers in this mission. At the last moment, Kohli and Bhangu too were assigned a supporting role in this project. This team reached Rishikesh on 24 August but could not proceed further for the next four days due to landslides caused by heavy seasonal rains. When Kohli and his team were stranded at Rishikesh, he got a coded message from New Delhi that the device on Nanda Kot had stopped working. Kohli was asked to immediately form another team which would determine the problem with the device and get the sensor to function again. Kohli was pushed in another covert mountaineering operation.

After returning to New Delhi, Kohli was asked to conduct an aerial reconnaissance of the Dome on the peak to get photographs of the place where the sensor was installed. Kohli took the photographs from a powerful lens camera. The ARC officials and Kohli examined the photographs with magnifying glasses but the Dome was found utterly smooth with no sign of the device on its surface. Another catastrophe seemed to be in the offing.

Some mountaineers had noticed a strange phenomenon on the peaks they climbed and the snowy tops they conquered. It was rudimentary and customary to leave behind a memento after scaling a summit. Usually a flag or pennant is put atop the mountain as a sign of victory and a signal for a future expedition. The mountaineers experienced that if a single flag post is installed, the snow would take an extremely long period to accumulate around it to its height level. If they returned there after some years, they could find the pole still fully exposed provided the wind had not swept it away. If they placed more than one flag post in close proximity, then there was a different scenario. Snow would intensely accumulate around these posts in the space in-between and would attain considerable height to bury all the posts in a short span of time. This theory was never kept in mind by the team members when the sensor was installed on the Dome on 30 May when snow was not relatively in abundance at that spot.

Kohli and his team members comprising of most of the old-foxes started another spying mission to detect the functional problem of the sensor. They started the expedition in the middle of September and on 1 October four Sherpas reached the Dome. They found the antenna and the generator in a subterranean cavity where warm sides around three feet radius had kept the snow at bay due to extreme heat of the nuclear device. When Kohli was radioed of the ground reality, he was not surprised at all in view of his climbing experience of the past. Although, the four components were elevated off the surface by posts, the close proximity helped snow to mount heavily around them and buried the entire apparatus under the surface. Kohli informed New Delhi of the situation, and he was asked by the IB bosses to remove the snow and make the device functional at the earliest. It was not an easy task to be done so easily. Kohli directed the climbers stationed at upper camps to dig the apparatus although it was a difficult job at such a high altitude.

For next two days, the team members were shovelling snow from the antenna and transmitters. On 3 October, several hundred pounds of snow powder were excavated and they managed to slice away the entire snowdrift and the antenna and transmitters were exposed just above the snow line. They removed the snow from atop the cavity where the generator was placed where it was stationed in a hemispherical position. While the climbers were engaged in this excavation, Kohli received a call from the technicians at Sandev that the device started sending signal back to the relay station as soon as the antenna was unearthed. CIA and IB were pleased with this development in view of the hidden agenda of monitoring Beijing's nuclear weapons and missile programs. China had conducted two nuclear tests in late 1966 and another thermonuclear in July 1967. However, the CIA and IB were more concerned about the more disconcerting missile program. It had been evidently proved that the China would test an intercontinental ballistic missile in the near future. Its range was roughly estimated as around 6,000 nautical miles, capable to touch the American soil. This test was expected at any moment and the re-functioning of the nuclear device at Nanda Kot was a big relief to both the Intelligence Agencies wary of the Chinese nuclear agenda. However, Kohli and his team returned to New

Delhi after finishing the cleaning operations of the device at the Dome.

The earlier Chinese nuclear tests were conducted when this nuclear device was not installed on Nanda Kot with the result that no missile telemetry data of any sort could be accessed. Moreover, the rocket tests did not send strong signals which could be intercepted by this device. Obviously, the CIA and IB were enthusiastic about the smooth functioning of the sensor in view of the hectic activities of the Chinese at the test range areas. However, it was a guess work open to suggestion and conclusion after this hindrance of the summer snowdrift which disengaged this mission in three months only and the winter snowfall would be much more dangerous to make this arrangement sustainable. Drawing room planners of New Delhi and Washington were the least aware that it was hazardous to clear away the snow deposits every now and then by the climbers and this nuclear installation was an experimental exercise without any fool-proof long-lasting strategy. Strange are the intelligence operations when some neighbouring enemy country is found dangerous to the security considerations and China was no exception to both India and America.

On the other front in the Sanctuary, the search operations for the missing device were continuing with guess and gosh. Initially, there was perennial shortage of local porters, with this result the SFF and ITBP assistance was sought. Rawat was conducting searches sometime under duress and at times in a hapless state of affairs. Coordination among the different working positions was missing which was sometime very disgusting and disheartening to continue the process anymore. The New Delhi operators were ill-conceived with many farce options which put the combing operations in a perilous situation. They engrossed themselves in erratic and haywire planning without assessing the ground realities at the operation places. One such futile exercise was wasting time and energy to search the device up the ridge and scrutinize the upper slopes along the south-eastern side facing a ridge named as Longstaff Col. This was a farce because the device would not be able to defy gravity by rolling dozens of feet over and across the Camp Four tent site before plunging down the south-eastern slope. It was evidently photographed that the rocky platform that had once supported the device had been strewn down the south-western and not the south-eastern slope where the New Delhi planners dispatched Rawat and his team and wasted more than a week's time under perilous hiking conditions. They faced death threats from the hurricane velocity of cold winds and snow during this vain and thoughtless endeavour. Finally, this route was closed down on 4 October and Rawat and the Sherpas returned to the Base Camp.

Two nuclear scientists who accompanied this search team, started their ice and scree testing operations with the alpha counter on 25 September. They decided to conduct tests on such accumulation where the nallahs emptied onto the moraine level because almost an entire year has passed since such tests were performed there. It was assumed that there were chances that any portion of the generator could have been stucked in the rocky nallahs and washed down in the interim. At initial stage their efforts brought no results. Their continuing efforts brought some tantalizing results on 3 October when the neutron counter gave an initial reading of 150 counts per minute in the air when the search team conducted the tests. It was slightly higher than the last year's recording of 105 per minute. It was not considered too dangerous. They further moved to nallah two which was marked on map as G-14 where the neutron counter shot up to 330 counts per minute and then settled to 200 counts per minute. They were given to understand that the generator's nuclear fuel would give off a reading of 1,000 counts per minute. In addition, passing a metal detector over the same area showed negative results.

When these facts were informed to the two scientists at Base Camp by the search team, they were scared of the unforeseen tragedy. Two more scientists joined the earlier two. Next day, the search team was again sent to reconfirm the counting of the previous day. Again, the neutron count registered about three times the norm. After assessing the results of the neutron counts of two days, these four scientists concluded that there was serious danger to human life because as per the norms available with them, the air was heavily contaminated with radiation. As a precautionary consideration, they had asked all members of the search team to wear snow goggles and gloves while outside the tents and wash all exposed parts of the body with soap and hot water. They further suggested immediate medical examination of the whole search team. Panicked on this new development, Intelligence Officials in New Delhi sent another counter to reaffirm the result of the first one. On 5 October, G-14 was again searched with the two neutron counters. This time the results were more baffling when the first counter shot up to 2.570 per minute and the new one indicated 225 counts. Although, the scientists were puzzled on sudden spike in the first counter, they ultimately concluded it to be defective. But the second counter too was showing readings higher than normal. It was considered a natural phenomenon because the temperature had fallen on the moraine abruptly which could have affected the mechanical counter.

However, the senior CIA and IB officers were obviously concerned with these developments which could trigger a major environmental disaster due to the hidden nuclear device. On 9 October, two senior officers of whom one was an eminent scientist of the Ministry of Defence, were rushed to the Base Camp. They concurred with the existing team and reached the opinion that the two counters were establishing inaccurate counts due to cold weather. They brought two new counters attached with tape recorders believed to be more forgiving of the low temperature. By that time the weather was very frigid in the entire region. The next day, the search team again visited G-14 area to begin the search anew. The tape recorders attached with the counter did not work due to extreme cold. Ground level too became very hard like marble in those conditions and digging to collect soil and rock samples was impossible. Dejected, the search team returned to Base Camp without any success. Scientists made some modifications to the neutron counters and the team again went to G-14 on 11 October. To their dismay, they found the devices giving unbelievably inflated readings of 2,000 of counts per minute. Jay Horace, US Atomic Energy expert, joined the scientists at Base Camp. Everyone was in a dilemma on this turn of events.

Indian and the US scientists reviewed the sequel of previous days and agreed that the defective neutron counters had made a reliable investigation impossible. They were also joined by several members of Nanda Kot mission who were also deployed for this search operation. It was decided to disassemble the Base Camp and tents were pitched on G-14 area itself. More than a week's time was spent on this new arrangement. They were waiting for the arrival of a new set of equipments for a fresh search. On 23 October, another pair of neutron counters was sent from New Delhi with the direction that these sets were fully calibrated and would function as devised for. The next day, both counters were taken to the nallah where the instruments indicated nothing abnormal. These tests were repeated at different places several times but the counters never flickered. When the progress was informed to New Delhi and any trace of the generator was not insight, they were asked to abandon the search operation the following day. This futile exercise of searches towards south-eastern slope and the conflicting signals recorded by the neutron counters at G-14 wasted more than two months of time of the search team which finally returned to New Delhi dejected and disgusted.

At the Sandev telemetry data receiving centre, the Indian technicians were duly monitoring the functional device atop the Dome on Nanda Kot after the 3 October clean-up process. After two months, towards the end of December, the sensor on the peak abruptly became non-functional again. In the meantime, China conducted its second nuclear test on 24 December 1967. Debris samples of this test produced evidence of thermonuclear fuel. It was concluded by the policy makers of US and India that China's progress to develop weapons of mass destruction was not disrupted despite the turmoil of the Cultural Revolution. The CIA authorities were obviously perturbed and the importance of having an operational sensor was their top priority. However, regular snow accumulation around the sensor and its cleaning operations at such a big height at regular intervals was not only impractical, but was only a temporary arrangement. Moreover, the CIA operatives were not included in this exercise.

Kohli was again summoned to review the modus operandi. The subject of discussion again focused on selecting another peak for such an installation which should be close to China border with easier access in order to ensure better maintenance of the device. There was limited scope in this new specification of the CIA operatives. Sikkim Mountains were perilous while the Nepal and J&K borders were as hazardous as Nanda Kot. However, in Ladakh region some mountains were found suitable despite the Chinese posts confronting from the northern side. Kohli and Bhangu were dispatched to Leh in the beginning of 1968 where they surveyed all available options for the new installation. Thereafter, Kohli briefed the CIA and IB officials in New Delhi about some peaks in the vicinity of Leh which were better than Nanda Devi and Nanda Kot in terms of accessibility. However, the weather here too was almost identical to the earlier two missions and any trekking outside the climbing season was impossible. All agreed to this suggestion and another mission in Leh was proposed later in 1968.

During this awaiting period, the CIA was working on the plan for the installation of a sensor near Leh. However, before venturing for the new mission, they were concerned about bringing back the non-functional device from the Dome on Nanda Kot. Unlike the Nanda Devi mishap, the CIA honchos were pretty sure that the sensor had stopped working due to heavy snow accumulation and could be retrieved easily. There was no inclination at the back of their mind that in case it was not traceable, they would hesitate to position a new device with already two done missing in this endeavour. However, in any case the non-functional sensor from the Dome had to be retrieved first despite such apprehensions.

As usual, Rawat, Bhangu and Wangyal, the most capable climbers along with six Sherpas and some SFF porters were entrusted with the new assignment to bring the sensor and other equipments. No American was included in this expedition. They started this work in the beginning of May 1968. The climbers made quick headway up to the Saddle. Surmounted beyond Saddle, they put up their final camp beyond it unlike the other mission so that the Dome could be reached easily. On 29 May, the team reached the Dome. To their utter surprise, there was no trace of the device anywhere on the Dome. They walked around the Dome's circumference and did not find any visible marks or anomalies wherein it could be concluded that the device was under the surface. It was only to be expected based on the previous experience when the device was buried during 1967 after a monsoon season. It was obvious that the device was beneath a big stretch of snow accumulated during the entire winter and spring.

Obviously, the exploring team had no option but to dig some spots where the sensor was expected to be installed the previous year. At such high altitude, such digging was life-threatening and the Sherpas in particular were bristled at this idea. After much cajoling, the Sherpas assisted the Indian climbers in digging the area at various places to locate the hidden device. In a last-ditched effort, a six-foot hole was made in the centre of the Dome. This hole led to a bore into a spherical cavity at the heart of the Dome. The snow had melted away in a five-foot radius and the walls had hardened into a crust from repeated melting and freezing. In the centre of the cavity, the generator was located by the team. Warm air was emanating from the cavity. The team was concerned that radiation might have erupted inside the hole. After discussing the possible pros and cons, ultimately, the device was removed from the post and brought to the surface. Subsequently, the antenna and transceivers were pulled out of the cavity. One transceiver which was buried further inside the snow was left to remain there. At the Base Camp, the expedition team sent a radio message to New Delhi about the success of the operation. Soon thereafter, a chopper arrived at the helipad near the Base Camp. Jay Horace, the US nuclear expert, emerged from it, took the generator and flew back from that spot.

The CIA operative took this device to Charbatia in Orissa where the ARC has its aviation facilities. In the first week of June 1968, Sam Currie, the CIA head at US Embassy, who was involved in placement of the device at Nanda Kot, contacted B.N. Mullik to accompany him to Charbatia where the sensor was taken by Jay Horace. Although, Mullik had retired by then, he enjoyed enormous influence in the IB hierarchy. In the meantime, the CIA had arranged a special air-craft C-130 from Norton Air Force Base, California to come to Charbatia to retrieve the device to USA. Mullik and Sam arrived at Charbatia the following day in an ARC chopper. The sensor was loaded into the C-130 aero-craft which took off to an unknown destination in the USA. At least, one hazardous apparatus with unknown intensity of radiation was off the Indian soil.

After this misadventure, the CIA and IB were again pushing the idea of placing another such device after the monsoon at a mountain nine miles north-west of Leh. Bhangu selected this mountain and climbed it in a single day in August that year. But the CIA informed IB that the device was not readily available at that time. It was learnt that the CIA was wary of the past controversy over the nuclear generator and had decided to use a trio of gag-powered generators for the power supply. The new device would be without any radioactivity hazard and could be easily serviced from the nearby areas. Since the new device was not available for positioning, the perennial search for the missing generator at Nanda Device was re-launched. Rawat was entrusted the task of an aerial survey of the slopes and moraine. Despite several days of searching with binoculars, he could not detect any trace of the lost device and abandoned it by late October. The sensor was still unavailable and the unforeseen danger was looming large on the population engrossed with various activities in the holy Ganges.

❑

# 6

# Eerie Silence Unravelled

After the hit-and-trial experiment on the Nanda Kot, when the second sensor was fortunately located by Rawat and his team, the CIA smuggled it out to USA on the spur of the moment fearing political and media repercussions. No trace of any toxic material was left with the Indians by the clever and dominating US officials. It was a pity that a hazardous killer material was lost in the Rishi-Ganga, a part of the holy Ganges and the second identical one was allowed to be taken to the US. Had that sensor been in the custody of the Indian authorities, there was every chance of getting it analysed by the Indian atomic scientists to determine the existing danger of the device lost in Rishi-Ganga. Later investigations and assessments were based either on hearsay or the printed material available on this subject matter. Whatever were the conclusions of the Committee of Scientists constituted in this regard was pure guess work based on these facts and nothing practically was placed on record. This was a sheer surrender by the Indian authorities before the powerful US administration when they could not deter the carrying away of the Nanda Kot device from Orissa in a US plane not clandestinely but bullishly. B.N. Mullik, the all-powerful former IB Director was present at the air-strip of Charbatia in Orissa to see them off without any hassles.

Though Kohli and most of his fellow mountaineers had given up hope of finding the device, the IB made a last ditched-effort to locate it before the onset of winter in 1968. Rawat made an aerial survey of the area where the device could have perished in the Sanctuary and on the slopes of the Nanda Devi. After several days of search operations by powerful binoculars, he called it off in October 1968 and returned to New Delhi. This was the last known effort in this regard. It was a forgotten story thereafter in every sense because of other compelling circumstances.

Indira Gandhi, who succeeded Shastri, had lived with her father Pandit Nehru after finishing her education abroad. This gave her immense experience to understand the politics of ruling and opposition Indian leaders. She had, thus, a good grasp of the complicated national issues as well as state matters. This apprenticeship served her in good stead to lead and control the ruling Congress party comprised of some old hawkish politicians clinging to various top positions. She squashed whoever tried to revolt against her among these stalwarts by sheer domination. In this pursuit, she took hard decisions in her administration. Y.B. Chavan, the then Home Minister, was the one aspirant to compete against her in the one-upmanship. She cut him to size to the core. The Home Ministry was pruned by her by divesting the Department of Personnel, responsible to administer the bureaucracy of IAS and IPS etc., and brought it under the Prime Minister's office. The Central Bureau of Investigation (CBI) too was soon removed from the Home Ministry to her fold. She further decided to bifurcate the IB and create a new Foreign Intelligence Department. R.N. Kao who was the then

Joint Director in IB was asked to produce a paper delineating the structure of the new Foreign Intelligence Agency. Kao produced his magnum opus, defining the proposed structure of India's CIA, The Research and Analysis Wing(R&AW), purportedly akin to the two Directorates of CIA i.e. Directorate of Operations and Directorate of Analysis. This name, sounding like some scientific entity proposed for this new organization by Kao, was approved by Indira Gandhi. In order to camouflage its structure like a civil department, ranks nomenclature started as Secretary as its head and Additional Secretary to Under Secretary to the bottom which was a prevalent feature of the Government of India Ministries. The R&AW was attached to the Cabinet Secretariat as its wing to maintain its secret working. K. Sankaran Nair, a brilliant Intelligence Officer of IB soon joined the R&AW as deputy of Kao. Sanjay Gandhi, the younger son of Indira Gandhi, later jokingly dubbed it as Relatives and Associates Wing when he was ruling the roost during the Emergency era of 1975-77.

With the formation of R&AW on 21 September 1968, all the foreign desks from IB were transferred to this new department. The then Director of IB, M.L. Hooja opposed the suggestions of Kao on formation of this external intelligence department with tooth and nail, but had to bite the dust in view of the sheer brilliance of Kao on all fronts. Most heads of important Ministries like Home, Defence and External Affairs gave their consent to the creation of this new Intelligence outfit. Initially, the Directorate General of Security or DG(S), responsible to control the ARC, SSF and SSB was not transferred to Kao, and Balbir Singh, the Joint Director of IB continued to head it after the creation of the R&AW. Subsequently, when A. Jayaram became the IB Director, the post of DG(S) was brought under R&AW and its Secretary was made the de-facto head. Another desk, the Directorate of Technical Laboratory was soon shifted to R&AW. Kao brought in the concept of separate Analysis and Operational Desks based on the CIA functioning. Soon, the newly recruited

R&AW officers fought back with fang and claw and got the R&AW firing on all cylinders within a year. After its pivotal role in the liberation of Bangladesh, R&AW was rated the best to the east of Suez and west of Macau on the international globe.

During this upheaval period of Indian Intelligence, the missing nuclear device in the glaciers of Nanda Devi was lost in the sight of the Intelligence Fraternity. B.N. Mullik had relinquished the charge of DG(S)in the beginning of 1968. He became a more devout Hindu thereafter, exchanging his "short at the back and sides" hairstyle for a braid or Chothi (the turf of hair that old conservative Hindus used to keep). Initially, Kao was not assigned the job of DG(S) and the IB echelons like Hooja were indulging in dirty games to frustrate Kao in his new assignment as the head of R&AW. This scenario continued for around two years. In this squabbling, though the IB continued to search places in Ladakh to place gas-powered sensors, the search for the missing device was totally ignored and it became an almost forgotten chapter with the passage of time.

Most of the climbers of the 1965 mission of Nanda Devi were settled in various other departments and agencies. Captain Kohli was initially chosen by Kao for a diplomatic cover assignment in Nepal but since his identity was too well known in Nepal, he was not considered for this covert job. He served as the Assistant Inspector General of ITBP from 1968 to 1971. Subsequently, he joined Air India and initially shifted to Mumbai and later to Sydney as the Station Manager of Australia, Fiji and New Zealand. All other team members of Kohli's team were formally absorbed in various paramilitary organizations under DG(S). In January 1970, a High Altitude Operations Training Centre (HAOTC) was established at Sandev where the telemetry relay station was opened during the Nanda Devi and Nanda Kot operations. Rawat was given the command of this station. He was assisted by many of the Nanda Devi veterans including Bhangu, Sisodia and Wangyal along with seven of the best Sherpas. This centre was assigned the task of handling all future mountaineering projects with the latest modern amenities. Rawat was later shifted to R&AW in its training branch to train the new recruits in military operations. Bhangu was posted to Leh where the Sandev collection station was shifted. Sisodia was also taken in R&AW on various assignments. Wangyal was selected to command the training centre at Gangtok which was posthumously named after Sonam Gyatso. Gyan Singh died four years later while climbing a peak at the south of Nanda Kot. The sanctuary, however, remained closed for climbing for the next eight years.

This tragic loss of a nuclear device remained a shrouded mystery for a long spell of time. Obviously so, due to the precautions taken by the two elite Intelligence Agencies of the world, the CIA and the IB to hide the repercussions of untraceable nuclear material dangerously hidden in the glacier. All the Indian mountaineers who participated in this mission were government officials who were bound to the oath of secrecy under the colonial Officials Secret Act of 1923 wherein a maximum penalty of 14 years could be imposed for its violation. The Sherpas and the porters were illiterate persons having no knowledge of what was transpiring in that expedition. Barring the CIA case officers on this operation, the US civilian mountaineers had sworn the oath of secrecy to CIA wherein they were liable to any psychological screening and lie-detector tests. They were all assigned pseudo identities based on some dead person. One of the climbers Dr. Robert Schaller's moniker was Norris P. Vizcaino. Schaller later admitted that he never knew who Vizcaino was, but the CIA claimed he was a real person. McCarthy was nicknamed as Jim by Pete Takeda in his book. Kohli too claimed that McCarthy was not on the mountain in this mission. He accepted the participation of Jim in the expedition. So, from these two different versions, it was evidently proved that all the US climbers were known to the Indian participants by their pseudo identities. Only after

Kohli and Takeda wrote books on this mission, were the real identities of the US and Indian mountaineers made public. Despite disclosure of the real identity of the US participants, only three out of eleven admitted their presence in this mission.

This practice of deporting agents on pseudo names to other countries is inhuman in many aspects. It was a cold war era phenomenon which continues even now. Numerous media reports in India and Pakistan revealed how agents are infiltrated on assumed monikers. Most of them are usually arrested and when they return to the respective countries, they are disowned as their agents. Their conditions become very pathetic since their traumatic past is not compensated with due remunerations. This is the most inhuman aspect of this cloak and dagger game which is stigmatic in open societies of the world in general and in India and Pakistan particularly.

Whiffs of this secret mission were getting obvious suspicion among the family members of the eleven US mountaineers because of their prolonged absence in mysterious circumstances. According to the wife of one such spy climber, it was a dangerous enterprise because she heard about the huge life insurance policies taken on these guys by the CIA. Many of these wives including that of Dr. Robert Schaller were separated from the mountaineers due to their undisclosed long absence during these missions. Their friends, dependants and fellow workers too floated unanswerable stories about their conspicuous disappearance and on return, found them in deteriorated health conditions. However, nothing came to public domain in view of the oath of secrecy affirmed by them to the CIA.

Although none of the other US climbers except Dr. Robert Schaller spoke about this mission, Schaller revealed his participation only after publication of the books of Kohli and Takeda. He said that he was a man happily married to his schoolmate and had two young children. He was happily practicing as a surgeon at the University Hospital at Seattle.

He was a climbing fanatic and had just returned from climbing Mount McKinley when the CIA approached him for the Nanda Devi mission. The CIA was obviously looking for a physician with some interest in electronics who also had a background in high-altitude medicine for a classified mission to place a listening device somewhere on the roof of the world. He was offered $1000 per month which was exorbitant at that time. He realized the real cost of this mission when he had to leave his family for months for training in tradecraft. He became aware of the clock and dagger policy when he was blindfolded and led through a canvas tunnel to an airplane with blacked-out windows. His fellow companions were college professors of Nuclear Science including some renowned Alpinists. The American operated with pseudonyms. Schaller was Norris P. Vizcaino, who was some dead entity.

The team was flown to undisclosed locations where they were trained in blowing up materials with C3 and C4, the plastic explosives. Jumping from helicopters was also part of this training. This initial training lasted for two to three weeks which he did not disclose to his wife. This was the beginning of keeping secrets. Schaller's cover was that he was training as a scientist-astronaut. Schaller revealed that the plutonium fuel cells placed in the generator at Nanda Devi were rigorously tested. He himself had helped drop them out of airplanes from 10,000 feet onto granite. According to him they were known to be sturdy and it was hard to imagine how they could ever be destroyed. But if the fuel cells burned their way to bedrock, could the massive tonnage of the glacier, grinding away for decades or centuries, destroy the core and release the plutonium to the environment? When Schaller returned to US after this mission, the CIA approached to see Schaller's journals and his film so that a report could be prepared for the govt. The material was handed over to CIA which was never returned to Schaller. He was awarded an Intelligence Medal of Merit for his contribution to the espionage missions when two CIA operatives came to his house and draped a silver medal on ribbons around his neck and then took away that medal. It was locked in a vault at the CIA's Langley Headquarters along with myriad other artefacts that officially do not exist and with his journals and photographs, of course.

Schaller's family life was ruined after this mission due to his long absence from home. He could not explain his long absence to his wife when he adapted to his clandestine way of life. He was divorced after 13 years of marriage. He married twice more and had seven children. He regretted the cost of his secret life which had a lot to do with the separation of his first wife. Subsequently, both his knees were replaced and his spine was fused. His height too was reduced by 4 inches than when he was as a young man.

After reports of this mission surfaced through books and other magazines, Schaller again tried to reclaim his records of these secret climbs. He appealed three times to the government through Freedom of Information Requests asking to return his personal diary and photographs from the Nanda Devi and Nanda Kot missions. Each time he was denied. "The CIA can neither confirm nor deny the existence or non-existence of records responsive of your request" the letters said. "Such information – unless it has been officially acknowledged – would be classified for reasons of national security .... The facts of the existence or non-existence of such records would also relate directly to information concerning intelligence sources and methods." He approached some Senate members but nothing happened in this regard. Schaller felt betrayed for not getting his personal diaries and photographs from the archives of CIA.

The presence of another American Jim McCarthy in this mission is too intriguing. According to Takeda, he claimed that he developed testicular cancer following his exposure to the SNAP's radiation. Takeda wrote that McCarthy selected for his climbing skill, had been instructed, as were the other Americans, in the use of explosives like C4 to excavate the set-up site. He had also been trained by the Atomic Energy Commission to handle the plutonium. According to him, it was, “Martin Marietta who trained me to place certain things in certain orifices”. Connotations aside, McCarthy’s reference is to his job of loading the SNAP generator with its deadly fuels. And it was he who ultimately loaded the glass-encased plutonium capsules into the battery pack. “In the Sanctuary, I was the only guy who handled the actual plutonium and I am the one who loaded the device. I had to straddle the fucking thing. Let me tell you, the fuel rods were wildly warm.” McCarthy further says, “No question, there was no shielding at all and I got a large dose of radiation.”

In 1971, while on a rock climbing trip to the Wyoming monument of Devil’s Tower, McCarthy had finished climbing a route with his new wife, when he first discovered his condition. “I was in these painter’s pants and was changing them when I noticed that one of my testicles is greatly engorged. We drove straight back to New York, found the very best doctor in the Metro area. He says, ‘This is not good.’ Two minutes later, I was in the OR.”

McCarthy recovered, as his the one-type of testicular cancer was treatable at that time. Kohli, as an expedition leader, says that there were safety precautions, including limiting the carrying time for the Sherpas to four hours and pinning radiation badges to detect leaks. McCarthy has no recollection of exposure limits for Sherpas. “I never saw the Sherpas carrying it on the mountain. I did see them fighting over who got to carry it.” He adds, “They had no idea of what it was. After it was loaded, they would put the thing in the middle of the tent and huddle about it.”

“There was absolutely no shielding”, says McCarthy. “It was a field operation and when I look back on it, I can’t believe I was not smart enough to believe these shitheads.” He adds, “If you challenge the Indians to prove any of these Sherpas are alive today, it can't be done. They are all dead. They were sleeping with the fucking thing."

To Kohli's assertion that there were radiation badges, McCarthy says, "There were absolutely no radiation tags-none whatsoever."

Schaller concurs, "I don't recall any radiation tag. There was some talk about them but I don't remember ever seeing one." He definitively adds, "I know that I never had one."

As far as official oversight goes, Conboy's book states and we can assume that these words are based on Kohli's recollections, "One additional American arrived with the rest (in the Sanctuary in early September 1965). Introduced only as Jim, he was from the US Atomic Energy Commission. Soft-spoken and polite, Jim would oversee the fuelling of the generator...." Regarding the presence of an official government technician to oversee the RTG, McCarthy scoffs. He states, "I was Jim, I was the guy trained to load the device."

What is disturbing is that if his words are true, McCarthy, the trial lawyer and rock climber, is the guy tagged by Kohli as the man in charge of safe handling of the device in the field. This means that when "oblivious to any danger, the Sherpas snuggled up to the device, warming their hands and patting their face", it was a climber, not a qualified safety technician, who was claimed by Kohli, to have given assurances of the device's safety. Indeed, spies in the Himalayas further states, "Despite Jim's assurances that the chance of dangerous radiation exposure was minimal, the 'Friends and Members' were not inclined to join the Sherpas."

According to Kohli, the first such rumour was floated by some American climbers who were sent on the first US expedition attempting to scale the K2 summit, the second tallest mountain in the world located on Pakistan's border with China.

This mission did not succeed due to hostile weather conditions. Members of this mission were criticized in the USA on return for their friction with the Pakistani counterparts. One American of the Alpine Club spread tittle-tattle that it was a CIA-sponsored programme to place a monitoring device on K2 Mountain. He had apparently heard some hints about the Indian sensor programme from other participants. It was sheer false propaganda out of personal grievances. Rob Schaller, the Nanda Devi mission participant, was also a member. Schaller swapped stories with a fellow team member Galen Rowell who happened to be an acclaimed photojournalist. Rowell had an inkling of Nanda Devi rumours. He was editor of American Alpine Journal and had written a story about the CIA's interest in climbing. According to Schaller, Rowell was inquisitive to know more details about the sensor missions during the K2 expedition. In 1978, when the USA prepared for a second expedition at K2, one climber who was denied participation in this mission floated stories that the expedition was conceived and funded by the CIA. Just when the Seattle Times was planning a story on this news, a law firm retained by one of the team members threatened the paper with a libel suit and got it blocked from publication. .

However, all hell broke when on 12 April 1978, Howard Kohn, the Associate Editor of Rolling Stone Magazine of USA, published the details of nuclear device missions at Nanda Devi and Nanda Kot in Outside magazine. Kohn described this mission under the auspices of the Air Force High Altitude Test Programme (HAT), an appropriate acronym since the special pack that left a warm spot on the back of porters was shaped like a stovepipe hat. Kohn mentioned that until the plutonium in the sensor deteriorates, which may take centuries, the device will remain a radioactive menace that could leak into the Himalayan snow and infiltrate the Indian River System through the headwaters of the Ganges. A biophysicist, Dr. Arthur Tamplin, who worked with the Atomic Energy Commission described it as a hazardous situation and demanded its recovery soon. Kohn blamed the US Government for the short-term feckless effort to search for the device. He affirmed that his article was based on information from eight of the fourteen mountaineers who participated in the project and from three sources in the US intelligence community. However, this whole story was concocted on the basis of the tittle-tattle emanated among some disgruntled US mountaineers during the K2 mission of 1975 in Pakistan.

Kohn's blaming the CIA for contaminating India's hallowed waters with plutonium, or even to have risked that possibility, was an unprecedented breach of the unwritten internal nuclear code. He described this incident as far more politically embarrassing to the US than the radioactive pollution the Soviet Union's Kosmos 954 satellite rained on northwest Canada in January 1978, except that the CIA was able to keep its mishap covered up.

In his article Kohn claimed that the CIA had unofficial cooperation of its Indian counterpart, the Central Bureau of Investigation (CBI) which was factually incorrect. CBI is the crime investigating agency of India and has nothing to do with such sensitive operations. It was the Intelligence Bureau of India which was working with the CIA in this mission. Kohli has given vivid description of this mission in his book wherein he disclosed the names of all IB officers who were involved with their CIA counterparts. Kohn indicated that Bill McNeff, the CIA case officer, was assisted by a demolition expert, a psychiatrist and a squadron of lesser strategists. The psychiatrist was stated to have used lie detector to quiz the group about drugs, homosexuality, and fidelity (marital and national) and with dedicated professional myopia, about any friends who might be communists. Kohn also described the climbers as former track stars and staunch patriots. Kohli gave a different version about the composition of US climbers which make this expedition more intrigued and questionable. He named William McKniff as the CIA case officer which did not corroborate to what Kohn wrote in his article.

Kohn exaggerated his findings by branding Indian mountaineers as CIA agents which Kohli strongly refuted in his book. All Indians were committed patriots who never needed any certificate from any Tom, Dick and Harry including Kohn.

When the device was lost in the glacier, Kohn related a different incident as to how the CIA tried to locate it by rushing to New Delhi and collecting several hoses of varying lengths to divert the water to wash away the snow and exhume the nuclear treasure below. Kohli did not mention such modus operandi in his details of the search operations. Kohn claimed that the CIA pressured IB (not CBI as he wrote) not to inform Prime Minister Indira Gandhi's Government. The CIA allegedly also concealed its decision from the White House. This claim was totally unfounded and lacked any confirmation in so far as the Indian part of the story was concerned. Kao confirmed to the author that Indira Gandhi was duly informed about the missing device. Even when Prime Minister Morarji Desai replied to a debate in the Indian Parliament, he made it amply clear that these operations were in the know of and with the approval of the highest political level of the Government of India at that time. These assertions of Kohn lacked any feet to stand on in such sensitive matters which Indian Intelligence have rarely kept secret from their political bosses. The CIA's notoriety in such misadventures was a matter of routine like the Gulf of Tonkin incident in war of Vietnam.

Further, Kohn gave his configuration about the Plutonium-238 which could remain dangerously radioactive for 300 to 500 years, and even if the SNAP generator had survived the avalanche intact, its outer shell would eventually corrode and release its poisonous core. Handling or inhaling plutonium could be fatal, and it would be impossible to retrieve the radioactive material once it escaped into the snow. If it reached the Ganges river system, it could cause cancer to anyone who consumes even microscopic amounts of the water or the contaminated fish. Other studies conducted on this subject too asserted what Kohn mentioned, but gave a little varied danger, which was obvious because different minds form conflicting opinions on all such matters and as such, Kohn's assertions in this regard sound unmitigated.

In the expedition to Nanda Kot, Kohn gave an interesting input wherein he narrated that the Indians were more security-conscious about the new recruits of CIA. One American, a CIA radio operator, had such arid, alabaster features that he was conspicuous in any crowd. After a hushed conference, the Indians produced a disguise, Man-Tan, an American drugstore potion that fabricates a suntan. It turned his skin a carotene-brown. Such revelations were nowhere found in the memoirs of Kohli who was team leader and accustomed with every American who was involved in this project.

In India, political imbroglio took its worst course during the seventies when Indira Gandhi proclaimed a state of National Emergency in June 1975, when all opposition parties demanded her resignation after the Allahabad High Court verdict deposed her from the Parliament seat. All opposition leaders were arrested and imprisoned by her to continue in power. However, in January 1977, she abruptly declared the general elections and released all the opposition leaders. A joint front was formulated against her by all opposition leaders as Janata Party which contested the March elections. Indira Gandhi lost miserably in the north region and she herself was defeated in this election. Morarji Desai, the octogenarian hard-nut of Indian politics became the Prime Minister. R.N. Kao was then head of R&AW. Morarji was apprehensive that R&AW was hand-in-glove with Indira Gandhi during the emergency and worked against her opponents. He summarily removed Kao and pruned the cadres of R&AW. Fortunately, the Nanda Devi episode was not in the news at that time, or else Morarji would have certainly made Kao responsible for that misadventure.

After the disclosure of Kohn, left-leaning media of India made a lot of hue and cry on this matter. This was the powder keg that the Kohn article lit in India at that time. Blitz, the leading Mumbai weekly, was fiery rhetoric in its publication. Another weekly depicted Sir Edmund Hillary as the CIA agent which was unfounded and absurd. Opposition Members of Parliament blocked the Parliament proceedings and demanded statement of Morarji Desai. Communist leader, Jyotirmoy Basu, raised this issue in Lok Sabha wherein the opposition Congress supported him and the debate continued for over an hour on Nanda Devi mishap. Prior to that, the US Ambassador was summoned by the Foreign Ministry to respond on this matter to which he replied that the State Department was looking into the matter. Thereafter, Morarji Desai made this statement in Lok Sabha on 17 April 1978:

"Mr. Speaker, Sir,

Honourable Members are quite understandably exercised over the reports that have appeared in the Press here on a news item which appeared in the United States about the attempt to locate a nuclear-fuelled power-pack on the heights of Nanda Devi. The failure in this attempt has raised just apprehensions about the possibility of contamination of the waters of our sacred river Ganga. I can assure the that House that all of us share concern of the Honourable Members as well as by the people at large at the possible hazards to our environment and people.

The House is aware that as soon as these reports came to our attention, we expressed our grave concern to the U.S. authorities and have subsequently been in touch with them in New Delhi and in Washington. We have also made thorough enquiries at our end to obtain as complete details as possible in the last few days. In the light of international situation prevailing at that time and scientific developments which were taking place both far and near, it was decided by the government of India and the Government of United States of America at the highest level that a remote sensing device with nuclear power-pack should be installed near the highest point of Nanda Devi with the object of securing information about missile developments. Accordingly, a mountaineering expedition manned only by the Indian mountaineers went up the Nanda Devi followed by a Joint Indo-American expedition scientifically equipped with the device with a view to installing it at a height of 25,000 feet.

When the expedition was approaching the summit, it was overtaken by a blizzard which made further ascent impossible and facing fatal hazards to the party, they were obliged to retreat to the lower camp at a height of 23,000 ft. In the precipitate descent under very trying and exacting conditions they had to leave the power-pack securely cached. With the onslaught of winter, no attempt to locate and retrieve the device was immediately possible and had to be postponed. Another expedition was mounted in May 1966 in the following spring, with the intention of retrieving and installing the device. However, the expedition party on arrival at the area discovered that a major avalanche had occurred around the area and the device could not be located. Every attempt was made by ground and aerial search aided with supersensitive scientific equipment to trace the power-pack but these efforts proved in vain. After all such attempts conclusions reached by our experts, which included scientists, was that if the power-pack was broken, it would have been detected through these means and the likelihood was that the device got buried into neighbouring crevice by the avalanche. Searches both on the ground and by helicopters were organized every year over a wide area and continued till late 1968 but without the equipment being sighted or detected by the scientific means.

Simultaneously, samples of the water were taken up to 1970 and were under observation for some years but no trace of contamination was detected.

In 1967, a new device was taken to the same area and was duly installed on a neighbouring peak. This functioned for a while but was removed subsequently in 1968 and the equipment was returned to the United States. These operations, as I said, were apparently carried out predominantly by Indian personnel but under joint auspices and were in the know of and with the approval at the highest political level of the Government of India.

After the news reports appeared, a few days ago, we have assembled relevant details and background of these expeditions with reference to available record and in consultation with both the US Government and the Indian Departments who were involved in this project.

We have tried to get as much technical information about the device as was possible. According to information obtained and published literature on the subject, the device comprises of a power system energized by 2 to 3 lbs of plutonium-238 metal alloy which is contained in several doubly encapsulated leak-tight capsules. The inner capsules enclosing the plutonium are made of 20 mil thick tantalum - a refractory metal. The primary function of tantalum is to inhibit corrosive action of the plutonium fuel. The outer capsules are encased in a Graphite heat block which along with the thermoelectrical modules in turn is encased in a cylindrical aluminium casing which is 14 inches in diameter and 13 inches high. The total weight of the entire assembly was 38 lbs.

According to the records, it is clear that at that time all aspects of safety, including the possible hazards to the operating hands and general public, were taken into account and conclusion was reached that no undue hazard existed. The tests, which have been carried out by the United States, indicate that even under extremely unlikely conditions of complete instantaneous fuel exposure to water, there is little, if any, possibility of pollution attaining unsafe limits. We understand that even in such an unlikely eventuality, a flow of 5,000 gallons per day would itself dilute the dissolved material to safe drinking water levels. It is also believed by scientists that the dangers of pollution on instantaneous exposure to air are also minimal. In brief, they claim that the design details and protective systems are such as to ensure the maximum possible safety against splintering and consequential contamination and environmental hazards.

Notwithstanding the safety factor in the design and the results of physical search and scientific detection, now that our government's attention has been drawn to it, we are making renewed efforts to make ourselves triply sure. It is proposed to appoint a committee of scientists to study and assess the problem and with the help of all possible expert advice, to recommend such further action as may be considered necessary to safeguard against future hazards to the environment and to the people. We have taken immediate action to obtain fresh samples of the water from the upper reaches.

As I mentioned, we have been in touch with the American Government. The US authorities had provided technical details, scientific co-operation and sophisticated equipment at the time when the search operations for the missing power-pack were being made in the summer of 1966.

Mr. Speaker, I can recall the critical situation with which we were faced during these days of concern, apprehension and anxiety. The authorities concerned in India at the highest level assessed the situation in terms of certain precautionary and effective devices to identify the various threats and contingencies and decided upon the measures which I have outlined above. It is clear from the records that as far as human agencies could provide against hazards, they were taken into account. It is unfortunate that nature intervened to present for the future as we now find it, a continuing source of apprehension and anxiety.

However, as far as I see, no cause for alarm on grounds of health or environmental hazards exists. The indirect evidence so far is that the safety precautions built into the pack may be as effective as has been claimed and if so pollution effects may not take place in future. It is gratifying that none have been detected so far. I would also like to assure the House that to our knowledge, no other device of this kind exists on Indian soil and no such operations which carry potential national hazards would be permitted by us."

Morarji Desai outlined the government version uninterruptedly for over half an hour heard in stunning silence by Parliament Members. Measures suggested by Morarji had no effect on the opposition MPs who continued to raise their voices on this hidden danger to the sacred Ganges. The Speaker tried to calm them down by saying that the Himalayas would not be going to be ruined in a day. However, many Members of Parliament were sceptical of accurate scientific assessment in this regard. K. Lakkappa, a Congress MP, lamented Indian scientists as gutless against the western pressure. He was concerned whether India should have independent thinking and understanding about the sophisticated science and technology that had been deliberated by the Indian scientists. Another Congress MP, K.P. Unnikrishnan was apprehensive of the fact whether the Government was revealing the entire story. He cited the presence of the CIA as a grave danger to the national security of India and other developing countries which was neglected by the government. He was concerned that the Nanda Devi mission was not a minor scientific expedition in search of something.

The Indian media added fuel to the fire. One commentator focused on the false allegation in the Kohn article that a disgruntled US team member assaulted an Indian intelligence officer which was termed as contempt of the CIA towards their Indian counterparts. There was no truth in such wild allegations of Kohn. Accusations of Indian mountaineers as CIA agents were also malicious and unfounded. The Indian participants were all Government officials and were patriots to the core and had no inkling about the background of the US team. But much damage was already done when Kohli was summoned from Sydney by the Prime Minister's Office on 10 May 1978. Initially, Morarji Desai personally sought a briefing from him on his memory about this mission. Thereafter, Kohli was asked to submit a report on the entire operation which he gave on 18 May. Kohli concluded that his gut feeling focused on two possible scenarios. First, the missing device could have hit the snowfields softly and landed intact on the glacier. The heat generated by the device would have caused it to sink to the very bottom of the glacier making it impervious to detection from the current generation of alpha and neutron meters. The less likely eventuality was that it had hit a rock on the fall, broken apart, and been strewn across the glacier. If that were the case, however, he was pretty sure that at least some debris or radioactivity would have been detected during their search missions. Kohli was the head of the expedition team to carry the device and install at the place determined by the Americans. He was neither a nuclear expert nor an environmental genius. He only outlined the possibility of the area where the device could have fallen due to the avalanche. He pointedly gave his assessment in this regard and was not supposed to brief about the components of device which was not his cup of tea.

Morarji Desai submitted his reply on 17 April 1978, i.e. just four days after the news article appeared in Outside magazine even when Kohli, who was the only eye witness to all events, was not consulted by the Prime Minister's Office. What Morarji Desai revealed in the Parliament was the handiwork of the bureaucrats of his office and available intelligence as well as opinion of the science fraternity of that period. Kao, who was Director of ARC responsible for this operation, had retired by then. He was a victim of the high-handedness of Morarji Desai. There were some serious discrepancies in the statement of Morarji Desai if the testimony of Kohli could be considered as the actual version which was available in May 1978. The statement of Morarji in

Parliament mentioned that the mountaineering expedition was manned only by the Indian mountaineers who went up the Nanda Devi followed by a Joint Indo-American expedition. Kohli stated in his book that the Americans were associated with them since the very beginning of the expedition. Again the statement said that the operations were predominantly carried out by the Indian personnel in contradiction to what Kohli wrote.

Morarji Desai further informed the House that, "The tests, which have been carried out by the United States, indicate that even under extremely unlikely conditions of complete instantaneous fuel exposure to water, there is little, if any, possibility of pollution attaining unsafe limits." There is no mention of such tests of the US authorities in the book of Kohli who even went there for initial training along with some other mountaineers. Morarji said that there was no cause of alarm on the grounds of health or environmental hazards existing as of then. It was preposterous in view of the fact that the statement was prepared in just four days after Kohn's article was published and no person who participated in the expedition was consulted while drafting such assertion to inform the House. It was all guesswork or misinformation provided by the bureaucrats. More so, the Prime Minister did not clarify as to how the samples were taken only up to 1970 and not beyond that year. It was a hastily prepared statement which was patchy, incoherent and unsubstantiated by any evidence which could focus on the authenticity of facts and circumstances.

John D. Dingell and Richard L. Ottinger, Members of Congress of the United States, wrote a letter on 12 April 1978 to Jimmy Carter, the US President and the Indian Ambassador to USA, Nani A. Palkhiwala, forwarding therewith the details of Outside magazine published by the Rolling Stone. They asked the US President to investigate this matter and provide them full details of his findings. They raised the concern that if the facts of the article were accurate, necessary steps have to be taken to resolve the serious and embarrassing situation for the USA. They also asked the Indian Ambassador Palkhiwala to provide them details available with the Indian Government relating to this issue.

The New York Times reported the same day of Morarji Desai statement that, "The (United States) State Department would neither confirm nor deny today's the statement by the Indian Prime Minister that the planting of a nuclear-powered device in the Himalayas had been a joint project of India and the United States." Senator Alan Cranston sought clarification from the CIA on this issue to which he got the following reply from an unidentified official:

"Thank you for your letter...I am advised that it is the policy of the CIA not to publicly comment on speculation about the intelligence activities which may appear in the media from time to time. You should be aware, however, that the CIA does report on its activities to oversight committees in both Houses. They are the Senate Select Committee on Intelligence....and the House Permanent Select Committee on Intelligence....These two committees and others in Congress maintain a careful scrutiny of the activities of the Central Intelligence Agency."

Hence two suppositions mentioned by Kohn's news report remained unanswered. The one about the SNAP's casing is based on Kohn's words, ".....would eventually corrode and release its poisonous core. Handling or inhaling plutonium can be fatal and it would be impossible to retrieve the radioactive material once it escaped into the snow...." Whatever Kohn wrote was correct on several accounts but what the CIA responded was unethical.

Kohli and other climbers of the mission had given complete details of extensive searches and findings of futile efforts to locate the missing sensor. It belied the insinuations of Kohn that feckless efforts were made by the CIA in this regard. While all these activities were hectic at New Delhi, R&AW quietly dispatched Rawat to Nanda Devi in the middle of June to make visual inspection of the south-western front of the peak. An American expedition was already under progress into the Sanctuary. Rawat was clandestinely represented as a liaison officer of the Indian Mountaineering Foundation to assist the expedition team. He surveyed the possible slopes in this disguise but found nothing in the end. This was the last known attempt by the Indian Intelligence to locate the missing device.

In 1982, the Indian Government declared the Sanctuary as a National Park in view of the fact that some environmentalists complained to the government about the region's unique and encapsulated flora and fauna which were decaying due to the garbage left behind by the expedition teams. In its small size and enclosed nature of the ecosystem of the region, the effect from even a small amount of trash was harmful. Thereafter, it was closed for all the climbing expeditions and trekkers. The entire Sanctuary, including the outer flanks of its walls on all sides, was placed on the United Nations Educational, Scientific and Cultural Organization's (UNESCO) list of World Heritage Sites in 1988.

However, while celebrating the Golden Jubilee of the College of Military Engineering, the Army's Corps of Engineers got permission to send a scientific and ecological expedition to Nanda Devi. It included army engineers and scientists of the Wildlife Institute of India. They were deputed to assess the impact of the long closure on the diversity of flora and fauna and clean up the junk of the past climbs. Five mountaineers scaled the summit of Nanda Devi. They brought about a ton of rubbish with them while returning to New Delhi. It included empty butane jars, hundreds of plastic food wrappers and rusting carabiners. In the reception held to celebrate this event, Kohli too was invited to examine the trashes. He found one olive-drab box used to bring the seven plutonium capsules into the Sanctuary. This box was checked for radioactivity but found negative. This box was used by the mission team to bring the plutonium canisters to the mountain which was left at the Base Camp after it was emptied in the generator. It was concluded that the supporting staff could have thrown it into a gully to lighten the load with him. The testimony of engineers too proved that it was found between the Base Camp and the Sanctuary helipad. Thereafter, this issue was closed for ever on the report of Kohli.

❑

# 7

# Nocuous Plutonium

Despite various theories about the word plutonium, it is widely assumed that coincidentally its origin is linked to the Latin name "Pluto", the God of the dead and ruler of the underworld and from the Greek word ploutos, i.e. wealth. Probably, like a supernatural power imbibed from this Godly connection, plutonium is considered the most deadly poisonous substance on this earth. Scientists have candidly admitted that no other substance is as lethal as plutonium is. This is because it came from Uranium which was named after the planet Uranus and neptunium which was named after the planet Neptune. Plutonium emits neutrons, beta particles and gamma rays. According to the scientist fraternity, plutonium-238 (also known as Pu-238) is a radioactive isotope of plutonium that has a half-life of 87.7 years. It is a very powerful alpha emitter. This makes the plutonium-238 isotope ideal for use in Tadioisotope Thermoelectric Generators (RTGs) and radioisotope heater units.

The Nuclear era of modern history was the by-product of intense rivalry among fascist governments in Europe during and after the First World War. The German weapon project was an impending danger among the scientists who lived as refugees from Nazi Germany in other fascist countries. This decade of thirties saw a strong mistrust among these fascist countries about the new discoveries in the nature of atoms, including the existence of nuclear fission. When apprehensions were going around among many war-affected countries that the nuclear weapons were theoretically feasible, the British and United States Governments decided to work on it tirelessly to be ahead of all such eventualities. In this background, this project was transferred to the authority of the US army and code-named as Manhattan Project. The portion of this project related to the development of weapons was assigned to the Los Alamos Laboratory in northern New Mexico under the directorship of Physicist J. Robert Oppenheimer, who is considered the creator of the atom bomb.

Plutonium is a radioactive silver metal which can be used to create or destroy. Initially after its discovery, it was used for destruction, but today the element is used mostly for creating energy throughout the world. According to scientific records, plutonium was first discovered in 1941 by scientists of the University of California, USA. This discovery was not shared with the rest of the scientist community until 1946, after the World War II. A paper related to this discovery was submitted to the journal, Physical Review, in March 1941 but it was removed when found to have mentioned that an isotope of plutonium, Pu-239 could be used to create an atomic bomb. However, it would be impossible to understand plutonium without understanding its origins, in a human context, as a bomb-making material. It is argued that plutonium is a man-made material. It could be a fact in a way but it is believed that plutonium existed before earth itself, in the depth of space as a by-product of supernovae, or exploding stars. This fact was further proved by the French Scientists in 1972 when they discovered in the uranium mines called Oklo in Gabon, situated in Central Africa, four tons of plutonium created by the natural reaction of thousands of years.

However, it was the outbreak of Second World War which gave plutonium a so deserving place; else it could have been relegated to the abstruse orbit of elemental obscurity if it was not discovered that it was more fissionable than the hard to produce uranium-235. It was concluded that plutonium was more appropriate to uncontrollable chain reaction which was an essential part for making a bomb. Knowledge of this property came into consideration in March 1941, after a few months of discovery of plutonium. It was a time when Japan's onslaught in Second World War over the US Navy was increasing immensely which later resulted in the attack on Pearl Harbour.

According to Los Alamos National Laboratory, soon after this discovery, this team of scientists was dispatched to the University of Chicago to lead the Plutonium Production Lab, also known as the Met Lab. Main purpose of the lab was to create plutonium as part of the Manhattan Project which was a secret venture during World War II that worked exclusively to develop an atomic bomb. This project achieved the big success and eventually produced enough plutonium for the "Trinity Test". Trinity, three-fold nature of God, was the code name of the first detonation of a nuclear weapon. It was given by the Director of Los Alamos Laboratory, and inventor of the Atomic Bomb, Robert Oppenheimer.

In March 1944, the E-9 (Explosives Development) group of scientists was assigned the task of planning of the first nuclear test by the US Government. Seven subgroups were formed to assist this team in this endeavour. These groups were comprised of experts from services, shock and blast, measurements, meteorology, spectrographic and photographic, airborne measurements and medical. The scientists wanted a flat area space suitable for this test to minimize secondary effects of the blast with a little wind to spread radioactive fallout. Eight sites were surveyed and finally the northern end of the Alamogordo Bombing Range, in Socorro County near the town of Carrizozo and San Antonio was selected for this nuclear blast. Soon thereafter, war scale preparations were made to construct the required paraphernalia in the vicinity of the proposed site.

In August 1944, the Alamos Laboratory's physics division known as "G" assigned the name Gadget to this project out of sheer euphemism for a bomb. Initially, it was not specifically referred, as the Trinity Test device was yet to be developed but once it was decided, it became the code-name. The Trinity Gadget was officially a Y-1561 device, as was the Fat Man which was later used in bombing of Nagasaki. These two were similar except for the absence of fusing and the external ballistic casing. The bombs were still under development and small changes continued to be made to the Fat Man design.

After completion of the bomb "Gadget" for detonation, it was hoisted on top of a 100 Feet (30 meter) steel tower. This height would give a better indication of how the weapon would behave when dropped from a bomber because the detonation in the air would maximize the amount of energy applied directly to the target and would generate less nuclear fallout. This tower was cemented 20 Feet (6.1 meter) into ground on four legs with concrete footings. On the top were an oak platform and a shack made of corrugated iron that was open on the western side. The Gadget was hauled up with an electric crane. A truckload of mattresses was placed underneath in case the cable broke and the Gadget fell down. A seven member team drove out to the tower to perform the final arming shortly after 22.00 hrs. on 15 July 1945.

The scientists wanted good visibility, low humidity and light winds at low altitude for the test. This quality of weather was predicted between 18 and 21 July. In the meantime, the Potsdam Conference was scheduled to be held in Germany between 18 and 21 July wherein the three Heads of USA, UK and USSR were to meet to decide on how to administer the defeated Nazi Germany. It was in the aftermath of Germany's surrender nine weeks earlier on 8 May, it was one of the terms of surrender. The main purpose of this conference was establishment of a post-war order, peace treaty issues and countering the effects of war. The US President was keen that this test should be conducted before that conference so that the USA could assert its total domination in this post-war scenario. Hence, the test was scheduled for 16 July, when the bomb components would be duly fixed for explosion. More so, USA wanted to rehearse before the world community what was in the offing for the ongoing confrontation with Japan.

The First atomic bomb "The Gadget" was thus exploded near Socorro near New Mexico on 16 July 1945 at 5:29:45 AM. The device exploded with an energy equivalent to around 20 kilotons of TNT. It was the beginning of the era of nuclear explosion. As a result of the data gathered on the size of the blast, the detonation height for the bombing of Hiroshima was set at 1,885 feet (575 metres) to take advantage of the Mach Stem blast reinforcing effect. The final Nagasaki burst height was 1,650 feet (500 metres) so the Match Stem started sooner. The knowledge that implosion worked led Oppenheimer to recommend that the uranium-235 used in a Little Boy gun-type weapon could be used more economically in a composite core with plutonium. It was too late to do this with the Little Boy meant for Hiroshima. Information related to the Trinity test was made public only after the bombing of Hiroshima on 12 August 1945. This test was also a prelude to the Fat Man bomb later detonated over Nagasaki, Japan, on 9 August 1945.

After the test, Oppenheimer said that the world would be the same hereinafter. Some people would laugh, a few would cry but most would be silent. He is quoted as saying that while witnessing the explosion, he thought of a verse from the Hindu holy book, the *Bhagavad Gita*(XI, 12):

कालोऽस्मिलोकक्ष्यकृत्प्रवृद्धोलोकान्समाहर्तुमिहप्रवृत:।
ऋतेऽपित्वांनभविज़्यन्तिसर्वेयेऽवस्थिता:प्रत्यनीकेषुयोधा:।।११-३२।।

*Transliteration:*

*Divi Surya Sahasrasya Bhaved Yugapad Uthithaa*
*Yadi Bhaaha Sadrusee Saa Syaad Bhaasasthasya Mahaatmanah*

"If the radiance of a thousand suns were to burst at once into the sky, it would be like the splendour of the mighty one". This famous Hindu scripture is: "Vishnu is trying to persuade the Prince Arjuna that he should do his duty and to impress him, he takes on his multi-armed form and says that, "Now I have become Death, the destroyer of worlds'." According to the Royal Society of Chemistry all they suppose all this thought, one way or the other. Hence, the new invention based on the deadly plutonium was made available to the world community by the US scientists and new agenda of future warfare was a cause of concern for major powers at that time.

Primarily, plutonium is a by-product of the nuclear power industry. According to the Los Alamos National Laboratory, around 20 tons of plutonium is produced nowadays . Even the spent nuclear fuel can be reprocessed to separate usable plutonium from other elements in the fuel. A survey of World Nuclear Association revealed that testing of weapons in the atmosphere in the 1950s and 1960s left tons of plutonium in the atmosphere of the earth which is lying even today.

After the havoc caused by this deadly element in Japan wherein millions of people were killed, wounded, crippled and caused deformation of future generations, properties of plutonium were declassified further by the scientists. Out of the five isotopes of plutonium, only two isotopes—plutonium-238 and plutonium-239 were practically used for anything at all. Plutonium-238, though deadly enough, was mainly used to generate electricity for space missions using radioisotope thermoelectric generators. These generators are used when the mission cannot get enough solar power because of being far away from the Sun. When concentrated enough, plutonium-239 undergoes a fission chain reaction which is used in nuclear weapons and some nuclear reactors. In fact, one of the biggest uses for plutonium is energy. According to the survey of the World Nuclear Association, over one-third of the energy produced in most nuclear power plants comes from plutonium. It is also the main fuel in fast neutron reactors. Indeed, it was plutonium's extraordinary response to shape and density that made it the material of choice for nuclear weapons. According to a Nobel Prize-winning scientist, plutonium is so unusual as to approach the unbelievable. In some conditions, it could be as hard as lead and brittle as glass and under other conditions, as soft as plastic. It will burn and crumble quickly to powder when heated in air or slowly disintegrate when kept at room temperature and could undergo transition in five phases up to melting point. It has four oxidation states and is toxic.

However, in the initial stages of this invention, the scientist community never realized the gravity of the danger hidden in the properties of the plutonium. The death of two scientists was perhaps a caution signal to handle this element with utmost care; else, its deadly effect was dangerous for survival of those who were involved with its further studies. It would be pertinent to understand how toxic this substance is when it comes into direct contact with a human body. These two scientists paid the price at the cost of their life while handling the project related to the plutonium studies.

**Harry Daghlian:** He was a physicist with the Manhattan Project which designed and produced the atomic bombs which were dropped in Japan by the US Government. During the course of an experiment on 21 August 1945, Daghlian was involved in building a neutron reflector manually by stacking a set of 4.4 Kilogram tungsten carbide bricks in a fashion around a plutonium core. The purpose of the neutron reflector was to reduce the mass required for the plutonium core to attain criticality. Daghlian was moving the final brick over the assembly. He was alerted by neutron counters to the fact that any addition of such brick would render the system supercritical. While doing so, he withdrew his hand and inadvertently dropped the brick inside the centre of the assembly. This assembly had already attained the critical state and the accidental addition of that brick reacted immediately into the prompt critical region of neutronic behaviour. A critical accident occurred thereafter. Daghlian made a futile attempt to take out the brick from the assembly. He disassembled a part of the tungsten carbide pile in order to stop the reaction. During medical examination, it was estimated that Daghlian had received a dose of 510 rem (5.1 Sv) of neutron radiation from a yield of 10 of 16 fissions. He was diagnosed with symptoms of severe radiation poisoning. He was in coma continuously before he died 25 days after the accident. He was the first known casualty caused by the radiation effect in this nuclear research related to the danger of plutonium density. After this accident, safety regulations were reviewed and it was decided to have at least two persons in such an experiment, use of at least two instruments monitoring neutron intensities with audible alerts and preparing a plan for operating methods and any contingencies that might occur during similar experiments. Daghlian was memorialized on 20 May 2000 by the city of New London with the erection of a memorial stone and flagpole in Calkins Park which was unveiled by his brother and sister. It read, "Though not in uniform, he died in service to his country."

**Louis Slotin:** He was a Canadian physicist and chemist who worked on the Manhattan Project at the Los Alamos National Laboratory. He was involved in the experiments with uranium and plutonium core to determine their critical mass values. On 21 May 1946, Slotin along with his seven colleagues was performing an experiment which involved the creation of one of the first steps of a fission reaction by placing two half-spheres of beryllium (a neutron reflector) around a 3.5 inch (89 mm) diameter plutonium core. In this experiment, Slotin used the same 6.2 kilogram (13.7 lb.) plutonium core which had irradiated Harry Daghlian. This core was later named as "demon core" for its role in these two accidents. Slotin grasped the upper 228.6 mm (9 inch) beryllium hemisphere with his left hand through a thumb hole at the top while he maintained the separation of the half-sphere using the blade of a screwdriver with his right hand, having removed the shims normally used. It was however an unusual exercise because screwdrivers were never a normal part of such experimental protocol. While doing so, the screwdriver accidently slipped and upper beryllium hemisphere fell which caused a prompt critical reaction and a burst of hard radiation. Slotin experienced a sour taste in his mouth and an intense burning sensation in his left hand. He at once, dropped the upper beryllium hemisphere on the floor. He was exposed to a lethal dose of neutron radiation. Slotin started vomiting which was a common reaction when exposed to extremely intense ionizing radiation. He was rushed to the hospital but the radiation damage was already done. Soon, Slotin's condition started deteriorating rapidly. Numerous volunteers offered to donate blood for transfusions while he was in intensive care unit. During the next nine days, Slotin suffered an "agonizing sequence of radiation-induced traumas", including severe diarrhoea, reduced urine output, swollen hands, erythema, massive blisters on his hands and forearms, intestinal paralysis and gangrene. He had internal radiation burns through his body which doctors described as a "three-dimensional sunburn". By the seventh day, he was experiencing period of "mental confusion". His lips turned blue and he was put in an oxygen tent. He ultimately experienced "a total disintegration of bodily functions" and slipped into coma. He died on 30 May 1946 in the presence of his parents.

Out of those seven present in the room where Slotin was conducting that experiment, one who was standing the closest to him also developed acute radiation sickness and was hospitalized for several weeks. Although he survived but lived with chronic neurological and vision problems. Another one too suffered from acute radiation syndrome but he recovered. Three of those ultimately died of conditions which were known to be promoted by radiation.

After this accident, Los Alamos stopped all hand-operated critical assembly work. Remote-controlled machines were used thereafter for the critical testing of fissile cores in the future experiments. Operators used to sit at safe distances while conducting such tests to prevent harm in case of accidents. However, the official version of the accident of Slotin hailed him as a hero for ending the critical action and protecting seven others who were present in his room. One of the survivors later said that Dr.Slotin's quick reaction at the immediate risk of his own life prevented a more serious development of the experiment which would certainly have resulted in the death of the seven men working with him as well as serious injury to others in the vicinity of that place. However, the other blamed Slotin of using improper and unsafe procedures, endangering the others in the lab along with himself. Whatever transpired thereafter, it was also concluded that Slotin had been fully exposed to an exploding atomic bomb at a distance of 4,800 feet. Slotin was ultimately decorated with an honour when in 2002, an asteroid discovered in 1995 was named 12423 Slotin after him.

"The Manhattan Project" was without any doubt the most concerted intellectual discovery by the US scientists. Its approximate cost was around $2 billion at that time. It is a historical fact now that this Manhattan Project was responsible for the destructive end of World War II, with the first time and till date, the only use of a plutonium nuclear bomb in warfare.

Hence, it was evident that without the happenings during Second World War, no one would have given much emphasis to plutonium. A new concept of chain reaction was discovered in March 1941, just after the discovery of plutonium. During this war, plutonium became a subject of national security in the USA. However, the patent for the atom bomb was claimed by a Hungarian-Jewish scientist Leo Szilard before this war when plutonium was an unknown commodity. It happened prior to the discovery of nuclear fission which is not only necessary for splitting of the atomic nucleus but also the foundation of all nuclear energy generation be it for weapons or for peaceful purposes. In this background, Szilard was the first scientist who foresaw the atomic bomb and stoutly opposed the use of nuclear weapons during the Second World War. He garnered the support of 155 scientists working on the atomic bomb and sent an appeal to President Truman of the USA to conduct a demonstration of the atomic bombs before using it against the Japanese population. However, his appeal was not heeded by the war-monger American Government and the result was a holocaust unprecedented in the history of any war.

## Atomic Bombings in Japan

In Europe, the second war ended when Germany signed the instrument of surrender on 8 May 1945, before the Allied forces. But in the Pacific, Japan was still fighting a stiff battle despite the devastating bombing of its more than 100 cities and towns by the US air force. Although there are different versions on the number of casualties, it was estimated that around 3,33,000 people were killed and 4,73,000 were injured in these air raids. More than 5 million became homeless. Once, the Allied forces attained supremacy in Europe in the final year of the war, they prepared for the bloody invasion of mainland Japan. In the Potsdam Declaration, while deciding the fate of Germany in July 1945, the Allied Forces called for the unconditional surrender of the Japanese forces and warned of prompt and utter destruction in case of defiance. However, Japan rejected this ultimatum and the war continued in the Pacific.

After the Allied threat, Japan planned all-out defence with little left for any subsequent defence operation. In all, around 2.3 million Japanese Army troops were prepared to defend the home islands which were supported by a civilian militia of 28 million men and women. Estimates drawn about the impending casualties were varying widely but were extremely high. Around 20 million Japanese deaths were predicted in this last phase of war. For the Allied Forces, a study from 15 June 1945, by the Joint War Plans Committee, estimated between 130,000 and 220,000 US casualties. The Americans were alarmed by the Japanese build-up, which was accurately tracked through Ultra-Intelligence. The Secretary of War, Stimson, was sufficiently concerned about high estimates of probable American casualties and conducted his own study in this regard. This committee estimated that the invading Allies would suffer between 1.7 and 4 million casualties in such a scenario, of whom between 400,000 and 800,000 would be dead while Japanese fatalities would be around 5 to 10 million. In view of this large scale human destruction, the Allies contemplated the use of other options which were readily available and assuredly could decrease the American casualties i.e. use of poison gas. Quantities of phosgene, mustard gas, tear gas and cyanogen chloride were moved to Luzon from stockpiles in Australia and New Guinea in preparation by the General of the Army, MacArthur, who ensured that Chemical Warfare Service units were trained in their use. Consideration was also given to using biological weapons against Japan.

The war equation suddenly changed the scenario in the Pacific after the success of Trinity test of July 1945 by the US scientists. On 26 July 1945, the Allied leaders issued the Potsdam declaration which was the final ultimatum to the Japanese which outlined that without surrender, the Allied attack would result in the inevitable and complete destruction of the Japanese armed forces, and just as inevitable would be the utter devastation of the Japanese homeland. An attack by atom bomb was not mentioned in this communiqué. Prior to this warning, millions of leaflets were thrown over the whole of Japan, warning of the impending danger in this final phase of war. A Target Committee already selected five Japanese cities namely, Kokura, Hiroshima, Yokohama, Niigata and Kyoto as the possible target of atom bombing. However, due to the personal intervention of Secretary of War, Stimson, Kyoto was replaced by Nagasaki because of his emotional bond having honeymooned there decades earlier. How the fate of a large city of Nagasaki changed to doom due to such personal choices!

This Target Committee proposed the demonstration of atom bomb inside the Japan territory which was considered as a suspected trickery. An atomic bomb was an intricate device at the embryonic stage. Such test in some neutral territory would hardly convince Japan's determined and fanatical military men as some mocking exercise. If such an open test were made first and failed to bring surrender, the chance to give a shocking surprise that proved so effective would be gone. Though the proposal of a demonstration that would not destroy human lives was convincing, no one could suggest a way in which it could be made so imperative that it would be likely to stop the war. Many US officials and scientists argued that a demonstration would sacrifice the shock value of the atomic attack and the Japanese could deny the atomic bomb was lethal, making the mission less likely to produce surrender. Allied Prisoners of War might be moved to the demonstration site and be killed by the bomb. They were also uncertain about the success of this demonstration because the Trinity test was of a stationary device and not an air-dropped bomb. In all totality, only two bombs were available at the start of August which cost billions of dollars to the USA and using one of it for a demonstration would be too expensive for an experiment. However, on 28 July, 1945, Japan media reported that Potsdam Declaration had been rejected by the Japanese Government. Japan was willing to surrender but it was conditional and not acceptable to the Allies forces.

## Hiroshima Bombing

The Little Boy bomb was the code name for the atomic bomb meant to be dropped on Hiroshima, the seventh largest city of Japan. It was the first nuclear bomb to be used in the warfare. Its component composed of highly enriched uranium-235 of around 140 lbs (64 KG). It was dropped at 08:15 am on 6 August 1945, from the aircraft at a height of 31,000 feet to a detonation height of about 1,900 feet above the city. It exploded after 44.4 seconds when dropped from the aircraft. It released energy equivalent to 16 kilotons of TNT. The radius of actual destruction was around one mile with resulting fires across 4.4 square miles. Around 70,000 to 80,000 people, nearly 30% of the population of Hiroshima were killed by this bomb and about 70,000 were injured. Approximately 20,000 Japanese soldiers were killed. A survey estimated that about 4.7 square miles area of the city was exploded and 76% of the buildings of the city were destroyed. Over 90% of the doctors and 93% of the nurses in Hiroshima were killed or injured. The Mayor of the city was killed while having breakfast with his son and granddaughter at his house. After this bombing, Truman issued a statement that the US spent two billion dollars on this greatest scientific gamble in history and won. Truman further warned Japan that if they would not accept their terms, they should expect a rain of ruin from the air, the like of which has never been seen on this earth. Japan was also warned of such attacks on other cities if the Potsdam Declaration was not accepted. However, the Japanese Prime Minister remained obstinate and continued the war. At this juncture, the Soviet Union too abrogated the Soviet-Japanese Neutrality Pact on 5 August and started the Manchurian Strategic Offensive Operation which was the official declaration of their war.

## Nagasaki Bombing

Bombing of Nagasaki, a city of population of about 240,000, was a sheer misfortune loomed on its citizens not by choice but by compulsion. The second bombing in Japan was scheduled for 11 August on the city of Kokura. This raid was re-scheduled to two days earlier in view of bad weather forecast to begin on 10 August. Three bomb pre-assemblies were transported to Tinian, labelled F-31, F-32 and F-33 on their exteriors. On 8 August, a dress rehearsal was conducted off Tinian. Assembly F-33 was expended testing the components and F-31 was designated for the 9 August mission. This bomb named as Fat Man was the second plutonium, implosion-type bomb. The first was the "Gadget" detonated at the Trinity side on 16 July, 1945. This bomb with a total weight of 10,800 lbs contained 6.2 kg highly enriched plutonium-239. Its efficiency was rated as 10 times that of Little Boy detonated over Hiroshima. The Intensity of plutonium explosion in such devastation was never known to the Americans before this target. On the morning of 9 August, the plane carrying the Fat Man with Kokura its primary target and Nagasaki the secondary choice flew for its mission.

The original departure time limit for this mission was delayed by nearly a half-hour due to clouds and drifting smoke over the city Kokura which emanated from a major firebombing by the US planes the previous day. Some industrial units of Kokura deliberately burnt coal tar to produce black smoke to hinder clear vision for further air attack by the US planes. This smoke covered over 70% of the area over Kokura, obscuring the aiming point. Three bomb runs were made over Kokura the next 50 minutes burning fuel and exposing the aircraft repeatedly to the heavy defences around Kokura but the bombardier was unable to drop visually. By the time of the third bomb run, the Japanese anti-aircraft fire was getting close when detected by the monitoring of the US experts. After three runs over Kokura when the bomb could not be dropped, the pilot diverted his aircraft to the ill-fated city of Nagasaki which was the secondary target. It was also decided that if the fuel was found insufficient to reach the target, the bomb would be disposed in the ocean, if necessary.

When these planes were sighted over Nagasaki, the Japanese assumed them for reconnaissance and no alarms were raised. At 11:01 AM, the Fat Man was dropped on the industrial valley of Nagasaki. It exploded 47 seconds later at 1,650 feet above a tennis court. This was a place nearly 3 km away from the planned hypocentre. The blast was confined to the Urakami Valley which protected the main city in view of the intervening hills.

Although, this bomb was much more powerful then which was dropped on Hiroshima, its destruction was much less in view of the hilly terrain of Nagasaki. The radius of total destruction was around one mile and fire effect was about 2 miles in the city. Even then, it was estimated that 35,000 to 40,000 people were killed and over 60,000 were injured. Although no definite figures were available, by the end of 1945, a range of 39,000 to 80,000 can be found in various studies. A Japanese report briefly characterized post-bombing Nagasaki as like a graveyard with not a tombstone standing. Unlike Hiroshima, the trains were still running evacuating the victims to hospitals in nearby towns. Medical teams and fire-fighting brigades from the adjoining towns assisted the local administration.

When one considers that all this was the fall-out from a small size component of the plutonium, it is not surprising to consider the consequences and elemental fear stirred by the mere mention of this material. Plutonium, thus, proved very complex and incomprehensible as it was found so powerful.

This destruction was the first inflicted by the deadly plutonium on the human population. There was no testing whatsoever of an uranium bomb in Alamogordo or anywhere else before Hiroshima. It was never visualized by the American scientists with regard to any estimate but was an experiment heaped on the Japanese population. The plutonium enriched for this bombing was beyond any imagination of the scientists with regard to its intensity, causes and other destruction effects. In view of this initial destruction caused by the plutonium, it has never been repeated till today considering its innocuous properties.

## More Atomic Attacks were Planned on Japan Before It's Surrender

The US Army generals were divided with regard to more atomic attacks on Japan. LeMay, who was the mastermind of air attacks on the entire Japan, was more emphatic about these attacks. Another Fat Man Bomb was made ready for an attack on 19 August, with three more in September and a further three in October. However, one of the generals declined to use further atomic attacks without the express authority from the President. This was in modification of the previous order when the target cities were to be attacked with atomic bombs "as made ready". Secretary Stimson suggested sparing the remaining cities on the target from any atomic attack. Anyhow, good sense prevailed after observing the devastation caused by plutonium enriched bombs on Nagasaki and further atomic bomb attacks over Japan were stopped by the US. On 15 August 1945, the Emperor surrendered which was notified on 2 September 1945. There ended the first ever atomic warfare related incidents of 20th century which would always remain a scare on humanity. It was, however, an eye-opener for the major powers that thereafter are scared to use this war instrument fearing the worst consequences and Korea and Vietnam wars were the best examples. The US fought these wars with maximum casualties but refrained from using any atomic weapon in this region. Plutonium, thus, proved introspective deadly element for these super powers.

Pete Takeda, author of book "An Eye at the Top of the World", is perhaps the only person who analysed the impending danger still looming over billions of Hindu population of India as a result of this fiasco. He climbed the Nanda Devi Kot to get some proof or new information on this mission but was not so successful. He however, gave some vital information in his book. According to him:

"Here are a few facts. The SNAP-19's plutonium is not like what you would find in a nuke, nor is it the thick green glowing waste depicted in The Simpsons. Rather, it consists of those seven fuel capsules, small rods inserted in a graphite block. They were arranged in a radial pattern—one axial rod in dead centre with the remaining six arranged evenly spaced and equidistant, like a compass with six cardinal points. The metal plutonium rods were doubly encapsulated as "leak-tight" casings with the first layer being a half-millimetre of tantalum, a highly corrosion-resistant; hard, blue-grey metal. Tantalum is used in surgical instruments and electronics. In this case, it was chosen to inhibit the corrosion of the plutonium fuel, which when exposed to air oxidizes rapidly and under certain conditions, ignites spontaneously. ......

Experts in radioisotopes point out that predicting the possible effects of the plutonium power-pack on humans is sketchy at best due to the number of unknowns. The material itself poses some questions, as it is an alloy primarily composed of Pu-238 with 18 percent of Pu-239. Pu-238 gives off far more heat than Pu-239, which in turn, is the fissile material that "explodes" in nuclear weapons. Pu-238 has a half-life of 87 years. Alloying the two yielded the most effective combination of lifespan and energy generation. The SNAP was expected to last decades whether in the depths of space or on a bleak mountaintop".

He is not unwarrantedly sceptical of the presence of such deadly substance in the Nanda Devi glacier. He spent considerable time and energy to find some relevant facts to help the Indian Government to trace this hidden poison which is an unending danger until located and removed.

The US scientists during 1954 began testing the practical applications of radioactive polonium in a nuclear lab called the Mound in Ohio. This lab was initially building parts for nuclear weapons but later successfully converted nuclear heat to usable electric energy. In 1958 this lab delivered the world's first radioisotope thermoelectric generator (RTG). After some years, the first satellite equipped with an RTG power source was successfully launched using polonium-210 as its fuel. President Eisenhower's farewell speech referred to this achievement in these words:

"When I say power source, I mean the RTG created by the electricity to run on-board electronics and later small propulsion motors. The RTG doesn't use self-sustained atom splitting or fission to create heat. They depend on natural nuclear decay. In other words, the RTGs do not blow up, melt down, or chain react. Still, polonium burned hot and fast, so much so, that it was soon supplanted by plutonium-238. The plutonium required less shielding from nasty penetrating ionizing gamma radiation—the invisible killer that generates the greatest fuss and panic when people think of radiation. Plutonium-238's half-life (the amount of time it takes for half of the atoms to decay) is far longer than polonium-210 by a factor of almost 230. That extended lifespan was a big bonus, especially considering the unprecedented power demands of the emerging Space Age."

This was the plutonium which the CIA used in the spy device which was meant to be installed on the Nanda Devi peak. This RTG principal was subsequently incorporated as the electrical power source for nuclear power and designated as System for Nuclear Auxiliary Power (SNAP). The SNAPs turned radioactive heat into electricity, through what is called the Setback Effect. The Nanda Devi SNAP called as 19C had seven such plutonium rods in its graphite core. Inside the SNAP lay the metal lozenges which could emanate orange heat of radioactive decay. This SNAP was fuelled by around 1,900 grams of alloyed plutonium—Pu-238, with a life span of about 100 years and Pu-239 with life of over 24,000 years. This combination was expected to provide power the four-part Nanda Devi sensor assembly for two years without any proper supervision.

## Kosmos 954 Disaster

On 18 September, the Soviet Union launched a reconnaissance satellite, Kosmos or Cosmos 954, from its launching site the Baikonur Cosmodrome on a Tsykhon-2 carrier rocket. Russians dubbed it as "Controlled Active Satellite" while the Americans called it as a 'RORSAT", i.e., radar ocean reconnaissance satellite. Its main purpose was to monitor ocean traffic especially of NATO vessels including nuclear submarines. Its launching mass was around 3,800 kg which was powered by about 50 kg of Uranium-235. The satellite was meant for long-term on-orbit spying but it faltered. A malfunction prevented safe separation of its on-board nuclear reactor when the satellite re-entered the Earth's atmosphere the following year. The US trackers noticed that it had begun deviating from its designed orbit. The Soviets tried to regain control of their wobbling spy satellite without any success. An apparatus designed to eject the reactor core into a higher safe orbit also failed. The Soviets secretly informed the US of the problem existing with the ejection mechanism. It would soon be entering the earth's atmosphere. The Soviets informed the US that the craft would disintegrate and burn up posing no real problem.

The North American Aerospace Defence Command noticed Cosmos 954 deviating from the altitude of its orbit up to 50 miles and became uncontrollable for the Soviets. In tracking the satellite, it was finally observed that it would come down with its radioactive core on north-eastward track over western Canada. On 24 January, a fireball was seen streaking across the northern sky. Kosmos actually did not burn up. Instead it broke into pieces and scattered material including bits of the highly radioactive core over some 124,000 kilometres of the Northwest Territories,

Alberta, Nunavut and Saskatchewan. The Canadian parliament raised a hue and cry as to why the Soviets and Americans were holding back such vital information. Nevertheless, a massive detection and clean-up operation was launched codenamed "Operation Morning Light". The American and Canadian aircraft flew over the vast area trying to detect radiation with a huge ground search and recovery. It continued for over three months when initially a large section of the satellite was found by accident by the civilians on an expedition in the Arctic while the military eventually recovered some 4,000 bits, many tiny and almost all radioactive, totally about 65 kg but only a tiny 1% of the fuel. In this search operation, they ultimately recovered 12 large pieces of the satellite; 10 of the recovered fragments were radioactive. One fragment had a radiation level which was sufficient to kill a person.

While other nuclear satellites had fallen from space, it was always in the sea. But the pertinent question about the nuclear safety in space was obviously a concern for all the major powers if the satellite was prone to spread its nuclear reactor over the living population. Existing terms for such disaster were brought under the terms of reference of the Space Liability Convention of 1972 which decided that a state which launches the object into space is liable for damages cause by that object. In this pursuance, the Canadian Government billed the Soviet Union C$ 6,041,17,470 for actual expenses and additional compensation for future unpredicted expenses. The Soviet Union paid the sum of C$3 million.

Russia launched its last nuclear-powered satellite in 1988. There are still 30 nuclear powered satellites in orbit out of which 29 are Russian and one American. The US "SNAP-10a" was launched in 1965 but stopped responding only 43 days later. It, like most others, should not re-enter the atmosphere for another 3,000 years, by which time the radioactivity will be relatively harmless. However, any one of these could be hit by other space debris or tiny space meteorites with uncertain results. A radioactive cloud is now orbiting in space after the reactor Kosmos 1900 was hit by something leaking its coolant. Kosmos 1900 was also a Soviet satellite which disappeared in this manner.

These radioactive particles are dangerous for human survival be it in the orbit or lying beneath the upper portion of the earth. In space, it could be a weird imagination beyond the control of the scientific fraternity but if it is lying on earth in a particular area, it should be a cause of grave concern. Whatever is the approximate quantity of Pu-238 and Pu-239 lost in the Nanda Devi glacier, it is more dangerous than the Kosmos-954 or Kosmos-1900 fiascos. That disaster was scattered over a large area but the Nanda Devi fiasco is well documented, highly debated and scientifically examined by the US and Indian experts. Even then, if both the countries are silently watching this hidden catastrophe of millions of Indian population, it is certainly a cause of worry if efforts are not renewed to locate it.

❑

# 8

# Factum Of Indian Nuclear Policy

*The atomic Bomb has deadened the finest feeling that has sustained mankind for ages. There used to be so-called laws of war which made it tolerable. Now we know the naked truth. War knows no law except that of might...The moral to be ultimately drawn from the supreme tragedy of the bomb is that it will not be destroyed by counter bombs even as violence cannot be, counter by violence. Mankind has to get out of violence only through non-violence.*

***– Mahatma Gandhi***

City: Jodhpur, date:18 May 1974, time: around 9 AM. This author, posted at Jodhpur office of R&AW, was returning along with some colleagues from his usual morning walk, exercises and indoor games. Suddenly, the sky towards west in the desert was completely covered with a dust storm. It was an unusual sight that day, despite the fact that flow of strong dust winds was a routine matter in that season at Jodhpur. All my colleagues seemed concerned on this heavily dust-cast sky on the western part of Rajasthan towards the desert of Jaisalmer. When all these fellows reached office routinely, Col. M.N.C. Dutta, in-charge of the Rajasthan sector of R&AW, called the seniors to his office and asked them to tune to Radio Pakistan. Col. Dutta had been mysteriously busy with the army authorities in Jodhpur for the last few days. He had not disclosed anything to his junior officers about this mystery. However, the Jodhpur-Jaisalmer highway had been closed for the public for a few days prior to 18 May 1974. The whole of Jodhpur city was under the close scrutiny of Intelligence and local CID persons. Every guest house and other public staying places were fully under their control. The same was the situation in Jaisalmer which is on the western side of Pokhran. Every Intelligence and local CID person was curious about such a tight security cordon but no one dared to ask for the reason. Since, only few could have been aware of the facts, everyone was watching with utmost anxiety. Jodhpur and Jaisalmer used to be hub of local Pakistani spies and everyone was apprehending some big catch. Such was the level of “Need to Know” during that period.

Col. Dutta was the uncle of J.P. Dutta, Director of the blockbuster film ‘Border’, based on the 1971 war. Col. Dutta was involved in that operation of the 1971 war in Jaisalmer which was scripted by J.P. Dutta in the film Border. The monitoring section of Jodhpur office was put on alert to catch any message related to the wind storm in the sky. At 1 PM, Pakistan Radio announced that India had conducted a nuclear explosion in Rajasthan. India became the sixth nuclear power of the world at 8.05 AM on that day. It was the best guarded secret operation of India wherein R.N. Kao, the founder of R&AW, played a pivotal role.

## Nehru Era (1947-1964):

This historic moment for India to become a nuclear power at the initiative of Prime Minister Indira Gandhi had its genesis on the day India attained independence in 1947. When Indira Gandhi got this nuclear test conducted successfully, the Congress Party had been ruling India all along since 1947. So, whatever nuclear progress India made till 1974 is credited to this ruling party. But it was the hard work of Indian scientists who succeeded in this indigenous endeavour. Among them was the highly nationalist Indian scientist, Homi J. Bhabha, who had had an inkling of nuclear proliferation, a nuclear power. In this background, he laid the foundation of the Indian nuclear programme in 1944 and founded the Tata Institute of Fundamental Research. This was done during the British regime in India which was a remarkable achievement. However, India's nuclear policy was effectively defined in 1948 by the late Prime Minister Jawaharlal Nehru when he presented the Atomic Energy Bill in the Constituent Assembly. Nehru stated in the Assembly:

"Unfortunately, the first use that atomic energy has been put to has somewhat clouded the other manifold uses that it is likely to be put in the future. Most people probably think of atomic energy in the sense of something producing atomic bombs for the destruction of human beings. But probably, even the great destruction of that atomic bomb will be forgotten, while the use of atomic energy may in future powerfully influence the whole structure of the world. No one can say when that use will be perfected or brought into the common man's life. But the tempo of change and progress is so great nowadays, that it is quite impossible that within our lifetime we may see the whole change because of the enormous power being released for human purposes. Therefore, it is not from the point of view of war that I am placing this Bill before this House but rather from the point of view of the future progress of India and the Indian people and the world at large."

Thus, in the initial stages, the nuclear programme of India was emphasized to meet the fundamental problems which newly independent countries usually were confronting in the pre-Cold War era. Jawaharlal Nehru and Homi Bhabha were the pioneers for development of nuclear power programme during the initial years. They foresaw the role of nuclear energy in the development and progress of India. Nehru, while suggesting its peaceful purposes, observed:

"Somehow we cannot help associating atomic energy with war. That is the present context of our lives. Nevertheless, the important thing today is that atomic energy is a vast source of power that is coming to the world and it is something even more important than the coming in of wars and the like ... The point I should like the House to consider is that if we are to remain abreast in the world as a nation which keeps ahead of things, we must develop the atomic energy quite apart from war indeed. I think we must develop it for the peaceful purpose. I do hope that our outlook with regard to the atomic energy programme is going to be a peaceful one for the development of human life and happiness and not one of war and hatred."

Dr. Bhabha, the founder father of the nuclear energy programme was of the opinion that the atom can be used to formulate the philosophy of Nehru into reality. When Bhabha returned to India during the Second World War, the Dorabji Tata Trust created a Chair for him at the Indian Institute of Science at Bangalore so that he could enjoy complete freedom and adequate facilities in his research programme. On the initiative of Bhabha, the Tata Institute of Fundamental Research was created for fundamental research in physics, mathematics and nuclear energy programme so that experts could be indigenously available for India. So, Bhabha was singularly responsible of the early emergence of nuclear India from the policy foundation to decision making, from executive to scientist and engineer and from building construction to designing processes. At his initiative, Nehru formed the Atomic Energy Commission on 10 August 1948 and Bhabha was obviously appointed as its Chairman. The Commission was assigned the following functions:

(a) To protect the interests of the country in connection with atomic energy.

(b) To survey the country for minerals useful in the release of atomic energy.

(c) To train and develop the necessary scientific and technical personnel for this work.

(d) To foster fundamental research in nuclear science in its own laboratories and in the university and research institutions in India.

(e) To work and develop such minerals on an industrial scale.

(f) To take steps leading to the use of atomic energy in India for industry.

The Atomic Energy Act of 1948 was the Bible of all future nuclear developments in India till date. Initially, the Commission was assigned following major tasks:

(a) To take up such steps, may be necessary from time to time, to protect the interests of the country in connection with atomic energy by exercise of the power conferred on the Government of India by the provisions of the Atomic Energy Act.

(b) To survey the territories of the Indian Dominion to locate useful minerals in connection with atomic energy, and

(c) To promote research in their own laboratories and to subsidize such research in the existing institutions and universities.

When Bhabha was alive, he took all the policy decisions which were approved by Nehru without any check. At a time when nuclear energy was thought of only in terms of its destructive capacity, Bhabha had the courage to strike a different note. He visualized a network of atomic power industries that would produce vast amounts of radioactive material useful in industry and food preservation. There was also the possibility of the use of irradiation for artificial mutation of plants and crops and its allied application in propulsion, biology and medicine.

Like Bhabha, Nehru also preferred to identify India with the spirit of humanity instead of aspiring for nuclear arsenal. He clearly indicated, while replying to the debate on the Objectives Resolution in the Constituent Assembly regarding the nuclear energy development:

"We hear a lot about the atom bomb and the various kinds of energy that it represents and in essence today, there is a conflict in the world between two things, the atom bomb and what it represents and the spirit of humanity. I hope that while India will no doubt play a great part in all the material spheres, she will always lay stress on the spirit of humanity and I have no doubt in my mind that ultimately in this conflict that is confronting the world, the human spirit will prevail over the atom bomb."

Nehru had very categorically stated that the vast potential of atom should be harnessed only for peaceful purposes. He said, "On the one hand, the nuclear bomb and the destruction of Nagasaki and Hiroshima illustrate the horrendous revolution that has taken place in military technology and on the other, the application of nuclear energy to peaceful and constructive purposes has opened limitless possibilities for human development, prosperity and over-abundance. This major challenge confronts our times with a choice between co-destruction and co-prosperity and keeps it imperative for the world to out-law war, particularly the nuclear war". A detailed report entitled "Nuclear Explosions and their effects" prepared by three eminent scientists, Homi J. Bhabha, D. S. Kothari and V.R. Khandolkar at the behest of the India's PM Nehru, was released by the Indian Government in 1956. In the preface of this study, Nehru said, "These peaceful uses will only prosper if they are divorced from the idea of war. There can be no doubt that people all over the world passionately desire some agreement among those frightful engines of destruction to put an end to the fear that haunts humanity." While stressing the imperative need for utilizing nuclear energy for peaceful and developmental purposes, Nehru clearly pointed out in the Lok Sabha on 10 May 1954:

"The use of atomic energy for peaceful purposes is far more important for a country like India, that too I say a country whose power resources are limited, than for a country like France, which is an industrially advanced country. It is important for a power-starved or power-hungry country like India or most of the other countries in Asia and Africa".

While inaugurating India's first nuclear Reactor 'Apsara' at Trombay on 20 January 1957, Pt. Nehru categorically declared that, "Whatever might happen, whatever be the circumstances, we shall never use this atomic energy for the evil purposes." Once again on 24 July 1957, Pt. Nehru reiterated the peaceful use of nuclear energy while speaking in the Lok Sabha. "We are not interested and we will not make these bombs, even if we have the capacity to do so, and in no event will we use atomic energy for those most destructive purposes ... I hope that will be the policy of all future governments who-so-ever is in charge." In order to achieve self-sufficiency in the field of nuclear energy, a conference of various distinguished physicists, chemists, industrialists and engineers was held at the National Physical Laboratory in Delhi to discuss the atomic energy programme, particularly about the choice of reactor, its place of establishing and the difficulties of setting up one indigenously. It was in this conference that Bhabha had announced the following three stages in the country's atomic energy development for peaceful purposes:

i. Building of heavy water moderated reactors which could produce power as well as plutonium needed to start the breeders,

ii. Utilising the plutonium produced from the first stage reactors in the fast breeders. This stage will continue until suitable thorium-uranium-233 reactors become available, and

iii. To run stage 1 type breeders until thorium-uranium-233 reactors become available.

Thus, the basic philosophy behind India's atomic energy programme is to make use of India's large reserve of thorium. It was in this conference that Bhabha also announced construction of India's first Heavy Water Plant at Nangal in Punjab. After the conference, a great amount of public opinion was created in favour of nuclear energy in the country. In order to achieve self-reliance in this sophisticated field of engineering it was necessary to set up research facilities. It was therefore decided, as early as in 1954, to build India's first research reactor. Within two years, a one megawatt reactor 'Apsara' was ready. Even today Apsara is used for various isotopic and physical experiments. The success of this research reactor gave confidence to the Indian scientists and engineers to build a much bigger reactor which could be used for various experiments. In July 1958, Nehru authorized "Project Phoenix" to build a reprocessing plant with a capacity of 20 tonnes of fuel a year which was equivalent to the size of the production capacity of CIRUS research centre of Trombay. This plant used the PUREX process and was designed by the American firm Vitro International. On 27 March 1961, plutonium plant was constructed at Trombay which was commissioned in 1964.

Subsequently, The Atomic Energy Act of 1962 was enacted by Parliament for the growing need of nuclear energy in India after rapid political and scientific developments took place since the initial enactment of 1948. This act granted enormous power to the government for development, control and use of atomic energy for the welfare of the people of India for peaceful purposes. It was, thus, the evolution of the nuclear policy of India. This act removed all obstacles related to the safety measures regarding radioactive substances containing uranium like payment of compensation, the right of patent in respect of inventions for the use of atomic energy and regulating the generation of power from nuclear energy and its supply. New expertise, foster research and development of new technology were the main agenda of the Atomic Energy Commission for the future development.

Before the Indo-China border crisis of 1962, Nehru always professed the peaceful use of atomic energy but thereafter he implicitly recognized the potential of India to manufacture nuclear weapons in view of the worldwide zest for proliferation of nuclear technology for this purpose. Nehru was facing vociferous challenge from various quarters to go nuclear in the wake of the Chinese aggression of 1962 which started a public debate about nuclear options. In early 1961, while briefing media in Delhi, Bhabha firmly declared that India could make an atomic bomb in two years if the government accorded permission. Bhabha was always eyeing the military advantages of nuclear energy and had great fascination for its destructive force rather than its philosophical and scientific challenges which were the primarily considerations in formulating the first Atomic Energy Act of 1948.

After the humiliation of the 1962 defeat by China and growing disillusionment among all and sundry in India, demand for nuclear options were generated among the elite class of India particularly in media and parliament. Euphoria over non-alignment had vanished into the blue and the general Nehruvian paradigm too suffered a serious set-back after October 1962. The Gandhian philosophy of non-violence looked questionable in the Chinese aggression. Consequently, the nuclear policy was reassessed after the 1962 conflict. There was a debate in the Parliament related to nuclear options. On 23 March 1963, Ram Chandra Bede, a Jan Sangh Member of Parliament proposed the development of nuclear weapons for self-defence. He emphasized, while lamenting over the Indian Communists, that only those who wish to see the Russians or the Chinese ruling

India will oppose the development of nuclear weapons. He urged Nehru to fully utilize the Indian research in Atomic Energy for nuclear options. Nehru unsuccessfully tried to persuade all Members of Parliament either economically or morally over the limited psychological advantage of India attaining a nuclear status, but it was a hot potato for whosoever professed peaceful use of nuclear energy. However, demand for India becoming a nuclear state in every field became a strong option among the majority of Indian analysts and general public. Although the official policy of the Indian Government was peaceful use of nuclear energy, full credit goes to Jawaharlal Nehru that he laid the strong foundation of atomic research so that when country decide to exercise the nuclear option, it could achieve it without much difficulty. However, this perception was changed due to two events in the sixties. The first was Sino-Indian war of 1962 and the second was the nuclear test by China in October 1964.

However, on nuclear weapons Nehru proved to be both an idealist and a pragmatist according to the leading journalist Raj Chengappa. While he was dead against the bomb, he believed that when India called for a nuclear-free world, it must do so from a position of strength. Nehru argued that it was not because India did not have the capability of making the bomb but because he believed that a nuclear arms race would only end in the annihilation of life on earth. While criticism is heaped on Nehru for his pacifist approach towards the defence of India, we must acknowledge that he laid the foundation for making India capable in nuclear energy in every sense.

## Indira Gandhi Era (1966-1977)

After the death of Nehru in 1964, there was no major shift in the nuclear policy of India. Even after the October 1964 nuclear test of China, there were voices of concern in the Indian Parliament but this test was dubbed anti-US by some so-called liberals. However, it was a psychological boost for China vis-à-vis India in the non-aligned world. Despite economic considerations and danger to democratic institutions, it was decided that India would remain non-nuclear. Even some critics blamed Bhabha for misleading about preparedness to build a nuclear arsenal and his attempts to influence India's nuclear policy. However, Lal Bahadur Shastri changed his stance after the Xinjiang explosions by China and directed Homi Bhabha to work towards minimizing the time-limit to develop nuclear explosives to three months after getting a go-ahead. He sanctioned the Subterranean Nuclear Explosion Project (SNEP) in November 1965. The US media reported that India was working in the strictest secrecy towards developing a nuclear device. One US columnist claimed that Home Bhabha, on his visit to the US in 1964, had discussed the possibility of setting off an underwater nuclear explosion to deepen the channel between southern-most tip of India and Ceylon. But in January 1966, Bhabha died in a plane crash in the Alps on his way to a meeting in Geneva. Shastri too died of a heart attack after signing the Tashkent Pact in January 1966. Indira Gandhi became Prime Minister of India in January 1966.

Indira Gandhi was the hostess of her father Jawaharlal Nehru at his official residence in Teen-Murti Bhavan all along his tenure as the Prime Minister of India. She was groomed in this political ambience when Nehru was at the zenith of his political standing nurturing the dream of a non-aligned world away from the influence of the US and USSR. She was witness to all internal and external policies of India concerning all major subjects, be those internal or external. She was the virtual shadow of Nehru in his political legacy. She had observed the humiliations which Nehru went through after the debacle of the 1962 Sino-Indian war. Nehru's health deteriorated drastically after this incident. She had all those memories in turbulent circulation in her mind when she became the Prime Minister of India. Though in theory she initially continued the nuclear policy of her father, her attitude was totally ambivalent. She instinctively considered it not only a matter of prestige for India but was also concerned for its deterrent outcome for the strategic value at the international level. Nuclear energy became her hidden agenda and with that objective, she always kept the portfolio of Ministry of Atomic Energy directly under her control.

During the initial stages of her Government, Indira Gandhi did not pursue an aggressive nuclear policy in view of the internal squabbling she confronted with the senior leadership of her party. More so, Dr. Vikram Sarabhai, the successor of Bhabha, was averse to aggrandize the existing projects. He even stopped Dr. Raja Ramanna from projects related to Peaceful Nuclear Explosion. Around this period, super powers were putting pressure on India to accede to the nuclear non-proliferation treaty which Indira Gandhi resisted. She professed that this treaty must obligate existing nuclear weapons states to freeze and then eliminate their existing arsenals and provide the guaranty of security to those who do not acquire nuclear weapons. The USA and USSR devised their Nuclear Non-Proliferation Treaty in 1968 which Indira Gandhi refused to accept. She still emphasized the peaceful use of atomic energy primarily due to the poor economic condition of the country.

However, by 1970, the nuclear debate intensified and three opinions emerged. The first one was averse to nuclear weapons. Second opinion advocated building a small nuclear arsenal which could be operated by aircraft and later by crude-liquid-fuelled ballistic missiles. The third group supported a steadier, less provocative long-term course to develop the capacity to deploy a small but sophisticated missile-based arsenal with attendant command, control and warning infrastructure. Most of the scientific intelligentsia were in favour of building the bomb. Defence Analysts like K. Subhramanyam and Samprooan Singh strongly favoured acquisition of nuclear weapons in view of the threat of growing Chinese capability. They stressed that nuclear power and political powers are correlated elements in world politics. More so, India was no more subscribing to the outmoded war-fighting doctrine. This growing demand was however confronted by the so-called non-violence theory advocates, which were not in plenty.

The US President Nixon was a paranoid, narcissist and insecure person. He used to call Indira Gandhi a bitch and referred to Indians as bastards. Nixon hated Indira Gandhi. He had a personal disliking for Indira Gandhi because she did not accord him a ceremonious welcome when he visited New Delhi in 1967. In view of this background, the Nixon-Kissinger duo formulated an anti-India policy in all political and other international matters. In this background, they dispatched the nuclear-powered 7th fleet Enterprise into the Bay of Bengal during the course of the 1971 India-Pakistan war. It was aimed at threatening Indira Gandhi in this war. This move had an overwhelming impact on Indira Gandhi that it was necessary to demonstrate India's power and technological prowess which finally culminated in the nuclear explosion of May 1974.

Indian scientists led by Raja Ramanna along with R. Chidambaram and P.K. Iyenger were put on the task of developing a nuclear bomb for explosion.

## Nuclear Bomb Explosion of 1974

*"The Pokhran test was a bomb, I can tell you now....An explosion is an explosion, a gun is a gun, whether you shoot at someone or shoot at the ground....I just want to make clear that the test was not all that peaceful"*, said Dr. Raja Ramanna, the former Director of India's Nuclear Program speaking to Press Trust of India on 10 October 1997. He was the head of the scientists who devised this explosion.

India maintained the utmost secrecy about the manufacture of its nuclear device which was dubbed as "Peaceful Nuclear Explosive" or PNE. The Prime Minister Indira Gandhi while visiting the Bhabha Atomic Research Centre (BARC) on

7 September 1972, verbally directed the scientists there to manufacture the nuclear device which was designed and prepare it for the test. Practical work of engineering to implement the paper design started after this authorization of the Prime Minister. Simultaneously, the process of locating, surveying and preparing the test site also began. No formal records of any kind were maintained on the development process or the decision making involved in its development and testing. Though it was intentional to preserve secrecy, this event was documented entirely based on oral reports many years later.

This project was overall supervised by the chemical engineer, Homi Sethna, Chairman of the Atomic Energy Commission of India. The head of the entire nuclear bomb project was Raja Ramanna, the Director of BARC. The designer and creator of the bomb was P.K. Iyenger who was assisted by the chief metallurgist, R. Chidambaram and Nagapattinam S. Venkatesan of the Terminal Ballistics Research Laboratory, Chandigarh, who had developed and manufactured the high explosive implosion system. The explosive material and the detonation system were developed by W.D. Patwardhan of the High Energy Materials Research Laboratory, Pune. Plutonium for the bomb came from the CIRUS reactor of BARC. Thir CIRUS reactor was assisted by Canada and the US where heavy water reactor technology was developed. This implosion-type design had a close resemblance to the American nuclear bomb called the Fat Man which was dropped on Nagasaki in Second World War. To upkeep the secrecy of this project, only 75 scientists and engineers were employed during the period from 1967 to 1974.It does not count the thousands of individuals required to build and operate the infrastructure supporting BARC and to produce the plutonium for the device. Except Indira Gandhi, her Principal Secretaries, P.N. Haksar and D.P. Dhar, were the only two civilians who were aware of these developments. Even Defence and Foreign Ministers were not kept in the loop about this project.

One Engineering Regiment in Jodhpur was assigned the task of digging the shaft for the explosion. Soldiers working on this job were informed that digging of this well was meant to supply the Pokhran test range. This digging was completed only a few days prior to 18 May 1974. The completed core, probably packed as separate pieces, was transported to Pokhran from Trombay under the direct supervision of Chidambaram. They rode in an army convoy carrying the plutonium core packed in a special case for the 900 km journey which was completed in three days. The explosive lenses and other components of the implosion system came from Chandigarh. The device was assembled on 13 May in a hut 40 meter, from the shaft. The assembly operation was completed after nightfall. The assembled device was hexagonal, yellow, about 1.25 meters in diameter and weighed 1400 kg. It was mounted on a hexagonal metal tripod and transported to the shaft on rails which the army had kept covered with sand. The team retired to an observation bunker about 5 km away from the test site on 18 May. The entire team of senior leaders and contributors to this project was present along with the then Army Chief General Bewoor.

The test explosion was scheduled for 8 AM but it was delayed by 5 minutes because one engineer sent to check the high speed cameras could not return due to break-down of his jeep. The army repaired the jeep in time and the firing button was pushed at 8:05 AM delaying the schedule by 5 minutes. Sethna tried to inform the Prime Minister about this successful explosion but the field telephone went dead and he was taken to Pokhran village from where he conveyed the message to D.P. Dhar. In the meantime, Gen. Bewoor had already conveyed this news to Dhar.

This test has been known as the "Smiling Buddha" but the origin of this appellation is considered mysterious. This test was not formally code-named at the early stages. The test was coincidentally conducted on the Buddhist festival day of

Budh Purnima. Perhaps this was code-named so thereafter. Chengappa wrote in his book that Sethna had passed on the message to Dhar with the code phrase "The Budha is smiling" is probably a myth. Ramanna claims that he had been told by Sethna that the code phrase had been used and that the phrase was Dhar's idea. Whatever is the truth behind such speculation, this test is code-named "Smiling Budha" in all write-ups and it is a part of history now. All the scientists involved in this operation were duly rewarded with civil honours in 1975. The popularity of Indira Gandhi was at its zenith after this explosion. The main opposition party Jan Sangh too hailed this achievement.

The plutonium used in this test was created in the CIRUS reactor supplied by Canada and using heavy water supplied by the United States. Both countries reacted against this test in the light of the then ongoing negotiations on the Nuclear Non-Proliferation Treaty and the economic aid both countries had provided to India. Canada, thereafter, stopped the nuclear energy assistance for the two heavy water reactors under construction in India terming this test as violation of a 1971 understanding between the two countries. However, the United States concluded that the test did not violate any agreement and continued to supply shipment of enriched uranium in June 1974 for the Tarapur reactor. Pakistan's reaction was obviously an anti-Indian tirade and vowed to react in a similar manner. Despite these reactions and other criticism, India became the first Third World Country to become a nuclear power and brought it at par with the five major countries of the World who were in possession of nuclear weapons. Prestige of India was enhanced in all major cold-war and NAM countries. South-East countries too welcomed the Indian achievement in the background of what had transpired in this region during the Second World War. One deterrent had appeared in this region and that was India.

## Indian Nuclear Scientists were capable to analyse the contents of sensors used by the CIA in the 1965 Nanda Devi mission

Although, there were conflicting reporting in the US media about the political consent of this operation in India, the then Prime Minister Lal Bahadur Shastri was duly briefed about this mission. This fact was corroborated by the late Shri R.N. Kao to the author. During January 1966, Shastri died and Indira Gandhi became the Indian Prime Minister. She too was aware of the events of 1965 expedition to Nanda Devi. The IB had a reference in their records which mentioned that Indira Gandhi was informed of the sensor missions in the Himalayas. She never raised any doubt about it. Hence, all news reports in the US media were rubbish and without any justification. It debunked the claims of the Outside article that the CIA had intentionally kept the climbs a secret from Indira Gandhi and as such Indian political leadership was fully informed about the secrecy of this mission.

However, the most pertinent question remained as to how the presence of PU-238 in this project was not got assessed for threat perception by the Indian Intelligence officers from the Indian Scientists who were at the helms of Atomic Energy Commission and other nuclear-related institutions. Dr. Homi Bhabha, who died in January 1966, was not less competent than Robert J. Oppenheimer, the US Scientist, who was considered the Father of the Atom Bomb Theory. There were eminent nuclear scientists in the team of Bhabha who were working on the nuclear energy programme in India and plutonium was their main source of subject. They were well aware of its deadly qualities for the human beings. Hence, while placing such deadly substance at a dangerous place and in adverse conditions, why the threat perception was not thoroughly assessed and analysed by the Indian intelligence officers and other bureaucrats responsible for this mission remains a mystery. This author had long discussions with Captain Kohli, the leader of this expedition, about the composition of this sensor. Kohli admitted that he was never informed by anyone that this sensor contains such nuclear material which could create havoc to the mankind. During the course of training in the USA, he and his team members were given rudimentary knowledge about the procedural installation of the SNAP which was later activated with dangerous PU-238. Had he been briefed about such danger, he would have never left this sensor in Nanda Devi when blizzards cut short this expedition in 1965. He got it tied with the rock with the simple reason that it was extremely difficult to take it back and bring back again in 1966. He was never aware that the nuclear-powered sensor contained such material which was similar in destruction to the Hiroshima and Nagasaki bombs. With this background knowledge, Kohli, a die-hard nationalist and humanist, would have certainly ordered the retrieval of the whole components to the base of this expedition. Unfortunately, this threat perception was never conveyed to him by anyone including B.N. Mullik.

Morarji Desai, the then Prime Minister, while informing the Parliament on 17 April 1978, admitted that a high level decision was taken by the Indian and US Governments to install this remote sensing device with nuclear power-pack near the highest point of Nanda Devi with the object of securing information about missile developments of China. Hence, Government of India at high level was aware of the fact that this device is nuclear power-packed and contains a deadly substance. Even then, in case of some tragedy, its dangerous results were not duly assessed and analysed and never conveyed to the leader of the expedition, Captain Kohli. More so, the American nuclear experts were present all along with this device while taking it for installation. When Captain Kohli decided to keep it along a rock with the aim to install it next year, no American objected to this decision and never briefed Captain Kohli of the impending danger.

Hence, it was the most major flaw as to why the leader of the expedition was not briefed about the presence of the deadly substance, PU-238, in this sensor. Had it been known to him, there was no reason for him to leave it unattended for more than a year of time in hazardous conditions. This question is a mystery which will haunt history.

❑

# 9

# Committee Suggestions

The Howard Kohn revelation on 12 April 1978 in the Outside magazine was perhaps the first major CIA-IB operation of post-Cold war era which created an obvious uproar in the Indian Parliament. The Indian Prime Minister, Morarji Desai, too had a tumultuous political legacy courting two warring factions of the erstwhile Congressman Jagjivan Ram and hot-headed agrarian and die-hard Congress opponent Charan Singh. Morarji had to contain both these divergent political opponents and made them the Deputy Prime Ministers under him to bury the hatchet and bring peace to a little extent. He had the tacit support of the left-leaners in the Parliament. His main opponents, the Congress, including Indira Gandhi, had lost Lok Sabha elections in the anti-Congress storm of post-Emergency (1975-77) atrocities and press censorship in India. Charan Singh was detained during the Emergency along with Morarji Desai by the Indira Gandhi Government, whereas Jagjivan Ram defected from the Congress in March 1977 when Parliament elections were announced. In this scenario, Charan Singh was even portrayed to become the Prime Minister of India. In a personal meeting with the author, Charan Singh claimed himself solely responsible for ousting the Congress regime in 1977 but Jai Prakash Narayan, the undisputed patriarch of this era, preferred for Morarji Desai owing to his senior status in political life. Charan Singh unwittingly agreed to participate, though he was always uncomfortable thereinafter. In this political scenario, Morarji Desai was faced with this Kohn reverberation not only in the Parliament but also in the media, particularly of left-leaning. The presence of CIA in India in such a sensitive operation further added fuel to the fire. One Member of Parliament mocked the statement of Morarji Desai citing Chinese monkeys, the famous three who hear no evil, see no evil and speak no evil and more so if it was about the CIA. Morarji Desai was then considered a pro-American and Seymour Hersh in his book "The Price of Power" had depicted him as a CIA agent. This reference had direct bearing on his right-wing approach during that period. The US President, Jimmy Carter, visited India three months prior to this disclosure. This visit by any President of the USA took place after a long gap.

Further to the statement of Morarji Desai in Indian Parliament on 17 April 1978, the government issued a notification formulating the Committee. As per the prevalent practice, it was published in the Gazette of India by the Cabinet Secretariat as resolution No. 1/1/3/78-CF dated 4 May 1978. Text of this resolution was as under:

1. "Pursuant to the assurance given by the Prime Minister in a statement in Parliament on 17 April 1978 on the planting of a nuclear device in the Himalayas, it has been decided to set up a committee of scientists to study and assess the problem, and with the help of all possible expert advice, to recommend such further action that may be considered necessary to safeguard against further hazards to the environment and to the people.

The composition of the Committee is as under:

1. Dr. Atma Ram, Chairman
2. Dr. H.N. Sethna
3. Prof. M.G.K. Menon
4. Dr. Raja Ramanna
5. Dr. V. Ramalingaswami and
6. Dr. A.K. Saha of the Saha Institute, Calcutta.

Dr. K.T. Thomas of BARC will act as the Secretary of the Committee.

2. The Committee will have powers to co-opt and other expert as and when required, and to obtain data and information, as well as carry out any experiments that may be necessary.

3. The committee should complete its inquiry and submit its recommendations within a period of three months.

4. Secretarial and other assistance to the committee would be provided by the Department of Atomic Energy.

Sd/- Joint Secretary to the Cabinet"

This Committee was headed by Dr. Atma Ram, the Principal Scientific Adviser to the Prime Minister along with Dr. H.N. Sethna, the Chairman of the Atomic Energy Commission who was responsible for India's first atomic test in 1974 and Prof. M.G.K. Menon, the Scientific Adviser to the Defence Minister and Director General of the Defence Research and Development Organisation (DRDO). Dr. Raja Ramanna, the Director of the Bhabha Atomic Research Centre (BARC) who had also designed and installed several of the India's nuclear reactors, was one of the scientists instrumental for the 1974 nuclear explosion at Pokhran. Dr. V. Ramalingaswami, the Director General of the Indian Council of Medical Research and Dr. A.K. Saha of the Saha Institute of Nuclear Physics were experts in their own field. M.G.K. Menon later became the Minister of Science and Technology in the V.P. Singh Cabinet. They were the six best Indian scientists in the nuclear and public health services in that era. The Committee was asked to complete its inquiry and submit the recommendations within a period of three months.

Although this Committee of Scientists was asked to complete its findings in three months of time, it submitted its 94-page report under the heading "National Committee on Science and Technology" on 22 April 1979 only, i.e. almost one year after it was constituted. It is the general practice in India that such Committees and more so, Commissions never stick to the timeframe prescribed for all such eventualities, whatever may be the consequences in this long period of time consumed by them. This Committee examined the following issues and gave their recommendations for future consideration:

A. Report of search attempts during 1966-69.

B. Technical descriptions of the Nuclear Device.

C. Tests reportedly carried out on the device by the US authorities and tests specified by International Atomic Energy Agency.

D. Environmental sampling carried out so far.

E. General features of the Nanda Devi region, and the site where the nuclear device was lost.

F. i) Hazard Evaluation - General Considerations.

ii) Thermal effects and rupture of the device and components under the accident conditions.

iii) Helium build-up and its consequences.

iv) Potential of the accident conditions for the environmental contamination.

v) Assessment of air contamination under the accident condition.

vi) A perspective of the radiological hazards of Pu-238 and the critical groups of population.

vii) Evaluation of hazards to the critical groups of population.

G. Summary of Hazard Evaluation.

## Search attempts during 1966-69

The Committee concluded that this account was based on the reports made by the climbers and others involved in the expedition in 1965 and in the search operations during 1966-69 and on the official records of the period. The climbers had secured the generator and the box containing electronic equipments and accessories on the ledge where Camp IV was established. It was 609 meters (2000 feet) below the peak. Prior to retrieving these equipments in 1966, an aerial reconnaissance was carried out on 26 April 1966 in the Nanda Devi area which reported that there seemed very little snowfall on the slopes of Nanda Devi and chances for recovering the equipments seemed to be good. In May 1966, an all-Indian recovery expedition comprising of four experienced mountaineers and 48 porters was organized and sent to base camp on 21 May 1966. A recovery party of one climber and four Sherpas reached Camp IV on 1 June 1966. They found the rock, where equipments were kept, broken and swept down by thousands of feet.

A second party of two mountaineers searched the Camp IV area with the help of a mine detector on 7 June 1966. This party concluded that the generator and device could have fallen down the slope to an altitude of 5486 meters (18000 ft.) where a flat area was visible from Camp IV. This party conducted searches with the help of mine detectors on 6 June 1966 between Camp III and IV. A partly consumed butane gas cylinder was dropped from Camp IV on 8 June 1966 which was later located between the Sanctuary and Base Camp. Ground search of higher rock bumps (5547 meters - 18,200 feet approx.), flat land below Camp IV fall (5486 meters – 18000 approx.), two steep nallahs going down to the glacier (5486 - 4572 meters and 18000 - 15000 ft. approx.) and the surrounding area was carried out on 9 June 1966. It was concluded that the generator was probably buried in the sandy slopes of one of the two gullies.

After this exercise, it was decided in Delhi to mount the search operation for the generator and monitor the waters of the Rishi-Ganga and other environs of Nanda Devi areas for radioactive contamination. Air support was given in these searches which were conducted in August-September 1966. The whole mountain face was divided into three zones:

1. Moraine level,
2. 4572 meters to 5486 meters (15000 to 18000 ft.), and
3. 5486 meters to 7010 meters (16000 to 23000 ft.).

Ground visual, aerial visual and ground technical measures were adopted for these searches at different levels depending upon the altitude including the two nallahs and numerous gullies. The following technical means were used for the search operations:

1. Metallic mine detectors
2. Neutron counters
3. Alpha counters
4. Infra-red detectors

Metallic mine detectors are used by the army in detecting the buried mines contained in containers. The neutron counter capable of detecting neutrons at a depth of one foot of solid ice or ten feet of loose snow was meant to find the emission of neutrons due to the spontaneous fission of Pu-238. The Alpha counter was meant to detect the emission of alpha particles due to the radioactivity of Pu-238. It was used to test the samples of water, mud, etc. to detect contamination from a possible breach of the capsule containing the radioactive material. The Infra-red detector was used to detect the heat to a depth of not more than one or two feet, possibly for infra-red radiation property of generator which was hot. A Questar telescope was used to visually locate the equipment.

All the reports of these methods were found negative. There was no indication of enhanced infra-red, neutron, or alpha radiation anywhere in the area.

A second search was mounted in 1967 consisting of five climbers, four scientists, a medical officer and ten Sherpas (all Indians). They reached the Nanda Devi area on 13 September 1967 and stayed on the mountain slopes up to 25 October 1967. Identical methods and techniques used in the previous search were again employed but with negative results only. In 1968, aerial search by helicopter was again carried out till late October.

This report contained information that after the loss of this generator, scientists of both India and the USA had examined the problem of determining the degree of hazard created by the possible breaking of the generator casing and the likely exposure of the plutonium content and the safety precautions to be taken immediately. Likelihood of breach of the capsule containing the plutonium was considered negligible and the corrosion resistance of the containers was considered to be quite high. Radioactive contamination of the river water was considered to be insignificant and the hazard involved was negligible.

## Technical description of the Nuclear Device

From the information and data made available by the US authorities and other information gathered from literature, the Committee noted that the nuclear powered device (RTG) is of SNAP 19C (System for Nuclear Auxiliary Power) type, capable of continuous output of 40 watts of electricity for a period of two years. This type of thermoelectric power generators, based on generation of heat during radioactive decay, can be used at remote locations where unattended operations are required for a long period of time. They have been used to power remote meteorological stations, light sources of buoys, remote radio-thermal systems, electric and electronic equipment of satellites, etc. This device was fuelled with an alloy of plutonium and zirconium (Pu-Zr). The plutonium was mainly Pu-238, with about 18% of Pu-239 isotope as an impurity.

The Committee determined following salient features of SNAP 19C:

| | |
|---|---|
| Total weight of (Pu-Zr) alloy | 1900 gm |
| Total weight of Pu-238 | 1386 gm |
| Total weight of Pu-239 | 348 gm |
| Total plutonium content | 1734 gm |
| Total radioactivity content | about 23500 curies |
| Total radioactivity content per capsule | 3360 curies |

The fuel was divided into seven capsules; each capsule was given an inner cladding of tantalum (0.5 mm thick) with sufficient space for accumulation of helium gas. The heavy-walled outer cladding of the capsule was of a 2.5 mm thick alloy - Hayes-25; this alloy is composed of nickel, cobalt, chromium and tungsten, and possesses high temperature and corrosion resistant properties as well as high structural strength. The fuel capsules were installed in a hexagonal graphite block along with accessories like thermocouples, thermal insulation material, etc. The whole assembly was encased in a cylindrical aluminium shell with a number of fins for heat dissipation. The Committee gave a full and detailed version of each and every component in this device. According to them, the radioisotopes commonly used for SNAP devices are Pu-238 (half-life 86.4 years and Sr-90 (half-life 28 years), the former producing heat from the energy of alpha particles and the latter from the energy of beta particles.

The Committee disclosed that they got details of the structural data and material of construction from the United States Government sources. But no detailed information on the thermal characteristics of the device was available with them. Extensive computational data on thermal analysis which was of great value for the evaluation of the hazard of the device under different environmental conditions was not presented. The major components of device were a hot fuel block, radioactive fuel capsules placed in the core of the block, thermoelectric generators mounted around the block, insulation material and the outer casing of the block. The Committee considered all detailed specifications of individual major components of the system on the basis of information provided by the US authorities and details made available to them. These included data for the hot fuel block, specification of fuel capsules, technical details of the thermoelectric generator, aluminium housing of the complete power system, properties of the materials used in the device and nuclear properties of Plutonium-238.

## Tests reportedly carried out on the Device by the US authorities and Tests stipulated by the International Atomic Energy Agency (IAEA)

Tests carried out and conditions of such tests as reported by the United States Government:

Tests made included chemical and physical analysis of incoming fuel capsule material, weld qualification, radiographic and dye penetrant examination of fabricated components, colorimetric examination, radiation leak checks and post-assembly weld evaluation. The purpose of the weld evaluation was to ensure 100% weld penetration; uniformity of grain structure; and the absence of porosity, cracks, voids and inclusions.

The integrity of the fuel capsules under credible aircraft accident conditions was determined by a series of thermal velocity impact tests. Test velocity used was 91 meters per second. Fuel containment can be assured if the capsule is able to survive the maximum force resulting from terminal-velocity impact on a rigid material such as granite. To test this ability, a large number (46) of finely-designed capsules containing simulated fuel were heated and impacted against granite targets at the impact angles ranging from 0 degree to 60° C. These tests were successful in determining the mean velocity for failure of a capsule of each altitude of impact and thus, the margin of safety for the capsule design. This margin of safety was found to be over 50 per cent.

In addition to the mechanical impact testing described, and in keeping with the absolute containment criteria, the fuel capsules must also be able to withstand safely all the temperature and pressure combinations which will occur during the lifetime of the fuel. Internal pressure results from the decay of the plutonium fuel. Emitted alpha particles capture two electrons each and form Helium. The continued formation of helium gas within the capsule causes the internal pressure to rise. A series of temperature-pressure tests were conducted, the results of which supported the analytical prediction that the capsules will withstand these conditions without failure.

Additional tests gave assurance that the fuelled capsule will maintain its integrity in an aircraft fire or when buried in the ocean. Fire test revealed a maximum equilibrium temperature of 815° C (1500°F), whereas the melting point of the nickel alloy exceeds 1315°C (2400°F). Sea water corrosion tests indicated that the refractory metal inner liner and the nickel alloy outer capsules will contain the fuel on the ocean floor for up to 900 years, by which time the fuel will have decayed to less than one thousandth of its original quantity.

## Tests specified by the International Atomic Energy Agency for the Radioactive Power Generator Capsules

**General :** The tests described herein-under shall be applied to samples or prototypes of capsules constructed for use in a generator except that their radioactive content may be stimulated by inactive material of the same or similar nature. This implies that subsequent to satisfactory conclusion of the tests, full inspection will be carried out during the production of capsules for operational use to ensure that the standards achieved by the samples or prototypes are maintained.

In addition, every loaded capsule shall be subjected to the leakage test mentioned below, prior to installation in a generator.

The capsule shall be subjected to each of the tests mentioned below, including those for corrosion and vibration where appropriate for the particular application.

If the tests do not require to be carried out at a particular temperature, they should be done at the operating temperature, if practical.

The tests shall be carried out in such a way as to ensure that the sample capsule suffers maximum damage.

After each of the tests, the capsule shall be shown to have retained its original leak-tightness within the accuracy of the chosen method.

A different sample or prototype capsule may be used for each of the tests except in the case indicated below.

## Test Methods

**Impact Test:** The capsule shall fall on the target from a height of 9 metres. The target shall be a flat, horizontal surface of such a character that any increase in its resistance to displacement or deformation upon impact by the capsule would not significantly increase the damage of the capsule.

**Percussion Test:** The capsule shall be placed on a sheet of lead which is supported by a smooth solid surface and struck by the flat face of a steel billet so as to produce an impact equivalent to that resulting from a free fall of 7 kilograms through 1 meter. The flat face of the billet shall be 2.5 centimetres in diameter with the edges rounded off to a radius of not less than 3 millimetres. The lead, of hardness number 3.5 to 4.5 on the Brinell scale and not more than 25 millimetres thick, shall cover an area greater than that covered by the capsule. A fresh surface of lead shall be used in each test.

**Thermal Test:** The capsule shall be heated to a temperature of 800°C and it shall be held at that temperature for a period of 30 minutes before cooling.

**Thermal Shock Test:** The capsule shall be heated to its maximum operating temperature and then plunged in water at zero temperature for a time of 10 minutes.

**Pressure Test:** The capsule shall be shown to be able to resist an external pressure of 1000 bars, i.e. $10^8$Newton per square meter.

**Leakage Test:** This test is done on the requirements mentioned above. Any commonly accepted leakage test may be used, provided it is of sensitivity comparable with the detection of leakage (STP) of $10^{-4}$ $cm^3$/sec. If this degree of leakage can be detected the test requirements are not met.

**Other Tests:** For certain specifications, corrosions, vibration, irradiation and creep, tests may be specified by the competent authority.

## Tests specified by the International Atomic Energy Agency for the Radio-isotopic Power Generator Fuel Capsule Housing

**General :** The following tests shall be applied to samples or prototypes of a particular generator design and shall be carried out at the operating temperature to the extent that this is practicable. This implies that, subsequent to the satisfactory conclusion of the tests, full inspection will be carried out during the production of generators for operational use to ensure that the standards achieved by the samples or prototypes are maintained. The tests need not be carried out if it can be shown by methods of calculation or model techniques that the requirements of the tests could be met.

For the purposes of the tests the fuel capsule housing must contain actual or simulating operating components (including capsule) of the generator.

The fuel capsule housing shall be subjected to cumulative effects of the mechanical tests of mechanical and thermal tests.

**Mechanical Tests:** The IAEA specified some mechanical tests about the dropping of the housing by two drops to a target. The order in which a fuel capsule housing is subjected to the two drops shall be such that on completion of the mechanical test, the housing will have suffered such damage that it will expose it to the maximum effect in the thermal test.

**Thermal Tests:** Any thermal test may be considered as satisfactory provided that the capsule housing is exposed to a thermal radiation environment of 800°C for 30 minutes with an emissivity coefficient of 0.9, assuming the surfaces of the capsule housing have an absorption coefficient of 0.8.

**External Pressure Test:** The capsule housing shall maintain its integrity of the normal operating pressures plus a safety margin to allow for operational or accidental contingencies. This may be demonstrated by the methods of calculation or model techniques.

**Other Tests:** Under certain conditions, corrosion, vibration, irradiation and creep, test may be specified by the competent authority.

**Radiation Safety:** Following each of the above tests, there must be no loss of the radioactive fuel from the capsule. The fuel capsule housing must retain sufficient amount of its radiation shielding properties to ensure that the radiation level at 1 m from its surface does not exceed 1000 mR/h, had the housing contained sufficient iridium-192 to produce 10 mR/h at 1 m from the surface of the housing, before being subjected to the tests.

## Environmental Sampling So Far Carried Out

From a study of the topography of the area and from the ground survey, it appeared likely that the generator had fallen to the foot of the mountain along its south-west spur and would have found its way along Nallah 1 or Nallah 2 to the glacier. On this basis, it was assumed that if any radioactive contamination occurs, it will find its way along the Rishi Gorge to the Rishi-Ganga waters. Based on this presumption, samples of water, sediment and soil were collected from the areas concerned and also water of Rishi-Ganga was constantly monitored at Reni, 5 miles from Tapovan. Scientists from several organizations of the government of India were involved in the collection of samples, monitoring and analysis work. Till 23 September 1966, about 271 samples were collected from the nallahs and glaciers and all of them were tested for radioactivity with negative results.

Monitoring of Rishi-Ganga water continued throughout 1966 and 1967 at Reni. Some of the samples collected during the second search operations in September-October 1967 were also sent to the Tata Institute of Fundamental Research whose report indicated that the radioactivity was several thousand times below permissible limits. Samples of the water were taken up to 1970 and were under observation for some years but no trace of contamination was detected.

Samples of silt and water were collected in April 1978 from location of the upper Ganga (Rishikesh and Haridwar) and also from the Sharda River for plutonium estimation. Sediments collected were only from near the bottom of the shore. No cross-sectional sample was made. Estimation of plutonium was carried out by radiochemical separation and Alpha spectrometry. Detection limits for Pu-238 in water is of the order of 0.001 pC1/litre (for 10 litres). The results of the sample analysis indicated that there was no radioactive contamination in the waters and soil.

## Nanda Devi Region

The Committee had summarized all features of Nanda Devi including its peaks, longitude, latitude; approaches types including ages of rocks and geographical as well as the geological details.

Unfossiliferous sedimentary deposits were said to be deposits of very ancient age of Precambrian, i.e. about 600 million years. It also gave details of confluences of various rivers and various other drainage points which carry water to the Ganga. According to them, Rishi-Ganga flowing from an altitude of approx. 4572 meters (15000 ft.) joins the Dhauliganga River near a place Reni, situated at an altitude of 1880 meters (6170 ft.). After this confluence, the river termed as Dhauliganga travels west and then north-west before joining the bigger river Alakananda at Vishnuprayag near Joshimath. The river Alakananda in its travel downstream passes through Chamoli and Karnaprayag before it finally reaches Rishikesh and Haridwar for the confluence with the Ganga. On the southern side of Nanda Devi the Pindar River collects the drainage from Pindar glacier and flows west and joins the Alakananda at Karnaprayag. Towards east of Nanda Devi, the river Gori-Ganga flows from north to south and finally converges to the Sarayu river. On the basis of the data collected over a period of time, the flow of water in Rishi-Ganga at Reni, Dhauliganga at Tapovan and Alakananda at Helong is considerable and is subject to seasonal variations. According to the assessment of the Committee, the Nanda Devi glacier is an extension of the Dakshini Nanda Devi glacier and leads to Rishi-Ganga which joins Dhauliganga and later joins the Alakananda River. Since the glacier is only of the several sources which feed water to the Ganges (Alakananda, Mandakini and Bhagirathi rivers being the major suppliers), its contribution to water flowing into the Ganges was expected to be small, possibly even less than 5%.

During the year 1978, the nearest point of human habitation in the neighbourhood of Nanda Devi was Paing along the Rishi-Ganga with a population of 108. The next human settlement was at Riniwalla having population of 145. Lata, which is north east of the confluence of Rishi-Ganga and Dhauliganga, had a population of 308. After the confluence, as the river travels west and then northwest, the major human settlements were Tapovan

(Population 780), Dhak (226), Barhgaon (495), Regaon (535) and finally Joshimath with a population of 3853.

Climatically, some of the important data were analysed on the basis of records available for nearby and similar areas like Lokpal (4330 meters) and Tapovan (1850 meters). These included annual precipitation, precipitation during monsoon months, glacier thickness, glacier temperature, glacier movement rate, glacier length, air temperature in the vicinity of the glacier and Camp IV and snow cover added during the winter which melts during the summer thereby maintaining equilibrium condition.

## Hazard Evaluation

The Committee examined general considerations of the hazard evaluation. These included Credible Accident Conditions, Incredible Accident Conditions and Likely Conditions of Fall of the device. According to this report, the postulated accident conditions were based on the assumption that the device fell from a height of a few thousand feet. It was important to consider the possible conditions of fall to distinguish between the situations requiring detailed hazard evaluation from those which might not present a hazard for a long time. These were examined in the following paragraphs.

If the device has fallen during early snowfall period, the glacier and other surface on the foot of the hill would be covered with soft snow which would provide very good cushioning effect. Structural damage may not be great and subsequently with the melting of the snow the device could be carried downstream.

During late winter and early spring, hardening of the surface and ice formation starts. The subjects falling on hard ice surface tend to bounce. Repeated bouncing would shatter the device to hard lumps, particularly due to the very large momentum gained during the fall. It is most likely that the individual capsules would be scattered by such a fall. If this happens on the surface of the glacier, hot capsules may go deeper in the glacier and subsequently get carried away in water flow from the glacier melt or under the glacier.

As would be shown by thermal analysis elsewhere, as long as the device with all the capsules or individual capsules are in the flowing water, the plutonium fuel alloy cannot melt due to rapid heat exchange with the ambient water. Therefore, no accident condition leading to plutonium contamination is envisaged till the plutonium alloy is exposed by slow corrosion of the outer and inner cladding or due to the remote possibility of rupture of the cladding as a result of excessive pressure build-up inside. The time involved for such a process is estimated to be few decades. Even after the fuel is exposed to water, its dissolution rate is too low for water contamination of any significance. In fact, the case of water contamination due to entire plutonium mass coming in contact with a small water body has been considered later as a condition of maximum credible accident.

Finally, we should consider the fall on soft soil rock. The device gets partially buried and subsequently covered by the extensive rock fall which is reported to be a common occurrence near the foot of the hill along the glacier-fed stream. This may lead to plutonium contamination under the dry soil conditions in the later summer.

It is also estimated that the thermal effects can cause rupture of the device and component under accident conditions. The internal and external temperature of the device along with the temperature stress and rupture conditions for ejected capsules were evaluated in the ambient air and water temperature. Details of computational method used for the calculation of the temperature distribution in the device and in individual capsule were given in the report. Helium build-up and its consequences were examined in detail. In the accident condition, possible contamination of food and water along with the migration of plutonium in soil and possible concentrations in drinking water sources from complete oxidation of 24,000 Curies of Pu-238 were duly examined with relevant data. Air contamination under the accident condition was also assessed with the procedural details. Basis for the radiological hazard assessment for plutonium along with maximum permissible concentration of plutonium was duly assessed with relevant factors. Evaluation of hazards to the critical groups of population and risk analysis for Pu-238 uptake through air, food and water were duly examined. Full tabulated data of all these hazard evaluations was mentioned in the report. Assessments, risk factors and conclusions were drawn under each and every condition in this portion of the report.

## Summary of Hazard Evaluation:

The Committee considered in detail the possible factors which could lead to the breaking and rupture of the device and possible fate of the radioactive isotope Pu-238 contained in it. Eight hypothetical accident conditions related to the loss of the device by being carried in a water stream, buried under the rock and soil, covered with snow during winter and exposed in summer, exposed to the air on land, completely shattered with the ejection of the fuel capsules, etc. were apprehended by the committee. Six of the accident conditions studied were considered as possible conditions (technically termed as 'credible') while the remaining two were considered to have extremely low probability of occurrence (termed as 'incredible'). Even though there could be other possible accident conditions, the risk associated with the hazard evaluation for the conditions studied included even the worst possible conditions (termed as 'Maximum Credible Accident or MCA'). The accident conditions which could lead to the spread of Pu-238 in water, soil and air were considered in detail to assess any possibility of a hazardous situation arising from such spread of plutonium in environment.

In dealing with the radioactive contamination, the hazard potential of the assessed contamination levels is generally judged with respect to the maximum permissible levels of the particular radioactive substance in the medium. If the assessed levels are very much lower than the permissible concentrations, the situation is considered safe. Thus in the present analysis also, the estimated contamination levels in each case were compared with permissible levels to assess the hazard potential of a particular accident condition. The probability of occurrence of a particular accident was also estimated as it indicates which of the hypothetical accident conditions were more probable.

Based on the above criteria, the study has shown that none of the credible accident conditions could lead to airborne contamination due to plutonium. They can give rise to contamination of soil and water in some of the conditions studied. However, the estimated levels of these contaminations were far below the permissible concentrations.

Amongst the credible accident conditions considered, one which could lead to maximum contamination of soil and water assumes falling of the device along the SW slope. It was further assumed that on impact, the contents of the device are compressed and the compacted device is buried under the rock and soil where it occasionally comes in contact with the subsoil water. If it remains buried under the dry soil and rock, it has been estimated that the temperature can rise so much as to melt the capsule and give rise to slow combustion of plutonium and its leakage into the subsoil water. If this material comes in contact with the underground water, it can give rise to the contamination of water. It has been estimated that the highest concentration of Pu-238 in drinking water under the conditions described above is not likely to exceed 0.001 nCi/litre which is less than one thousandth of the permissible concentration. Since plutonium gets strongly bound to the soil and its uptake by the plants and vegetation is extremely low, the levels of Pu-238 expected in these will be negligibly small.

One of the incredible accident conditions studied in detail assumes that one or more of the fuel capsules are expelled after hard impact of the device on a rock or ice and blowing up of the aluminium casing. The capsules thus exposed, make a further heavy impact on a hard rock such that the fuel along with its cladding is expelled. It is further assumed that the cladding also gets ripped off and the active alloy is exposed to air where it burns and gives rise to fine particles of plutonium in the air. This accident situation, though incredible as seen from the sequence of events assumed, is of interest as it can give rise to air contamination, which is not likely to result from any of the other conditions studied. In this case, it has been estimated that even under the most unfavourable atmospheric and weather conditions, the risk to the population will not exceed 1 in 2000. This risk should be considered along with the fact that the probability of such an accident occurring has been estimated 3 in 10,000,000, giving an overall risk of less than 2 in $10^{10}$.

Analysis of the likely conditions of fall based on topography, conditions of fall, etc. indicates that, whether the device has fallen on the glacier ice or is buried under the rock, it may result, at the most, in local contamination of soil and is not likely to present any significant contamination problem for the water or air. If one considers the safety features incorporated in the device that regards its capabilities of withstanding pressures and shocks, the actual position is likely to be very safe.

Plutonium is considered highly toxic only if present in air in the form of fine suspended particles which can be inhaled, and for intake through food and water, the toxicity of plutonium is lower than that of many other radioactive substances. The permissible concentration of Pu-238 in air is only one micro-curie per cubic meter of air. It is for this reason that in all accident situations assumed, efforts were made to ascertain if it is likely to give any air contamination through rupture of the capsule. The permissible concentration of Pu-238 for water is 5 nCi/litre which is about

500 times more than the permissible concentration of naturally occurring and known to be hazardous radium-226 which is found in large concentrations in spring waters, well water and most of the drinking waters.

The percentage of Pu-239 present in the device does not present any special hazardous situation.

Relatively high permissible concentrations of plutonium in soil and water are due to extremely low solubility of plutonium in water and its strong binding to the soil. Its transfer coefficients from soil to vegetation and then vegetation to man are extremely small. It is due to these factors that the permissible concentration of plutonium is 500 times more than the naturally occurring Radium-226. The environmental level of Ra-226 in water is around $10^{-3}$ nCi/litre and values higher by factors of 100 – 10,000 that are found in many spring waters and well in high radium areas. These high values are sometimes even more than its permissible value. In comparison, the maximum activity of Pu-238 likely to be found in accident conditions studied is only a fraction of the permissible value and is comparable to the normal value of Ra-226 in drinking water.

In conclusion, the detailed analysis of hypothetical accident conditions reveal that Pu-238 source lost near Nanda Devi hills is not likely to present any radiation hazard.

It can thus be stated conclusively that the future hazard potential, if ever/any, due to radioactivity in the water route, would be such as to involve concentrations that are one thousand times less than the permissible concentrations.

In the incredible situation of: (i) capsules totally getting damaged leading to instantaneous exposure of the fuel which in turns leads to its combustion due to its pyrophoric nature and (ii) smoke of fine particles containing Pu-238 getting exposed to a critical group, leading to the risk of lung cancers after a long time of exposure; it is estimated that even in the extremely low probability of three tenths in a million, the risk is only one in 2000 under the most improbable atmospheric condition of lowest dilution. With the passage of time, this effect will be further reduced due to the decay of radioactivity. The Committee is, therefore, of the view that the future potential hazard is negligible."

Notwithstanding the above, as a measure of abundant caution and in the larger public interest; it was considered important that a continuing monitoring programme be undertaken for detecting the appearance of any abnormal radioactivity in the air, soil, water, flora and fauna of the area.

❑

# 10

# Fallacies

This author met many former senior Intelligence Officers who had accessed the details of this operation from the embryonic stage till search the operations and subsequent deliberations in the Indian Parliament. No one, including Kao, had an answer to the question on how such a big secret operation was conducted without the proper assessment of political, scientific and risk factors. These inadequacies certainly had a direct implication on this monumental failure which is still looming large as a radioactive catastrophe hidden in the Himalayas which could create havoc to the entire religious activities of the Hindu population of India from Haridwar to Kolkata. Millions of Hindus assemble in two places, Haridwar and Allahabad, for the Kumbh congregations on the river Ganga. Allahabad is the next place to host it in 2019. Initially, the CIA portrayed this nuclear device as a most hazardous toxic radiation for human life but when the Indian Government sought details through the scientific committee, they tried to dilute the initial affirmation by contradicting the initial version of the gravity of this danger. However, it would be in the best interest of our future planning of any such operation that the political, scientific and risk assessment perspectives of this mission are properly reemphasized.

## Political Perspective

When the CIA conceived this mission after the Chinese nuclear explosion in October 1964, Lyndon B. Johnson was the President of the USA and Lal Bahadur Shastri was the Indian Prime Minister. Neither the media report of 1978 by Howard Kohn nor any other news article ever revealed that the decision about this mission was approved at any political confabulation of the two countries. Pete Takeda in his book has mentioned that, "The CIA did give President Johnson a general outline of the project, but that Agency also asked him not to notify the Gandhi Government. Whether aware or not, Indira Gandhi's Government certainly inherited the espionage plot. She became the Prime Minister in January 1966. By that time, plutonium had already blighted the Himalayas." Kohli, in his book, claimed that the CIA first broached this plan with Kao, who was the then Director of ARC. He was stated to be off-guard on the gravity of the plan. "I was not authorized to sanction such an important mission", recalled Kao. "So I passed the message to B.N. Mullik". A sensor mission in the Himalayas fell under his purview, and after listening to the concept, he was agreeable in theory. However, Kohli confirmed to the author that he had no idea as to whether Shastri was kept in the loop or not by Mullik in this operation. However, Kohli wrote in his book that the Indian intelligence officials had found in their files a letter sent to Indira Gandhi soon after she took over as the Prime Minister. In the letter, she had been informed of the sensor missions in the Himalayas. Significantly, she had never voiced any opposition to the project. This debunked the charges in the Outside article that the CIA had intentionally kept the climbs a secret from Gandhi. The Indian Intelligence officials privately testified that Lal Bahadur Shastri under whose brief administration the climbs started had also been informed of the operation.

However, Morarji Desai, in his statement in the Parliament on 17 April 1978, did not mention any political concurrence between the US and Indian Governments of this mission. He stated that, "In the light of international situation prevailing at that time and the scientific developments which were taking place both far and near, it was decided by the governments of India and the United States of America at the highest level, that a remote sensing device with nuclear power-pack should be installed near the highest point of Nanda Devi with the object of securing information about the missile developments." It was intriguing why Morarji Desai neither gave specific information in the Parliament about the highest level of diplomacy between the US and Indian Governments nor he openly declared the name of the country whose missile developments information was to be monitored as China. It is evidently beyond any imagination to conclude that no political decision was mutually taken by the two governments. This plan was conceived and put in the pipeline by the CIA and IB officials with informal approval from the President of USA and the Indian Prime Minister. Even the Committee of Scientists did not mention of such political collaboration between the US and Indian Governments in their report. Hence, from the Indian perspective, no collective political decision was taken in the Cabinet Committee to authorize this sensitive operation in collaboration with the US Government. At the same time, the US authorities did not provide any documentary evidence to the Committee of Scientists which was appointed by the Indian Government to probe the underlying repercussions of this fiasco.

Hence B.N. Mullik, the all-powerful IB honcho, was the highest authority who had authorized the installation of this nuclear power-packed device. B.N. Mullik ruled had the IB from 1950 when he succeeded the first Director, Sanjeevi Pillai, till his retirement. The British intelligence considered Mullik an expert on Communism of three dimensions, i.e. Indian, Soviet and Chinese. He was an upright officer. Mullik became the favourite of Nehru due to this reason as well as his brilliant political assessments. When Mullik became the IB Director, the army top brass thought, wrongly, that he was feeding wrong information to Nehru about possible military coups so as to make the PM rely on him more and more. It was a far-fetched illusion. Mullik was a workaholic and a hard task-master. He was a devout Hindu and an anti-Communist. After his retirement, he became even more devout than when he was in service, exchanging his 'short at the back and sides' haircut for a "Choti" (the tuff of hair that old conservative Hindus used to keep). How the time changed such stalwarts, who ruled the roost and become species of unwarranted attraction because of their stubborn attitude without heeding anyone in life which continued till their death! Though Mullik had retired in October 1964,he was re-employed as the Director General of Security. The ARC was under his command during those days. So, Mullik was solely responsible from the Indian Government to approve the Nanda Devi sensor installation. Surprisingly, there is no mention of the fact in the Committee report as to who from the CIA, whether the Director himself, coordinated with Mullik. It is beyond any stretch of imagination now as to how a few intelligence officers of these two big democracies of the world authorized such a coveted, dangerous and hazardous operation under the suspicious circumstances.

Although, there is no mention of the date and time of the approval of this operation in any Indian write-up, it is believed to have been decided between October 1964 and May 1965 when Lal Bahadur Shastri was the Prime Minister. Neither Nehru nor Indira Gandhi had anything to do with this mission because the former had already died and the latter became the Prime Minister much later. Shastri was considered too weak and meek a person to indulge with defence and intelligence authorities of India at that time. However, no such details are part of any official publication. This author perused this matter with many retired directors of ARC but no political approval could be found on any official paper or any available record. Over 53 years have elapsed since this operation was organised and like the Henderson-Bhagat report of 1962 war, these records would never be declassified for the public consumption. Kohli too has denied any idea to the author as to who has approved this expedition at political level.

The Committee report was submitted to Morarji Desai on 22 April 1979. Around this period, his government was plagued with the internal frictions. His Deputy Prime Minister, Charan Singh, was given tacit support by the Congress party to revolt against Desai and become the Prime Minister thereafter. An upright Desai avoided horse-trading tactics and preferred to demit the post of the Prime Minister. He resigned on 28 July 1979 and Charan Singh became the interim Prime Minister. Charan Singh could not muster the majority for vote of confidence in the Parliament and in the ensuing Parliament elections of 1980, Indira Gandhi became the Prime Minister with a very thin majority. Due to this political upheaval, the Morarji Desai Government could not bring this report for discussion in the Parliament due to an abrupt change of guard in the South Block. Thereafter, the Indira Gandhi Government of 1980 too did not prefer to gauge the priority of this poison hidden in the Ganga. The rest is history now. No other government thereafter, tried to look into this most hazardous radiation in the glacier above the confluence of the river Ganga, a danger to a very large Indian population, the enormity of which is still unknown.

Morarji Desai made a statement on 17 April 1978, i.e. just five days after the news report of Howard Kohn. In his statement, Desai tried to placate the angry Indian politicians by stating that no undue hazard existed due to the loss of the nuclear device. He further said that the tests which were carried out by the US indicated that even under extremely unlikely conditions of complete, instantaneous exposure of fuel to water, there would be little, if any, possibility of the pollution attaining unsafe limits. Further, it was assumed that in such an unlikely eventuality, a flow of 5,000 gallons per day would itself dilute the dissolved material to safe drinking levels. This was a too immature statement issued without analysing the contents of the material inside the device and its possible danger in view of other such exposures which took place during the Second World War, the Kosmos disaster and other radiation-related accident. More so, the possible threat perspectives too were not apprehended and analysed before making this statement in the Parliament. This was a bureaucratic jugglery of the South Block to soothe the agitating Members of the Parliament. Morarji Desai almost corroborated the contents of the news report of Howard Kohn with regard to the component and its material justifying thereof what he wrote on the basis of the American sources.

## Scientific Perspectives

Surprisingly, the scientific perspective of this operation is not only intriguing, but also questionable. No US scientist broached this theory with his Indian counterpart as far as the facts available in the documents in public domain are concerned. According to Kohli's book, Barry Bishop, an avid US mountaineer and staff photographer of the National Geographic of USA conceived this notion that if a nuclear-powered sensor could be installed at some vantage position atop a mountain in the Himalayas, from there the ranges of nuclear testing of nuclear and missile programme in the China's Xinjiang province could be monitored through remote telemetry signals. The US Air Force had designed some ground-based dishes which could pick up these telemetry signals which were considered the blueprint of a delivery system related to pressure, temperature, direction and fuel consumption. The telemetry data was essential to gauge the range, speed and payload of the Chinese missile. Bishop discussed this option with Curtis LeMay, the US Air Force Chief of Staff who was also the architect of the US nuclear missile programme. This was stated to be the beginning point of this covert mountaineering operation in the Himalayas. Kohli admitted that the idea seemed sound. The CIA probably jumped into the fray on the direction of LeMay. However, Kohli did not agree to this installation on the Kanchenjunga peak, which he considered a ridiculous proposition due to the many existing problems. Kohli suggested the shifting of this installation to any of the three mountains namely Trishul, Nanda Devi Kot and Karnet. On the CIA's insistence, the plan was shifted to Nanda Devi to which Kohli reluctantly agreed. Kohli suggested Nanda Devi Kot as an ideal suggestion which worked well later on the second expedition. According to Kohli, Kao informed him initially that the Americans felt Nanda Devi Kot was too low and unworkable. So, the focus shifted to Nanda Devi despite the opposition by Kohli.

Kohli in his book revealed that the mock-up of the monitoring device was demonstrated by the CIA officials when he went with his team to the McKinley expedition trial in the USA. However, Kohli mentioned that the seven capsules in the device contained 1,734 gram of plutonium. He told the author that theirs was a mountaineering mission and other details were out of his purview. But this team, on the return from the USA, would have certainly given a report of their mock trial and plutonium must have form part of it. So, the IB was aware of the presence of plutonium in the ensuring mission. However, Kohli denied any knowledge when asked as the nuclear-powered device devised by the US authorities was a handiwork of their scientists, technocrats, CIA officials and private mountaineers. He also had no idea whether any Indian official was involved in the mechanism of this device or any logistical support was taken from the Indian Government. He also denied knowing if any details about the material components i.e. Pu-238, were disclosed to India.

Around this time, the Indian atomic energy programme was at its pinnacle and the best scientist of the world and founder father of Indian Nuclear programme, Homi Bhabha, had laid foundation of any nuclear option for the Indian Government. Plutonium was readily available in the nuclear arsenal materials of the Indian scientist fraternity. After the Xinjiang nuclear explosion of October, 1964 by China, the Indian Prime Minister, Lal Bahadur Shastri directed Homi Bhabha to make options to develop nuclear explosives within a period of three months. Nehru had given a time limit of two year in this regard to Homi Bhabha. The US Government too had apprehension of such development.

Despite these facilities to test any nuclear related material, B.N. Mullik did not care to put the nuclear device for fundamental research on its impending repercussion in case of some unforeseen tragedy, which did happen later. This pertinent negligence was either due to the CIA domination to go ahead without any government hindrance or sheer stupidity prevalent due to the arrogance and stubbornness of his working style. The US authorities were fully aware that though SNAP systems had powered remote buoys and satellites in outer space, the Nanda Devi unit was apparently the device's first earthbound deployment. This fact too was ignored by the CIA. The most important thing which Kohn revealed was that, "The American undercover agents....co-opted Indian intelligence, setting up the arrangement on an informal basis to preserve the CIA's absolute authority over the project." It was shocking that the CIA insisted on keeping this affair a secret from the political as well as bureaucratic set-up of the Indian Government.

Had the dangers of nuclear radiations been measured by the Indian scientists prior to this mission and Kohli duly informed of that, there was absolutely no reason for him to secure the sensor with a shelf in the mountain while returning due to the bad weather conditions. Kohli also admitted that neither the IB officials nor the Indian climbers had experimented with the functioning of the device. It was a monumental error of judgment on the part of Mullik and his team of advisors which led to this fiasco. On the part of the CIA, it was absolutely a risky possibility to launch a nuclear-powered device on the experimental basis and tantamount to unprecedented breach of the unwritten International Nuclear Code. Kohn alleged in his news report that the top CIA officials were anxious to keep the agency's misadventure buried as was the device. They did not inform the Prime Minister Gandhi's Government and they pressured the IB officers, who were compromised by their earlier conspiracy, to maintain their silence. The CIA allegedly also concealed its decision from the White House. These assertions of Kohn were not out of place but had absolute bearing on this whole episode. Both the CIA and the IB would have remained mute for years had Kohn's revelation not surfaced after ten years of silence of these agencies.

## Risk Assessment Perspectives

Notification dated 4 May 1978, issued by the government to formulate the committee clearly mentioned that that it would study and assess the problem, and with the help of all possible expert advice, recommend such further action that may be considered necessary to safeguard against future hazards to the environment and people. Hence, this committee was not empowered to fix the responsibility or accountability for this failure. This is the general tendency in this country. Even the details of most serious issues like the 1962 Chinese war debacle are biting dust in the cupboards of the South Block. However, the committee did not peer into the past demeanours of this sensitive operation which could play havoc with the life of millions of Indians. Leave aside the political and scientific perspectives; the committee should have assessed the risk perspectives for such type of future assignments.

## Sustainability of Installation at the Peak

The first and foremost question on the risk perspective was the sustainability of the proposed nuclear device on a height of more than 25,000 feet on Nanda Devi where the condition of the terrain had never been assessed in the past by any scientific, environmental or ecological examination. The atmospheric condition was unimaginable and beyond the reach of any human reach. The worst possible blizzards, vast snow deposits and other hazardous weather conditions were the order of the day. Installation of a device atop the proposed area was an experimental matter because no concrete type base could be established there. Although this installation did not take place on Nanda Devi, it was done on Nanda Kot devising a primitive method. Underlying physics was that the water would be heated to a sufficient temperature which would be dripped to bore four holes of the measurement, the size of the pole of the device into the snow-cap. Posts of the main components of the sensor would be inserted into these holes and then the cold water would be poured into these holes which would harden this area into icy cement. This was not a field-test theory but a temporary arrangement due to non-planning for such installation by the CIA or IB top brasses. This stop-gap installation was done for the device at Nanda Kot. This arrangement ultimately failed and all the instruments were dislocated under the snow after some time. Rawat located them with a lot of hard work; else another disaster was in the offing.

According to Kohli, the mountaineers had long noticed a strange phenomenon on the mountain peaks. It was customary for climbers to leave behind a memento after reaching a summit, such as a flag or pennant. If this was limited to a single flag post, the snow would take an extremely long time to accumulate, they could often return years later and, provided the wind had not blown it down, find the pole still fully exposed. If they placed more than one flag post in close proximity, however, there was a totally different result. Snow would almost immediately accumulate in the space in between, burying all the posts in short order. Although the four components were elevated off the surface by posts, the posts' close proximity made them a choice target for the snowdrift accumulation. A single season of monsoon snows was all it took to bury the entire apparatus under the surface. This is what exactly happened for the Nanda Kot nuclear device. When it stopped functioning and the climbers restored that capability, for how long was anybody's guess. Kohli as a mountaineer rightly wrote that laymen sitting in the comfort of New Delhi and Washington might think it feasible to hike atop and clear away the powder every quarter, but it did not sound like a sustainable arrangement. Ultimately, his assessment was correct; the device at Nanda Kot too was buried under malicious snowdrift.

Hence, even if the expedition team of Nanda Devi was able to reach the peak it had to deploy the same mechanism to install the nuclear device as was done at the Nanda Kot. So, there was no chance of its sustaining for long and its fate was none other than to either be submerged under the ice there or skid away to the same position as happened due to the avalanche. This was the major flaw in this operation which both the CIA and IB did not apprehend while conceiving this mission. Even the expedition team should have taken cognizance of this fact because they were to face the ground realities while installing this device atop the Nanda Devi. This stupidity was neither highlighted by the committee nor the political bosses when the entire details were placed before them. Even Kohli has admitted that their objective was to successfully install the device and nobody thought of how long it would continue working. More so, Kohli had only logistic duties and never mandated to its operational functioning which was the brainchild of the nuclear scientists of the USA or the CIA officials. In view of this flaw, although the Indian officials could not escape their negligence, the US officials were entirely responsible for this disaster.

## Contradictory Facts

Although it is not so relevant, as a matter of record, Morarji Desai informed the Parliament on 17 April 1978, that these operations were apparently carried out predominantly by the Indian personnel but under joint auspices. This was a totally false and baseless statement. No Indian scientist or other official was involved in the assembly of the device. It was devised and assembled by the US authorities. Only logistic support was provided by the Indian Government. There too, an American team of climbers, atomic energy experts and even doctors was involved all along in both the expeditions. Most of the US climbers were private personnel. Only during the retrieval of the device from Camp IV on the Nanda Devi, the Indian climbers were deployed and the Americans were waiting at the Base camp to receive the device. These facts were revealed later by Kohli in his book.

When the weather conditions deteriorated at Camp IV on 16 October 1965, it was decided to secure the five loads in all, i.e. four cardboard boxes containing the sensor elements and one containing the generator. It was Kohli's decision and all including the US experts, agreed to it. Why the US authorities did not anticipate the danger of leaving such dangerous material unattended almost for nine months under the adverse atmospheric conditions is a mystery. Kohli was unaware of the various radiation-related facts and he could not be blamed for securing it there. This was an American blunder. Had they asked the Indian climbers to retrieve it, there was no reason from them to defy such a decision. However, the Committee of Scientists is totally silent on this aspect of safety and did not elaborate anything, for obvious reasons.

The committee report mentioned that the second search conducted from 13 September 1967 to 25 October 1967 to locate the device comprised of only Indians including the scientists. This finding too was patchy without proper corroboration because it could construe some misgivings to the Americans. Jay Horace, an American expert from the Atomic Energy Commission, was present with the other contingent till this search was abandoned. This fact was later disclosed by Kohli.

It was concluded by the committee that the neutron counter used to measure the emission of neutron due to spontaneous fission of Pu-238 was capable to detect neutrons at a depth of one foot of solid ice or ten feet of loose snow. Another reaction was the emission of alpha particles due to radioactivity of Pu-238 for which alpha counter was used and found the only appropriate apparatus. The generator was expected to be fairly hot and therefore would give out infra-red radiation. The infra-red detector was to detect the source of heat to a depth of not more than one or two feet. All reports were found negative at that time. There was no indication of any of the enhanced infra-red, neutron, or alpha radiation anywhere in the area. This was the subject matter of re-examination by other bunch of scientists from USA and other international atomic experts which was never got done by the Indian Government. Hence, whatever the committee concluded became a final version of this scientific examination and thus questionable.

## American Version Questionable

According to a report, this nuclear device, a thermoelectric power generating system, was stated to be discovered by the Americans by "Setback Effect" over 150 years ago. This report says that these generators based on radioactive decay heat were in use for over twenty years, i.e. in 1978. They were used at remote locations where unattended operations were required for long periods of time. These were remote meteorological stations, light sources of buoys, remote radio-transmission system and electrical and electronic equipment on satellites. Such devices named as SNAP (Systems for Nuclear Auxiliary Power) were manufactured by the contractors for the US Government. This device was classified as SNAP 19C on the basis of some specifications which were known to the Americans only. Indian scientists had no knowledge of its components and intensity of danger it could cause in the event of some mishap. More so, such generators were never used in such difficult operations without proper testing. Even when the Indian climbers were sent for training in the USA prior to this mission, they were never shown details of its inside or hazardous after-effects. According to the report, the radioisotopes used for these devices were Pu-238 (half-life 86.4 years) and Sr-90 (half-life 28 years).

The US Government sources made available some structural and construction materials data to the Committee. No detailed information was given on the thermal characteristics of the device. Indian scientists made their analysis on this half-baked information provided by the US sources. Whatever specifications of individual component of the system were given to the Committee were considered for evaluation and examination. Hence, the Committee concluded their assessment on the basis of the US data. In this report nearly 1734 grams of plutonium (mainly Pu-238 isotope) was stated to be used as an alloy with zirconium. Description of placement of all components of the generator was given in the report. Composition of the alloy was given as under:

| | | |
|---|---|---|
| Pu-238 | - | 72.95% |
| Pu-239 | - | 18.31% |
| Zirconium | - | 8.74% |
| Total | - | 100% |

Zirconium and its salts generally have low systemic toxicity. It is one of the radionuclides involved in the atmospheric testing of nuclear weapons. It is considered one of the long-lived radionuclides that have been produced and will continue to produce increased cancer risk for decades and centuries to come. Such dangerous radioactive material is also part of this alloy used in the capsule. Although presence of Pu-239 was considered as negligible, from the hazard evaluation point of view, it should not be undermined considering the past historical event of the Second World War bombing in Japan where it was used in the Hiroshima disaster. These details were already revealed by Kohn in his revelation and as such no accurate material was provided by the Americans to the committee. Whatever weight of the alloy mentioned by the committee in the report was also given by the US sources and had no corroboration for cross-check.

Although tantalum, a refractory metal was used in the inner cladding of the fuel capsule, pollution linked to human use of the element has not been detected till now. But it appears to be a very conservative element in biogeochemical terms and its cycling and reactivity are still not fully understood by the scientist fraternity. Hence, it is also a matter of concern so far as hazard evaluation is considered when the fuel capsules are lying in the adverse atmospheric conditions. The Committee did not evaluate this factor. The capsules are stated to have been tested against an impact on a granite surface when moving with a velocity of 91 meters per second. The corrosion rate of Haynes-25 used in the outer cladding of the capsules is stated to be less than 0.002 mm per year in the sea water. This is contrary to the fact that the capsules are lying in highly cold conditions whereas the sea water has much more temperature in comparison to it. The Committee never compared this aspect of the impact of outer cladding of Haynes-25. Pu-238 activity in each capsule, stated to be 3360 curies for generating nearly 114 watts of heat energy, was also a subject matter of corroboration from other available material on such similar incidents which was not found mentioned in the Committee report.

According to this report, sufficient details about the size of the thermoelectric modules were not available and for the thermal analysis an average value of thermal conductivity was assumed. Other most important consideration in the operation of thermoelectric generators was the temperature difference between the hot junction and the cold junction. This too was not specified in the details made available to the Committee.

Hence, in view of above facts and circumstances, this American version reproduced by the Committee is patchy and inconsistent to the real facts. Whatever data provided by the Americans for technical description and its hazard evaluation was a dictated scientific version of the committee members without any such corroboration from actual facts or reports with the US authorities.

## International Atomic Energy Agency (IAEA) Safety Standards

The IAEA's Statute was approved on 23 October 1956 by the Conference on the Statue of the IAEA held at the United Nation Headquarters, New York. It came into force on July 29, 1957. The Headquarters of the IAEA was situated at Vienna in Austria. Its principal objective was "to accelerate and enlarge the contribution of atomic energy to peace, health and prosperity throughout the world". India was member of the IAEA like the USA. From 1978 onwards, the IAEA published various publications for the member countries which had to be adhered to while conducting any nuclear related activity for any specific purpose. The IAEA Safety Standards as defined in "The Agency's Safety Standards and Measure' were approved by the Agency's Board of Governors on 25 February 1976. These Standards and Measures were mandatory for the Agency's own operations and all members of this Agency. These standards comprise the Agency's basic safety standards, the Agency's specialized regulations and the Agency's codes of practice. The IAEA Safety Guides supplement the IAEA Safety Standards and procedures to implement them were also issued from time to time by the IAEA. The latest in this series were issued as the Regulations for the Safe Transport of Radioactive Material 1985 which was amended in 1990. There are various sections in these publications which formulated the policy for various nuclear activities including radiation protection, procedure for preparation, requirements and controls for shipments and for storage of these nuclear materials. Also, there are requirements for radioactive materials and for packaging and packages. Another important factor is the test procedures to be adopted by every member of the country. In these test procedures, demonstration of compliance, tests for special form of radioactive material and tests for packages were prescribed. There are specific guidelines for approval and administrative requirements for all these activities.

## Tests Purportedly Done By the US Authorities & Tests Stipulated By the International Atomic Energy Agency (IAEA)

The Committee in its report has prescribed test methods for Radioactive Power Generator Capsules and Radio-isotopic Power Generator Fuel Capsule Housing. In its report, the Committee did not specify these procedural specifications of the IAEA but gave only the generalized version which might be available at the time of preparation of their report. Since the IAEA had approved these guidelines in 1978 and there was no readily available procedure as it is on date, the committee was not perhaps aware of the IAEA Safety Standards. The US authorizes too did not give details of these standards to the committee as mentioned in the report. The Committee mentioned test methods of impact, percussion, thermal, thermal shock, pressure, leakage, etc. tests in their findings without quoting reference numbers of the IAEA Safety Standards. It also gave findings based on the mechanical tests, thermal test and external pressure test. Some findings of the committee were irrelevant and questionable like the impact of aircraft accident conditions because no aircraft was used for installation. The sea water corrosion tests was stated to contain the fuel of the capsule on the ocean floor for up to 900 years by which time the fuel would have decayed to less than one thousandth of its original quantity. This too was a futile exercise because the device was lost in the glacier where temperature is much low and not in the sea water where temperature is much warmer. Safety margin for the capsule design was found to be only over 50 per cent. It was an alarming evaluation in view of the final assessment of the radioactive contamination findings of the committee. Temperature-pressure test was doubtful because the device was under extreme cold conditions. According to the committee report, the IAEA test says the capsule shall fall on the target from a height of 9 meters whereas this capsule got blown from a height of around 25000 feet. These specifications mentioned by the committee are thus irrelevant and an eye-wash. According to the Committee, the US authorities had provided information on tests of chemical and physical analysis of incoming fuel capsule material, weld qualification, radiographic and dye penetrant examination of fabricated component colorimetric examination, radiation leak checks and post-assembly weld evaluation. The purpose of the weld evaluation was stated as ensuring 100% weld penetration; uniformity of grain structure; and the absence of porosity, cracks, voids and inclusions. These specifications were never in conformity with the guidelines the committee itself mentioned in the report. Thus the US authorities provided very few details of the device and other tests purported to be conducted by them which were total violation of the guidelines of the IAEA. It was all humbug and subterfuge to conceal the factual details.

## Summary of Hazard Evaluation

After the study of topography of the area and from the ground survey, the committee concluded that the generator could have found its way to the glacier through any of Nallah 1 or Nallah 2. On this assumption of radioactive contamination, samples of water, sediment and soil were collected from the areas concerned and the water of Rishi-Ganga was monitored at Reni, 5 miles from Tapovan. Scientists from various organizations of the government of India were involved in the collection of samples, monitoring and analysis work. These scientists had collected 271 samples up to 23 September, 1966 from the nallahs and glacier and all of them were tested for radioactivity with negative results.

Monitoring of Rishi-Ganga waters continued throughout 1966 and 1967 at Reni. Some of the samples collected during the second search operations in Sept.-Oct 1967 were also sent to the Tata Institute of Fundamental Research whose report indicated that the radioactivity was several thousand times below permissible limits. Samples of the water were taken up to 1970 and were under observation for some years but no trace of contamination was detected.

Thereafter, the Indian bureaucracy discontinued this monitoring perhaps for ever because this sampling restarted in April 1978 when this operation was highlighted in the media of U.S.A. The re-sampling soon started from the locations of upper Ganga (Rishikesh and Hardwar) and also from the Sharda River for plutonium estimation. Sediments collected were only near shore bottom sediments. No cross sectional sample was made. The results of the sample analysis indicated that there was no radioactive contamination in the water and the soil.

The Committee did not indict anyone as to why the sampling was discontinued after 1970 in view of the fact that the generator was still active in the glacier. Another most controversial assessment made by the committee was that water contribution flowing from the Rishi-Ganga into the Ganga was less than 5% of the total confluence. This assessment is weird because the flow of all the tributaries is inconsistent depending upon various atmosphere conditions. The author consulted many experts in this matter and none of them will certain about these calculations. Also, many write-ups on contribution of water flows in the Ganga were consulted but nowhere was this finding of the committee corroborated. Such assumption was perhaps the handiwork of someone who wanted to indicate that the presence of the generator would in least affect the quantity of water coming to the plains and flowing into the sea. This is totally haywire and disturbing aspect of this Committee report to undermine the presence of this dangerous device.

For the purpose of hazard evaluation, the committee gave five categories of credible and incredible accident conditions about the fall of device into the glacier. The report admitted that by the thermal analysis, as long as the device with all the capsules or individual capsule are in flowing water, the plutonium fuel alloy cannot melt due to rapid exchange of heat with the ambient water, Therefore, no accident condition leading to plutonium contamination was envisaged till the plutonium alloy was exposed by slow corrosion of the outer cladding and the inner cladding or due to the remote possibility of rupture of the cladding as a result of the excessive pressure build-up inside. The time involved for such a process is estimated to be a few decades. Even after the fuel is exposed to water, its dissolution is too low for the water contamination of any significance. Another assumption of the committee was that the device could be partially buried and subsequently covered by the extensive rock fall which was a common occurrence near the foot of the hill along the glacier-fed stream. This could lead to plutonium contamination under dry soil conditions in late summer. Both these accident conditions mentioned by the committee are contrary to the fact that the fuel dissolution is low for water contamination or not in extraordinary circumstances because their assessment is based on ordinary situations. Hence, all such assessments are now a subject matter of further review in view of high scientific research on this subject thereinafter.

The committee separately examined the various other hazard evaluation of different types in normal and accident conditions. These include the temperature gradients inside the device depending upon the thermal conductivity of different materials including the gaseous component, the nature of contacts between different components, insulation losses and several other factors. In these conditions, estimated temperature of the device and individual capsule was examined at various locations related to the ambient air, water/ice, soil, etc. at various degrees by computational method used for the calculation of temperature distribution in the device and in the individual capsules. Build-up of Helium gas and its consequences were also examined by various calculations. Nothing abnormal was found by the committee in all these examinations. Similarly, possible contamination of food and water under various accident conditions was also found not so significant. This assessment needs re-examination in view of the new scientific developments in this field.

Perspective on the Radiological Hazards of Plutonium and the Critical Group of Populations was also examined by the committee in details. According to International Regulations on Radiation Standards, following categories of exposed groups of individuals have been prescribed as the Critical Groups of Population for hazard evaluation:

(a) Persons occupationally exposed,

(b) Individuals and groups exposed while residing in the vicinity of a nuclear operation, and

(c) Large population.

Critical group of population in the above groups was recognized among the (b) category where people use drinking water from a stream passing through the contaminated area. According to International Regulations this population is permitted only 10% of the level of exposure permitted for the occupational category. Since the hilly area around this site is very thinly populated, probability of significant exposure was stated to be extremely low. However, there is no mention of its danger to the large population which is using this water at the lower areas where this stream passed through in various places.

## Danger of Cancer

According to the assessment of the Committee when Plutonium is ingested through food or water, a small fraction enters the bone and if the ingestion is continuous, plutonium tends to concentrate in the bone, In radiation protection terminology, bone is thus called the 'critical organ' for soluble plutonium.

Similarly, lung is the 'critical organ' for insoluble particles of plutonium. However, if soluble particles are inhaled, they also provide a mode of uptake by bone.

The Committee mentioned that the risks of bone cancer and lung cancer in mankind from the uptake of plutonium are based on limited data from animal experiments and same data on the risks of radium uptake. There is no information whatsoever on the direct biological effects of low doses of plutonium since no injury caused by uptake of plutonium has yet been detected in mankind. Therefore, hazard evaluation is carried out in terms of dose to the critical organ and statistical risk or cancer induction in the critical organ. If a group of population is exposed to the uptake of plutonium, only a small fraction of the individuals exposed to the same level are susceptible to the injury due to large variations in tissue sensitivity amongst the persons exposed. Therefore, the risk of cancer is expressed in terms of persons affected per thousand or per million.

Mankind is subjected to radiation dose from natural sources such as cosmic rays and natural radioactivity; and also from the radioactive fallout. Therefore, hazard evaluation may also be based on the comparative risks of different exposures. In the present case, hazard evaluation is based on the computed dose to the critical organs and the likely incidence of cancer amongst the exposed population group. The hazard is found to be negligibly small. The computed values are presented even though they do not suggest a hazardous situation in any of the cases studied.

This assessment of hazard evaluation related to cancer was not based on the report of medical fraternity but scientific version largely from the experts of nuclear field. After around four decades from the date of this report, the medical researchers in cancer and other diseases related to nuclear radiation exposures have found new details which could be contrary to the findings of the committee on this issue. Hence, this assessment is meaningless as on date and whole area around the place where the device was lost has to be regularly monitored by medical experts also.

## General Conclusions

In this analysis, the committee concluded that various possible modes of contamination of air, water and food were considered for different accident conditions leading to release of Pu-238 from the capsules. Only two accident conditions were identified which could lead to the contamination of air and water respectively. The case of accident leading to air contamination has shown that if a large group of individuals is exposed to the radioactive cloud at the point of maximum concentration, the lung cancer risk involved is only one in 2000 under the worst atmospheric conditions. This type of accident leading to extensive air contamination is in itself a most unlikely accident assessed to have an extremely low probability of three in ten million. In the case of water contamination, the maximum Pu-238 levels in drinking water are less than one thousandth of the permissible concentrations.

The report further stated that the large safety factor for air contamination is due to very large dilution by the atmosphere. In the case of the accident assumed, the fuel burns in a short time and forms a particulate cloud dispersing widely in the atmosphere. It does not become a continuous source and therefore the hazard potential is low. Even the likelihood of the accident condition assumed is remote.

It further mentioned that a large safety factor in the contamination of water arises partly due to very low solubility of plutonium oxide in water and partly to very large soil/water exchange coefficient.

These health-related hazards were the guess work of the nuclear scientists and not by medical experts of that era. Be it what may, the whole of the nuclear studies and medical researches of four decades back are irrelevant today. All such accident conditions, hazard evaluation based on possible nuclear disasters and possibility of not only cancer/lung diseases but also of other diseases which are new discoveries in the modern medical science should now be explored in this region. No efforts have been made at any level to look into the grave danger looming on the large population of this country due to this nuclear device which is still elusive.

In the summary of overall hazard evaluation, the committee was of the opinion that the detailed analysis of hypothetical accident conditions revealed that Pu-238 source lost near Nanda Devi hill was not likely to present any radiation hazard. It further concluded that the future hazard potential, if ever/any, due to the radioactivity in the water route, would be such as to involve concentrations which are one thousand times less than the permissible concentrations. The Committee was conclusively of the view that the future potential hazard is negligible.

The Committee concluded in its finding that notwithstanding the above, as a measure of abundant caution and in the larger public interest, it was considered important that a continuing monitoring programme be undertaken for detecting the appearance of any abnormal radioactivity in the air, soil, water, flora and fauna of the area.

Scrutiny of source material considered by the Committee indicated that only scientific literature related to nuclear radiation, ecological behaviour of plutonium, etc. were used in this report. Radiation related other medical and biological materials were not fully examined by the Committee. Ostensibly so, because no medical and ecological experts were included in the Committee by the government. Perhaps the bureaucrats of that era did not foresee the repercussions of the radiation danger that arose after the device was lost. This Committee was routinely formed when the word 'nuclear radiation' became a focal point of worry and only nuclear scientists were included in the Committee. However, Committee too could not pre-empt the other impending dangers beyond the radiation only. Overall, this report was to some extent a real hard work by the scientists of that era to analyse various aspects of this tragedy but looking from the angle of today's perspective it should be reviewed again.

❑

# 11

# Government Apathy

Indian political system including the Executive is a unique culmination of default and choice. Politicians are intently circumvented by the Executive which is generally a rudderless and least risk-taking community. In a nutshell, this evasive nature combination has utterly brought this working culture into a state of limbo. Although political will, awareness and initiative are the main causes of this concern, bureaucratic stumbling has its major attribution in this scenario. In this vacuum, usually the other two pillars of democracy, i.e. media and judiciary are playing the major role in various policy decisions. This is the ridiculous state of affairs of Indian democracy. We have seen numerous Committees and Commissions appointed on many national disasters which usually consumed considerable time and energy without giving any conclusive and blunt findings. In this case also, the Committee submitted its report when the Morarji Desai Government was in "Intensive Care Unit" and did not survive long. So, the report was thrown into the cupboard of some government office. Thereafter ten Prime Ministers came and went. The eleventh is still in office but none of these ever knew if this type of report is gathering dust or they did not think it is a matter of serious concern. This author's main objective in writing this book was to highlight this apathy of the government.

According to this report, when the nuclear device was found to be missing in 1965, efforts were made to trace it till 1970. Thereafter, utter secrecy was maintained about this hidden danger. This is a funny example of political awareness and bureaucratic stumbling. Had Howard Kohn not published his news report in the USA, there was no chance of its recurrence at any level in India. When this exposure took place in April 1978, every pillar of democracy except the Judiciary was on the heels. Thereafter, there were debates in Parliament, numerous news reports appeared and to silence all and sundry, a Committee was appointed by the Prime Minister. This is the usual practice of our democracy: to settle for a temporary reprieve from some existing danger of national importance.

The Committee concluded its report with the direction that as a measure of abundant caution and in the larger public interest, a continued monitoring programme should be undertaken for detecting the appearance of any abnormal radioactivity in the air, soil, water, flora and fauna of the area. This precaution was given in April 1979 and even after around four decades, no efforts have ever been made by any government to look into this dangerous aspect of impending nuclear disaster. Perhaps the system is waiting for it to happen and to act thereafter.

This author sought information under the Right to Information act from the office of the Prime Minister on this matter. A questionnaire of thirteen queries highlighting various issues related to this nuclear device was sent to the Prime Minister's office on 7 September 2015 (Appendix I). The Questionnaire is as under:

i. What was the weight and quality of plutonium which was sent for placement on Nanda Devi Mountain in this operation? By quality, I mean Plutonium 238 or 239 or some other variety.

ii. How was this plutonium assembled in some equipment before placing on the mountain?

iii. What is the chance of the plutonium leaking in the mountain region?

iv. If high, what sort of radioactive radiation could develop in the region where this plutonium was lost?

v. What is the time period in terms of years, for which this device containing plutonium could remain radioactive?

vi. How much danger could it impose on the river Ganga if the device containing plutonium is bared open and plutonium is mixed in the Ganga water?

vii. What could be the danger to the Indian public in case this plutonium is found in Ganga Water?

viii. What were the findings of the Committee appointed by the government in 1978 to investigate this operation?

ix. Please give me a copy of the findings of this Committee report.

x. What measures has Government of India taken in this regard since 1966 to locate the lost plutonium-fitted device so that it might not mix with waters of the river Ganga? Please give me copies of details of these measures, if any.

xi. Has the government devised any mechanism to monitor regularly the efforts to trace these lost equipments?

xii. Has the US Government helped India in this regard? If so, details thereof may be furnished.

xiii. Is it the same plutonium that was used in bombs which were dropped in Hiroshima and Nagasaki cities of Japan by the USA during Second World War? If so, how many people were killed in these bombings?

As usual, no reply was received for three months from any quarter. Disgusted, this author brought this issue to the personal notice of the Prime Minister on 29 December 2015 (Appendix II). Even thereafter, the National Committee of Planning Wing of the Department of Atomic Energy sent only a scuttled reply on 3 March 2016 (Appendix III). This letter contained reply to only four points out of the thirteen which were mentioned in the questionnaire. This author again wrote to the Prime Minister's office in June 2016 and to the Prime Minister personally in July 2016, requesting to send replies to the remaining queries but did not get any response thereafter. Strange indeed are the ways of functioning of the Indian bureaucracy even after seventy years of independence.

Strangely, the Department of Atomic Energy has informed that it does not have any information regarding the Committee or the findings of the Committee appointed by the Morarji Desai Government in 1978. Hence, the department is unaware of the components of nuclear device, likely place of disappearance and threat perceptions analysed by the Committee of scientists in 1978. Without having any information to five relevant facts of the device, the Department of Atomic Energy, however, replied to the following two queries:

i. How much danger could it impose in the river Ganga if the device containing plutonium is bared open and plutonium is mixed in Ganga water?

ii. What could be the danger to the Indian public in this case if plutonium is found in the Ganga Water?

The Department of Atomic Energy informed in response to these two queries that pursuant to missing of the power source consisting of Plutonium-238 (Pu-238) for powering a nuclear device installed at Nanda Devi sometime in 1970s (*it was lost in 1966*), extensive sampling of water and sediments was done by a Committee covering the stretch from the Gangotri to downstream of the Ganga River. Analysis of the sample results done by the Health Physics Division, Bhabha Atomic Research Centre (BARC) of the Department did not reveal contamination in water or sediments. It was reported that the missing radiation source, i.e. Plutonium-238 was a sealed source and it emits only Alpha. Alpha can be totally stopped even with paper; therefore there is no danger of leaking out or giving radiation to either marine species or polluting water of the Ganga. Such sampling was conducted on six-monthly basis upto December 2011 and since there was no outcome, the same was discontinued. In a subsequent query, the Department of Atomic Energy affirmed that in the absence of any details about the device manufactured in the USA, there are no records available with them to respond to the other queries sought under the Right to Information Act.

This reply of the Department of Atomic Energy did not specify as to when the extensive sampling of water and sediments was started and why it was discontinued with valid reasons in December 2011. The device was still lying in the glacier of Nanda Devi and this abrupt suspension of sampling in December 2011 still poses a grave danger to the water and sediments of the Ganga. If the device is dismantled for certain unknown reasons, to what extent the contents of Pu-238 would flow and mix in the Ganga is a disturbing matter. The Department of Atomic Energy did not specifically mention as to who was responsible to order the discontinuance of this monitoring. How could the country afford to allow such a tragedy which has not been resolved to some conclusion, happen?

The author asked a very pertinent scientific query from the Department of Atomic Energy whether the same plutonium was used in the bombs which were dropped in Hiroshima and Nagasaki cities of Japan by the US during Second World War.

And, if so, how many people were killed. The Department of Atomic Energy did not give any reply to this query.

The Department of Atomic Energy has mentioned that the missing radiation source, i.e. Plutonium-238 was a sealed source and it emits only Alpha which can be totally stopped even with paper. Hence, there is no danger of leaking out or giving radiation to either marine species or polluting the water of Ganga. This is absolutely ludicrous. The Committee of Scientists duly analysed the Nuclear Properties of Plutonium-238 wherein particles/ radiation of Alpha too were tabulated with facts and figures. That Committee has nowhere mentioned that Plutonium-238 emits only Alpha which can be stopped even with paper and there is no danger of giving radiation to either marine species or polluting the water of the Ganga. Hence this reply of Department of Energy does not corroborate the assessment of the Committee of Scientists. In the absence of availability of the findings of Committee of Scientists, this reply of Department of Energy does not substantiate the impending danger of radiation which is claimed negligible.

This reply of the Department of Energy lacks credibility in view of the fact that the American Scientists gave their observation about properties of the device when it was lost. These two American experts of Atomic Energy Commission along with a CIA technician had assembled at the Base Camp in 1966 after the disappearance of the device in the glacier. They tested the gravel, water sample and steel ring for emissions of Alpha particles. One of the Indian mountaineers, Bhangu, who was assisting them in this job, asked these US nuclear experts about the impending danger if there was abnormal amount of radioactivity. One of them named as Sleeper, the nuclear expert, replied in a pained tone that the water to Calcutta could become poisonous, and that millions of Hindus taking baths in the holy Ganges would be in grave health hazardous situation. This opinion of the American Nuclear experts sounds perfect because this device was assembled in the USA and its contents were known only to them and not to any Indian. The plutonium capsules have longevity of over a hundred years. Even the leader of the expedition team, Captain Kohli, has admitted in a media report that the lives of millions of Indians will be affected, especially those living along the Ganga right up to Kolkata if radiation is emitted at any time. One US Climber of this mission, Jim McCarthy too claimed that his exposure to radiation had led to his subsequent testicular cancer. In another media report, it was mentioned that nine Sherpas who carried this device died of cancer due to radiation. All these facts and circumstances debunk the reply of the Department of Atomic Energy that there is no danger of leaking out or giving radiation to either marine species or polluting the water of the Ganga.

So, according to the Department of Atomic Energy, in theory there was no big problem. However, it is hard to be sure with Plutonium-238 when it was initially used as RTG fuel in the early 1960s. Plutonium is perhaps the most erratic and inconsistent of elements. Atomically, a single chunk of plutonium exists as a stew of twenty different isotopes continuously decaying and splitting, forming different elements, recombining to its original form, changing again, ticking with radiation as it swirls impatiently through its permutations. Physically and chemically, plutonium is equally problematic. David Fishlock of the UK Group of Supporters of Nuclear Energy described this element as under:

"It has six allotropic forms or crystal structures; more than any other element. One is so brittle that it shatters like glass. Worse, it has a perplexing tendency to switch from one to another with significantly different properties, as the temperature changes. Finely divided, as swar or fillings, it can catch fire spontaneously. No one seems to know the colour of the flame, but magenta is a good guess. All this makes it infuriating to work with. Too much in one place can 'go critical' as a weak but deadly kind of nuclear explosion that releases gamma rays."

So, in real sense, plutonium is very dangerous. As explained earlier, in the early years of the nuclear age, plutonium displayed an alarming tendency for confounding, eluding and even killing those who experimented with it. Beyond the Nagasaki disaster and instant deaths in the two separate incidents of the two scientists Harry Daghlian and Louis Slotin, while manipulating blocks of plutonium in order to ascertain its critical mass during the Manhattan Project, the annals of early plutonium health physics are an alarming litany of blue flashes, exploding glove boxes, irradiation and the occasional emergency amputation. If incinerated, injected into the atmosphere as micro-particulates or inhaled, and thus lodged in the lung, a few micrograms can cause cancer.

The US government documents from the 1960s also reveal that Pu-238 slurries displayed an alarming tendency for radiation excursions while stored in tanks. This led to guidelines that limited the quantity stored in one place to not more than four pounds. So, this amount of plutonium was loaded into the RTG on Nanda Devi. Nevertheless, after the Second World War bombing of Japan, the US Government was eager to use plutonium in defence, power generation and terrestrial and celestial RTGs and convince the public that enhancing the environment's meagre bounty of transuranic elements was not a particularly dangerous or reckless thing to do.

Like the Indian Government's Department of Energy, plutonium defenders debunked the canard that "plute" is, gram for gram, the deadliest substance on earth – radium, sarin and ricin are reputedly worse. To support their case, they cited the manageable risk of Plutonium-238's routine emission – the alpha particle.

Alpha particles are deadly but lumbering. Basically the nucleus of helium atom, their positive charge drives them away from other nuclei and limits the damage they can do. Alpha particles can be stopped by paper, plastic or the thin layer of dead skin covering the human body and will wreak havoc only if inhaled or ingested. In an RTG, they are safely buttoned up inside the fuel cell's tantalum and alloy cladding. The Department of Atomic Energy's conclusion that there is no danger of any radiation to either marine species or polluting water of Ganga was based on this theory. However, there is no apprehensive assertion that if these alpha particles are mixed in the Ganga water if the cladding is broken due to some unknown accident conditions, this would lead to lung cancer, according to all reports.

However, theoretical Plutonium-238, a dependable, single-minded emitter of alpha particles and real world Plutonium-238 are two different things. This was revealed in nuclear-related documents once made public by the Los Alamos National Laboratory but withdrawn in 2002. However, due to efforts of two researchers, Gregory Walker and Carey Sublette, these documents are now available on the website of the Federation of American Scientists.

Real-world Plutonium-238, especially in its early 1960s' incarnation, was abuzz with neutron radiation. Neutrons are everybody's least favourite particle because they are heavy, carry no charge, are not stopped at the skin and can bounce to and fro like a ping-pong ball freely through the human anatomy colliding and combining with nuclei, eliciting secondary radiation and cell damage. Neutron radiation is classified as highly penetrating, demands an immense amount of shielding and is subject to a health effects multiplier. Exposure to the same energy of neutron radiation is considered to be ten times more dangerous than beta and gamma radiation and as dangerous as inhaled alpha particles.

Plutonium-238's natural decay emits a few neutron particles, i.e. about 2,100 per gram per second. However, for the Nanda Devi RTG, hidden in the matrix of plutonium physics and chemistry was another, much more significant source of neutrons – the alpha-neutron reaction. Plutonium-238 fuel is considerably more complicated than pure Plutonium-238. It hosts an admixture of approximately this quantity of five other plutonium isotopes formed during the creation of Pu-238 in the reactor, each with its own radiation profile. It also contains significant quantities – as the parts per millions and parts per billion levels – of light element impurities such as fluorine, beryllium, boron and aluminium.

The alpha-neutron effect occurs when the alpha particles emitted by the decay of the Plutonium-238 atom collide with susceptible light element impurities inside the metal itself. The impurities absorb the alpha particles and release neutrons instead. Light element impurities were a fact of life in the 1960s as scientists and technicians struggled with enormous challenges of physics, chemistry, process design and safety to generate Plutonium-238 in reactor fuel rods and extract, purify and reduce it to metal.

When the plutonium fuel cells destined for Nanda Devi and Nanda Kot were fabricated, apparently all the problems were not examined. To a certain degree, light element contamination was built into the process. A key step involved reacting of plutonium with fluorine, one of those light elements, to produce plutonium tetra-fluoride. It also produced an abundance of neutrons, enough to justify the full radiation safety paraphernalia of counters and badges, remote handling equipment and 16-inch thick Lucite shielding to protect the technicians.

After the PU-238 was reduced to metal and the fuel went into space on probes and satellites, a certain amount of light element contamination and neutrons inevitably went with it. The RTGs had to be packaged in graphite containers attached to booms so their radiation as well as their heat would attenuate before reaching the mission electronics.

In 1967, Los Alamos evaluated the existing RTG plutonium for use as a power source in heart pacemakers and tests showed that the fuel emitted unacceptably high levels of neutron radiation due to light element contamination and the alpha-neutron reaction. How much radiation? As much as 150 times as many neutrons as should have been expected based on a pure Pu-238/Pu-239 mixture! In a four-pound RTG fuel array, that is not enough neutron radiation to cause acute radiation sickness but is enough to present a genuine cancer risk to humans. So, RTG radiation safety was not simply a matter of alpha particles buzzing harmlessly against the alloy cladding of the fuel cell like bewildered bumblebees in a jar. Neutrons were most certainly there in the mix and a good number would unavoidably have gone streaming through the minimal alloy and graphite shielding into the atmosphere and into the tissues of whoever was standing nearby.

Clearly there was knowledge of the neutron issue among specialists in the RTG program in the 1960s, but that awareness does not seem to have filtered down to the Himalayan expeditions. Accounts of fuel and radiation safety issues differ markedly between the Indian and American mountaineers. American counterparts did not discuss anything on this subject with the Indians. More so, the Indian mountaineers were trained only for logistic support to install the equipment on Nanda Devi. Nothing more or less of it is factual.

The American version of the impending danger of this nuclear device SNAP 19C was contradictory on two different occasions. When the device was lost in 1966, the CIA informed the IB that people up to Calcutta could be vanished if the contents were dissolved in the Ganga water. Subsequently, the CIA maintained an eerie silence about this danger. When in 1978, this operation was disclosed to the media, the CIA diluted the initial version of its danger and informed the Committee of Scientists that it was significantly less alarming. The CIA affirmed that the generator was not a major nuclear threat in general. It could pose minor danger only to those who would come in direct contact with radiation in this region of Nanda Devi Glacier. Further, if the material is swept into the Ganga Basin, the Committee was informed that it would be diluted to a very low concentration. Even if this theory of the CIA is to be believed, the impact of low levels of radiation is never apparently detected and slow reaction of its properties could cause deaths at slow rates. Medical facilities to check such unknown nuclear products in the rural areas of the Ganga Basin are rarely available leave aside the fact that it is not found in major towns and cities.

An Indian Journalist thoroughly investigated the causes of deaths of Sherpas in their native village. Villagers of Reini, from where the porters were hired by Kohli team to carry the nuclear generator on shoulders, confirmed that all of them had died while still in their 30s and 40s. Their peers were still alive up to the age of 80s. However, after such a long gap of time, it was impossible to definitely prove that their cause of death was due to the effect of radiation from the generator. Only circumstantial facts now cause concern that these deaths could be by radiation of generator.

So far as the version of Indian Nuclear Scientists is concerned, this generator is buried and inconclusive of its danger. But the glaciologists disagreed on this theory. Glaciology is a nascent discipline in India and only a few experts are available to analyse this subject. According to them, unlike the deserts in Rajasthan where India conducted its nuclear tests under the earth, the Himalayan glaciers are not standing still. They are on the move. The Nanda Devi glacier shifts a few centimetres every year. The contrast between the deserts of Rajasthan and the Himalayan glaciers is even more dramatic from a seismic point of view. Not only do these glaciers move regularly, but they are located in an area with a history of earthquakes and tremors.

Seismologists identify the Himalayas as a 'seismic hazard' area. When the Indian plate continues to hit the Asian plate, a massive tremor is inevitable on the Gangetic Plain according to a prestigious journal on this subject. This journal pointed out that:

"Over centuries immense pressure has built up over the underground faults beneath the front ranges of the Himalayas, and one or more earthquakes will occur in India in the near future. The dates indicate that the slope zone located about 12 kilometres underground between the Indian and Asian plates is comprised of hot stream-like fluid. The temperature pressure and the amount of fluids affect the entire seismic system."

According to that journalist who interacted with a senior Nuclear Scientist and discussed all these implications, no fruitful assurance was given on these impending dangers. These fellows try to be away from such complications to save their own skins. Their approach is resolutely single-minded, and they have no interest in the insights provided by seismologists and glaciologists. They still believe that the lost device would never resurface.

The Department of Energy probably did not analyse the features of RTG and alpha-neutron radiation on the above guidelines. Their reply is a routine exercise prevalent in the Indian bureaucracy system. However, the above facts and circumstances should be got re-examined by the Indian Government through a new team of experts from all fields on this subject.

Presently, the Indian Nuclear Regulatory authorities are in abundance to outwit each other on such danger posed by this unknown tragedy by the unsecured nuclear material. Prominent among these authorities is the Principal Scientific Adviser (PSA) to the Government of India and Chairman of the Scientific Advisory to the Cabinet of the Federal Government. Other such authorities are the Atomic Energy Commission (AEC), Department of Atomic Energy (DAE), Bhabha Atomic Research Centre (BARC), the Atomic Energy Regulatory Board (AERB), the National Disaster Management Authority (NDMA) and the Defence Research and Development Organization (DRDO). Most of these departments are headed by Nuclear Scientists or technocrats. These nuclear fraternities should be given the task of re-assessing the danger posed by this nuclear material in the Nanda Devi Glacier and impending danger to the Ganga River. The Government of India introduced the Nuclear Safety Regulatory Authority Bill in 2011 to convert the functional independence of the national nuclear regulator, the Atomic Energy Regulatory Board (AERDB) into 'de jure' independence and set up a Nuclear Safety Regulatory Authority (NSRA). This bill was subsequently referred to the Department-related Parliamentary Standing Committee on Science and Technology, Environment and Forests. This bill will give more teeth to regulate the nuclear-related matters to NSRA. Hence, renewed efforts should be made by this authority to take efforts to trace the lost device.

M.G.K. Menon, one of the scientists who were members of the committee appointed by Morarji Desai, revealed later that the committee relied on the documents provided by the US authorities. He affirmed that the committee had limited mandate to find out what the generator had in its components. Was it a nuclear material, the committee was never informed. Menon also disclosed that there was no evidence on record that the government had conducted risk-assessment reports before ordering the operation in 1965 although such assessments were mandatory. Menon too agreed, more than four decades after this mission, that if the device leaks and plutonium gets into the water, it can kill people because plutonium is not something you want to get into the human system. It is toxic and radioactive, and if enters the body, it ends up in the bones. He again suggested terrain mapping because roughly the area of this operation is known to the government. This revelation of Menon who was a member of the scientific committee of 1978 further debunks the reply of Department of Atomic Energy that the contamination of plutonium would have negligible health effects.

Captain Kohli has admitted to the author that he did not know the wider ramifications of the nuclear-powered generator's loss into the glacier. Only after it was lost, he heard that millions of Indians could be affected if the contents of nuclear materials were mixed in the Ganges water. The gravity of such a possible disaster was never disclosed to the Indian mountaineers, Even B.N. Mullik, the then Director of IB was not perhaps aware of such circumstances because he did not suggest any pre-emptive measure to check such fiasco. This is the biggest flaw and immature diplomacy of that period in this mission.

❑

# 12

# Thwarting Unknown Disaster

Secrecy is the biggest enemy of nuclear safety. Story begins like this. The Americans proposed the installation of an unknown disastrous material atop an Indian mountain near to the China border. India agreed, sceptical at what level. This material was left unattended for one year in a cavity of mountain around 23,000 feet above sea level. When relocated, it was found missing and swept into the glacier. It melted into solid blue glacial ice and disappeared beneath the surface, never to be found again. It was revealed by the leader of the expedition that he was never aware that the device containing nearly 2–3 pounds of plutonium would be enough to poison millions of Indians if it swept into the glacier and then mixed-up with the Ganga water. This man-made poison to kill a large portion of the Indian population is still lying untraced for more than five decades. How funny it looks, like a filmy drama, but alas it could be, it is a real story. It is strange how the Indian administration was befooled by the Americans in this misadventure. Surprisingly, even today everyone in the power-centre is sitting awkwardly to watch the catastrophic events to happen any time in future, unaware as to when and where? Let God give them some senses to look into it; else our future generations would never forgive us.

It has been more than 56 years now when the nuclear device was buried in the Nanda Devi glacier. This device SNAP 19C was not a bomb because it did not have a trigger to explode. But it was powered by the radioactive Pu-238 and Pu-239 along with other alloys which were toxic to any human being which could cause cancer and cripples the bones. Even plants could be affected by this radioactivity. According to the US Government, the outer cladding of the capsule is made of many alloys which have corrosion resistant properties lasting around 100 years or more. Agreeing to this assumption, 53 years are already gone and Indian Government should not wait for another 47 years to persist with this assertion and not remove this unknown disaster to its population. Even the Scientists' Committee submitted its report four decades back and nothing thereafter has been done to trace this dangerous device. Science and other technical researches have vastly improved in these four decades but the succeeding Indian Governments did not consider this hidden danger to its millions of population of any significance. Most intriguing aspect of this incident was that it happened in 1965 and everyone in India was tight-lipped for more than twelve years until this news was published in a magazine in the USA during April 1978. How irresponsible were Indian bureaucrats or to larger extent the politicians who were aware of this tragic incident but did not make further efforts to trace it in the glacier!

Prof. M.G.K. Menon, who was one of the members of the Committee of Scientists which gave its finding in 1978, admitted that the committee had no option but to rely on the documents provided to them because their mandate was very limited. He affirmed that the generator was to power "something." They had to look into that. The Committee never knew what that "something" was or if that "something" had any nuclear material in it. What that consisted of was not told to them. Menon also admitted candidly that he did not see any evidence that the government had conducted any risk assessment before ordering this operation in 1965, though such assessment was mandatory. He specifically admitted that, "If this device leaks and plutonium get into the water, it can kill people. Plutonium is not something you want to get into the human system. It is toxic and radioactive, and if it enters the body it ends up in the bones." This statement of a scientist who was part of the Committee that gave its report is ample proof of the hidden danger buried in the glacier of Nanda Devi.

Though in 1978, the International Atomic Energy Agency (IAEA) formulated safety regulations for radioactive materials but nuclear disasters continued to happen even thereafter which were too rampant earlier. In the instant case, the radioactive material is lying beneath the surface of a glacier which is solely the first case of impending danger of this form. Most of the other nuclear disasters occurred over the earth surface whereas this one is looming under it. Hence, the Indian and US Governments in consultation with the IAEA and other nuclear-monitoring agencies would have to engross in a deep exercise to locate and dismantle this poison lying in India under the earth surface.

## Nuclear Accidents

The US bombing in Japan during the Second World War was the experimental testing of nuclear power because the bombs dropped at Hiroshima and Nagasaki were hurriedly manufactured and no previous testing of such bombs was done to measure the intensity and ultimate disaster to be happened to humanity. The impact of nuclear accidents became more relevant for assessment after the USA established its first nuclear reactor in 1954. Although effective steps were taken to minimize the risk of accidents and contain the radioactivity release in the environments but human errors are the main causes of such accidents. Since 1954, more than 100 nuclear accidents of varying impacts have taken place at various places in the world. More than two-third of such accidents occurred in the USA only. The US citizens were the worst affected by such accidents and they sued the government time and again for medical compensations as a result of hazards of the fallout. Ultimately, the US Government passed the Radiation Exposure Compensation Act of 1990 for the affected citizens and also for the employees in nuclear weapons facilities. In India too, Nuclear Safety Regulatory Authority Bill was introduced in 2017 to safeguard the necessary statutory backing for various purposes. Elsewhere in other nuclear-powered countries, no such compensation provisions were found to have been enacted.

Although human error is the main reason in nuclear accidents, there are other factors also involved in it. Nuclear meltdown is a severe nuclear reactor accident that results in reactor core damage from overheating. Other category is critical accidents which occur when a nuclear chain reaction is accidently allowed to occur in fissile material. Decay accidents happen where the heat generated by the radioactive decay causes harm. While transporting radioactive materials, the accident could cause release of radioactivity (direct irradiation) which could occur due to contamination. Equipment-failures could be another factor for such accidents. Lost-source accidents, also referred as orphan sources, are accidents in which radioactive material is lost, stolen or abandoned. The Nanda Devi device could be categorized in this category because it is lost in the glacier though no accident has yet taken place due to any radiation release.

Some of the major nuclear accidents are summarized as under:

## Texas City Accident (16 April 1947)

A French cargo vessel, the Grand Camp, was carrying ammonium nitrate commonly used in atomic weapons. Accidently, a lit cigarette left by a worker sparked fire on the dock which ignited the ammonium nitrate which exploded and also engulfed another vessel High Flyer which was carrying sulphur. It was damaged badly and exploded next day. The entire city of Texas was caught in poisonous fumes thereafter. Over 500 people were killed in this accident including 28 fire-fighters sent to diffuse the fire.

## Kyshtym Nuclear Incident (29 September 1957)

In a town Mayak in Soviet Union a plant was established to manufacture six materials essential for the development of weapons-grade plutonium. Workers of this plant were not informed by the Soviets about the serious possibility of radiation-poisoning from radioactive materials. When one resident got radiation burns and his legs were amputated, wastage of this plant was dumped into the Techa River which got contaminated. Thyroid cancer rate is three times higher than other areas even today. People here still suffer from birth defects, radiation burns and seven rare forms of cancer which is uncommon elsewhere here.

Even after such serious effects of contamination, the Soviets continued to work on this plant which caused a chain reaction due to structural failure in one of the cooling systems. A massive explosion took place in one of the radioactive waste tanks. The radioactive material spread in a population of around 300,000. Around 10,000 ethnic Russians were stated to were have been evacuated and the rest of the population was left there to test the effects of contamination. Declassified Russian documents later revealed that this was known as the Muslumov experiment. Mayak and its surrounding area are still considered as the most contaminated place on earth.

## Goldsboro B-52 Accident in USA (24 January 1961)

A US aircraft, B-52G bomber, which was based at Seymour Johnson Air Force Base in Goldsboro had a rendezvous with a tanker for aerial refuelling. It was carrying two 3–4 Megaton Mrak-39 nuclear bombs. When the tanker crew noticed a fuel leak in right wing, the refuelling was aborted. However, the exercise continued till the pilot reported that leak has worsened. The aircraft was directed to land at the Base immediately. The pilot lost control at 10,000 feet and ordered the crew to eject. Three crew members died before the plane landed and broke apart around 1000–2000 feet above in air. Wreckage of aircraft spread around 5 square km of area in the tobacco and cotton farmlands near Goldsboro.

The first bomb that descended by parachute was found intact and standing upright. The Pentagon initially claimed that there was no chance of an explosion because the two arming mechanisms had not activated. The US States Department too claimed that the bomb was unarmed and could not explode. However, the information released in 2013 as a result of a Freedom of Information Act revealed that a single switch out of four (not six) prevented detonation. The second bomb plunged into a muddy field at around 700 miles per hour and disintegrated without detonation of its conventional explosives. The tail was discovered about 20 feet below ground. Although the bomb was partially armed when it left the aircraft, an unclosed high-voltage switch had prevented it from fully arming. It is a fact that had these bombs been harmed by the pilot in the aircraft before they were released, millions of lives would have been lost in no time.

## Palomares Hydrogen Bomb Incident in Spain (17 January 1966)

In a military exercise known as Operation Chrome Dome, 12 B-52 bombers were carrying hydrogen bombs to Allied countries in Europe to prepare for a first-strike-opportunity against the Soviets during the Cold War. While refuelling in the air over the southern coast of Spain, one bomber collided with a KC-135 tanker. A major midair explosion took place wherein seven crew members were killed. The aircraft and bombs fell on earth near the fishing village of Palomares. Three bombs were recovered on land and the fourth which fell in the Mediterranean Sea was recovered three months later. The two non-nuclear bombs detonated upon impact with the ground were spreading radioactive plutonium across the area which contaminated the land and water supplies around the town. It was the first time the US military had shown a nuclear bomb to the public. Around 2.6 km area was contaminated with radioactive material. This area included residential areas, woods and farmlands. In 2004, a study revealed that there was some significant contamination present in some areas. In 2006, Reuters reported that higher than normal levels of radiation was detected in snails and other wildlife in the region, indicating there still may be some dangerous radioactive material underground. This discovery was detected by the Spanish and US Department of Energy. In 2009, Times Magazine rated the Palomares accident as one of the "worst nuclear disasters". The surviving US Air Force officials, who were sent to clean up the contamination after the accident, were found to have long-term occurrence of cancer and other health defects. These officials were refused compensation due to this secret type of operation and were rather accused that adequate safety measures were not adopted by them to protect themselves.

## Three Mile Island Disaster in USA (28 March 1979)

The Three Mile Island incident is considered as the most terrifying nuclear disaster in the US history which took place at a nuclear facility in Pennsylvania. This accident occurred when the employees did not notice that a mechanical failure in the cooling system was causing a massive increase in the core temperature of the reactor. There were no warning systems or sensors at this centre. Reactor staff had shut off the emergency inflow supply thus supplying no coolant to the reactor. It got overheated and half of the uranium core melted. There was a small release of radiation which was not considered so harmful to the local population.

However, this plant was considered most hazardous to the two millions of population residing nearby. There were protests from the anti-nuclear energy activists. President Jimmy Carter personally inspected the plant to ensure that no such incident take place in the future. Clean-up started in August 1979 and ended in December 1993.

## Titan II Missile Fire at Damascus, Arkansas (18 September 1980)

This accident took place near Damascus, Arkansas, with a repair-crew member dropping a 4-kilogram (9 lb) socket from the missile platform and puncturing the lower fuel tank of the missile. One airman did not follow a technical order given by the US Air Force to use a torque wrench instead of the previously-used ratchet when making a repair. When he observed the fuel vapour leaking into the silo, all silo crew members evacuated to the surface. When other expert members were called to inspect the damage to the missile, they found that the oxidizer tank was quickly losing pressure. They returned to the surface and opened the silo to vent the gas. Soon after their returned, the silo exploded and the warhead of the missile flew into the air. The US Military started a search operation and found the 12-kiloton bomb in a ditch few hundred yards away from the site. The missile was the largest nuclear weapon in the US arsenal and would have resulted in a blast 600 times lethal than that of Hiroshima. One US Air official died and 21 were injured in this blast. The US Government maintained that it was a human error through the one who accidentally used a wrong device without proper knowledge.

## Chernobyl Disaster in Ukrainian Soviet Socialist Republic, Soviet Union (26 April 1986)

The Chernobyl accident is considered the most disastrous nuclear power plant accident in history, both in terms of cost and casualties. It occurred at the Chernobyl nuclear facility near Pripyat, a town 104 km away from Kiev, capital of Ukraine, then a part of the Soviet Socialist Union. This nuclear energy accident is classified as a Level 7 event (the maximum classification) on the International Nuclear Event Scale.

This accident took place during a late-night safety test which simulated a station blackout power-failure, in the course of which safety systems were intentionally turned off. The Soviet government had issued a detailed instruction list for the workers to follow for the safe execution of the test. A combination of inherent reactor design flaws and the reactor operators arranging the core in a manner contrary to the checklist for the test, eventually resulted in uncontrolled reaction conditions. The intense heat from the core caused a massive stream of explosions, blowing away nearly one-third of the building and releasing lethal amounts of radioactive material into the atmosphere above Asia and Europe. This fire produced considerable updrafts for about nine days. Fire crews battled the flames and collected raw radioactive material from around the site to avoid any further contamination. Even today, there is a molten pile of radioactive sludge beneath the core of the reactor. If someone stands next to it for 30 seconds, he would get radiation burns and if he stayed for more than four minutes, he would have only a few days to live.

After the accident, 134 servicemen were hospitalized with acute radiation sickness (ARS) of which thirty-one died. Additionally, approximately fourteen radiation-induced cancer deaths occurred among the survivors. The Russian Government sent in over 500,000 rescue workers to respond to the emergency. Pripyat's population of 50,000 was evacuated. The reactor was later sealed with a steel and concrete structure called "the sarcophagus." Even today, it is difficult to determine the extent of the damage caused by the Chernobyl meltdown. But victims continue to be affected by higher than normal rates of thyroid cancer and birth defects. The city of Pripyat is a ghost town which can be visited only with the permission of the Russian Government. A few residents were granted permission to live there in their old age. Although the area was deemed to be unliveable for the next 50,000 years, the Russian Government did not shut down the facility until the early 2000s. Before then, they shuttled in workers from outside the exclusion zone. The accident motivated safety upgrades on all remaining Soviet-designed reactors of which eleven continued to power the electric grids as of 2013.

## The Fukushima Daiichi Disaster, Japan (11 March 2011)

Like the Chernobyl disaster, the Fukushima Daiichi disaster was the second disaster to be given the Level 7 event classification of the International Nuclear Event Scale. It was an energy accident at this nuclear plant in Okuma, Fukushima Prefecture in Japan, triggered by the tsunami following the Tohoku earthquake. The massive wave travelling at several hundred miles per hour caused extreme damage to the cooling and venting systems of the plant. These systems are integral part of the process to control the temperature in each reactor. This resulted in immediate release of radioactivity into the local area.

Fukushima Nuclear Accident Independent Investigation Commission (NAIIC) confirmed that the causes of the accident were foreseeable and the plant operator Tokyo Electric Power

Company (TEPCO) had failed to meet basic safety requirements such as risk assessment, preparing for containing collateral damage and developing evacuation plants. The TEPCO too later admitted that it had failed to take necessary measures fearing lawsuits or protests against the nuclear plants.

After a month of assessing the damage to the local population, the Japanese Government declared a 20-kilometer (12 mile) restricted zone on 19 April 2011. The residents were evacuated and relocated. The government declared all six reactors to be decommissioned which were shut down one year later. It is observed that even today the area is extremely contaminated and radiation is still venting. The Japanese Government has not found any solution to this tragedy.

## Nuclear Accidents in India

Although there have been many nuclear accidents in India, these cannot be termed as disastrous in so far as human deaths are concerned. But economic loss has certainly cost the exchequer the most due to these accidents. The first such accident occurred on 4 May 1987 at Kalpakkam in Tamil Nadu when refuelling process was going on for fast breeder test reactor which greatly damaged the reactor core. The nuclear reactor was shut down for two years thereafter. A total of 300 million dollars was spent on the repairs.

Two accidents took place at Tarapur power plant in Maharashtra in 1989 and 1992. Leakage of radioactive iodine was the reason of the accident. Repairing work continued for one year which had cost around 78 million dollars. In second accident reactor tube released radioactivity due to its malfunctioning but no untoward incident took place. In 1993, a fire at the turbine blades caused an accident at Narora atomic power station in Uttar Pradesh. All important cables were burnt in this incident incurring 220 million dollar loss. There was no damage to the reactor.

In the Rajasthan atomic power station at Kota helium gas leaked in 1995. The heavy water was mixed with water at the Rana Pratap Sagar River. The power station was closed for two years for repairs. The loss was estimated at 280 million dollars for this repair work. The Kalpakkam fast breeder reactor leaked the radioactive sodium which damaged the valves and systems in another accident in 2002. This has caused 30 million dollars loss.

In 2010, a major radioactive disaster took place at Mayapuri scrap market in New Delhi. In 1968, the chemistry laboratory at Delhi University imported a nuclear power-pack from a Canadian firm with Cobalt 60 as its main nuclear material. After a few years of use, it was abandoned on the university campus where it laid open for several decades. In 2009, the university sold it to a scrap dealer who had no inkling of its contents. He melted it down and broke it up, releasing radiation into the entire scrap market. Even the Atomic Energy Regulatory Board had no idea that the nuclear material had passed into civilian hands. The worker at the Mayapuri scrap market who broke open the material died after being exposed to a high dose of radiation. Two others, the owner of the shop and his friend, who kept tiny parts of the fancy-looking nuclear material in their purses, survived because they were lucky enough to get their burns diagnosed as nuclear radiation. Local papers carried front-page stories and government agencies were under pressure for this disaster. Later the government approved a set of recommendations for stricter standards for such purpose.

## Modern Technology to Detect Lost Nuclear Device in Nanda Device Glacier

Last search operation to trace the lost nuclear device in Nanda Devi Glacier was conducted in 1965–68 by the Indian and US experts. It was a panic-ridden futile exercise in a very secretive manner. The only technology deployed at that time was the use of metal detectors and neutron sensors which proved ineffective in view of absence of any knowledge about the exact location of lost device. Thereafter, five decades' time has gone and science and technology have advanced considerably in this field under the supervision and expertise of the International Atomic Energy Agency. Even some Indian Nuclear Scientists have admitted that technologically it is viable provided the Indian Government takes initiative in this regard. The Americans, of course, should be asked to provide all materialistic participation including the financial sharing in this new venture because till date they have officially neither accepted this expedition nor denied the loss of nuclear device in the glacier. Their dubious role since the beginning when their expedition members entered without immigration entries at airport and subsequently taking away Nanda Kot device in a secret plane were ample proof to this discreet nuclear catastrophe of this mission in India. The Americans never participated in any investigation after the 1968 search mission. Even the Scientist's Committee did not indicate American participation what-so-ever is indicative of the fact that they do not want the failure of this mission to be attributed to them.

There had been voices from some activists in India on this sensitive issue but the government has not initiated any renewed plan to locate the nuclear device. Media suggested overtly that new searches should be done with new technology of ground-penetrating radars and hyper-spectral imaging to locate the device beneath the glacier in rocks and ice. Intriguingly, the Nuclear Controls and Planning Wing of the Department of Energy of Indian Government informed the author that sampling of water and sediments was conducted on six monthly bases up to December 2011, and later it was discontinued since there was no outcome. Hence, for the last seven years there is a complete silence in this matter as far as the Government of India is concerned.

As already envisaged in the previous chapters, the International Atomic Energy Agency was created in 1978. It formulated the basic safety standards, specialized regulations and codes of practice with regard to radioactive material. Both the USA and India are founding members of this regulatory body. Hence, this matter has to be accorded serious concern and the lost device should be searched with new available techniques and researches.

The IAEA has published many safety standards with regard to regulations of uranium exploration, ore processing, its chemistry etc. According to such manuals, intensive worldwide efforts for uranium explorations have been stimulating research on and development of new exploration techniques and field equipment. It is widely recognized that borehole logging is one of the most effective ways of estimating uranium resources. Logging for uranium, which once was an auxiliary technique subordinate to chemical analysis and drilled core examination, has become one of the most powerful and efficacious methods of measuring, directly or indirectly, uranium at depth. This exploration includes in-situ analysis, lithological identification, stratigraphic correlation and information on density and moisture. In search of nuclear fuel, millions of meters is drilled and logged by exploration firms and governmental organizations by member states.

The joint Nuclear Energy Agencies/IAEA Group of Experts in Research and Development on Uranium Exploration Techniques, aware of the importance of this particular subject, recommended the preparation of a manual that could be of use to both developing and industrialized countries. Accordingly, the IAEA convened a workshop to discuss problems related to borehole logging and later organized an international consultative group charged with the preparation of such a manual.

The IAEA formulated 17 analytical methods that have been accepted in the international uranium industry. These include

Uranium Exploration wherein area selection, reconnaissance phase, follow-up plan and deposit development were included. In Analytical Requirements in uranium ore processing, uranium extraction technology, development projects and plant operation were outlined. Properties of uranium compounds and its analytical methods were mentioned in the analytical chemistry of uranium. Most relevant descriptions related to this device were analyzed by determination of uranium in water using a scintrex UA-3 analyzer which includes measurement and calibration methods. Another technique specified was determination of uranium in ores, rocks and mineral processing solutions by XRF analysis which include analysis of aqueous and organic solutions using bromine as the internal standard. Most relevant facts were analysed in determination of uranium in ores and other samples by UV/VIS spectro-photometry.

In view of the details published by the IAEA and other nuclear-related agencies, the Indian Government should again form a committee of scientists from various Indian nuclear agencies including Principal Scientific Advisor to the Government of India, the Atomic Energy Commission (AEC), Department of Atomic Energy (DAE), Bhabha Atomic Research Centre (BARC), the Atomic Energy Regulatory Board (AERB), the National Disaster Management Authority (NDMA) and the Defence Research and Development Organisation (DRDO). Indian Nuclear organizations are a big asset which the government should utilize in this renewed effort to locate the nuclear device. Indian Government should also take help from the IAEA, USA, Canada, UK and other countries who could provide all possible help in this context so that this hidden danger is unearthed for the sake of the Indian generations to come.

❑

# Annexures

## Annexure I

**Application for Seeking Information Under Section 6(1)/7(1) of the Right to Information Act, 2005**

**Central Public Information Officer,** **7 Sept., 2015.**
**Prime Minister of India Office,**
**South Block, New Delhi.**

| | | |
|---|---|---|
| Name of Applicant | : | R.K.Yadav, former R&AW officer and author of book Mission R&AW. |
| Address | : | 84, Jwalaheri, Paschim Vihar, New Delhi-110063. |
| Subject | : | Disappearance of Nuclear Device slated to be planted on Nanda Devi Mountain during October, 1965. |

## Brief Facts:

During 1964, India and the US Govt. decided to plant a Nuclear-powered Monitoring Station on Nanda Devi Mountain in the

Himalayan region to monitor nuclear and air-force related activities of China. In this pursuit the IB and CIA developed a plutonium fitted device to be installed along with a generator on the peak. A six feet tall antenna was to be placed on this mechanism to collect data from the Chinese test site. The generator was meant to covert radioactive heat into electricity. It is informed that the generator was powered by radioactivity which was toxic to human beings. The device was manufactured by the US scientists and Indian Govt. was to assist it on the peak of Nanda Devi mountain for monitoring inside China.

The expedition team comprising of Indians and Americans started its mission to install this monitoring unit on 24 Sept. 1965. On 16 October 1965 the expedition was called off just short of the actual destination due to adverse weather conditions. The expedition team was asked to secure the equipments at a safe place so that this mission could be completed next year in good weather conditions. According to mission team, these equipments were placed in a rock cavity and tied there with nylon ropes. Mission was thus abandoned.

In May 1966, the expedition team again started its mission to track and place this device at the proposed destination. When the team reached at the place where these equipments were placed and tied with the rock, they found the equipments missing and the rock too was not there. It became evident that the avalanche had swept away the rock to which the equipments were tied.

When this disclosure appeared in media in 1978, the then Indian Govt. appointed a committee to investigate the details of this expedition.

## Information Sought

i. How many kilograms weight of plutonium and of which quality was sent for placement on Nanda Devi mountain in this operation? Quality means plutonium 238 or 239 or some other variety.

ii. How this plutonium was assembled in some equipment before placing it on the mountain?

iii. What is the chance of the plutonium to be leaked in the mountain region?

iv. If so, what sort of radioactive radiation could develop in the region where this plutonium was lost?

v. What is the time period in terms of years, this device containing plutonium could remain radioactive?

vi. How much danger it could impose in river Ganga if the device containing plutonium is bared open and plutonium is mixed in Ganga water?

vii. What could be the danger to the Indian public in this case if plutonium is found in Ganga water?

viii. What were the findings of the Committee appointed by the govt. in 1978 to investigate this operation?

ix. Supply me the copy of the findings of this Committee report.

x. What measures the Govt. of India has taken in this regard since 1966 to locate the lost plutonium fitted device so that it might not mix in river Ganga? If so, please supply the copies of details of these measures.

xi. Has the govt. devised some mechanism to monitor regularly the efforts to trace these lost equipments?

xii. Has the US Govt. helped India in this regard? If so, details thereof.

xiii. Is the same plutonium was used in bombs which were dropped in Hiroshima and Nagasaki cities of Japan by the US during the Second World War? If so, how many people were killed?

A fee of Rupees 10/- is enclosed herewith vide postal order 23F 478801.

**(R.K. Yadav)**
Applicant

## Annexure II

29 December, 2015.

**From**

R.K. Yadav,
Author of book "Mission R&AW", Former Officer of R&AW,
84, Jwalaheri, Paschim Vihar, New Delhi-110063.

**To**

Shri Narendra Modi,
Hon'ble Prime Minister of India, South Block,
New Delhi.

**Subject :** Disappearance of Nuclear Device slated to be planted on Nanda Devi during October 1965.

—00—

**Sir,**

Kindly refer to my letter dated 7 Sept. 2015 (Copy enclosed) on the above subject. You are requested to kindly direct the concerned authorities to supply me the relevant information as it is of national interest. This nuclear device is missing for the last 50 years wherein plutonium (which was used in the bomb dropped by the US in Japan in the Second World War) was placed in a box to be installed on Nanda Devi to monitor Chinese nuclear and air activities.

With kind regards,

Yours Sincerely,
**(R.K. Yadav)**

# Annexure II

डॉ. के. एल. रामकुमार, अध्यक्ष
**Dr. K. L. Ramakumar, Head**

नाभिकीय नियंत्रण एवं आयोजना स्कंध
**Nuclear Controls and Planning Wing**

सत्यमेव जयते

भारत सरकार
परमाणु ऊर्जा विभाग
अणुशक्ति भवन, छत्रपति शिवाजी महाराज मार्ग,
मुंबई - 400 001.

**GOVERNMENT OF INDIA**
**DEPARTMENT OF ATOMIC ENERGY**
ANUSHAKTI BHAVAN, C. S. M. MARG,
MUMBAI - 400 001

No. 33(2)/6/2009/BARC/R&D-I/3073 March 3, 2016

Sub : Disappearance of Nuclear Device slated to the planted on Nanda Devi Mountain during October, 1965.

Dear Mr. Yadav,

This has reference to your application dated September 7, 2015, for seeking information under Section 6(1)/7(1) of the Right to Information Act, 2005 addressed to Central Public Information Officer, Prime Minister's Office, South Block, New Delhi, which was referred to Department of Atomic Energy for response on September 11, 2015.

Pursuant to missing of the power source sometime in 1970s, consisting of Plutonium-238 (Pu-238) for powering a nuclear device installed at Nanda Devi, extensive sampling of water and sediments was done by a Committee covering the stretch from Gangotri to downstream of Ganga River. Analysis of the sample results done by the Health Physics Division, Bhabha Atomic Research Centre (BARC) of the Department did not reveal contamination in water or sediments. It was reported that the missing radiation source i.e. Plutonium 238 was a sealed source and it emits only Alpha. Alpha can be totally stopped even with paper therefore there is no danger of leaking out or giving radiation to either marine species or polluting water of Ganga. Such sampling was conducted on six monthly basis upto December, 2011 and since there was no outcome, the same was discontinued.

The above response is based on the information available with the Department. The Department does not have any information regarding the Committee or the findings of the Committee appointed by the Government in 1978.

With regards

Yours sincerely,

( K.L. Ramakumar )

Shri R.K. Yadav
84, Jawalaheri
Paschim Vihar
**New Delhi – 110 063.**

दूरभाष / TELEPHONE (91) (22) 2204 3041 फैक्स / FAX (91) (22) 2204 8476 ई-मेल / E-mail : ramakumar@dae.gov.in